Letters from Helen

A Canadian Student in Germany on the Eve of the Great War

Helen VanWart
edited by Douglas Lochhead

Leipzig Largest station in Europe   *Der neue Hauptbahnhof*

Der neue Hauptbahnhof in Leipzig ist der größte Bahnhof Europas. Es münden 26 Geleise nebeneinander ein. Im Jahre 1902 wurde mit den Bauten begonnen. Die linke Hälfte (preußischer Teil) ist seit 1. Mai 1912 im Betrieb. Die vollständige Inbetriebnahme erfolgt 1915. An den Gesamtkosten — ca. 150 Millionen — trägt der sächsische Staat 50 Millionen und die Stadt Leipzig ca. 17 Millionen Mark.

"The new main train station", Leipzig, begun in 1902, in service since 1912. It was still not completed when Helen saw it in 1913-1914. The Hauptbahnhof Leipzig is still the largest in Europe and looks very similar to what it did in Helen's day.

(Mount Allison Archives, Lochhead Fonds, 8701.)

Letters from Helen

A Canadian Student in Germany on the Eve of the Great War

Helen VanWart

edited by Douglas Lochhead

SYBERTOOTH INC
SACKVILLE, NEW BRUNSWICK

Litteris Elegantis Madefimus

Edited by Douglas Lochhead
Copyright © the Estate of Helen VanWart Lochhead 2010
Photographs copyright © the Estate of Helen VanWart Lochhead 2010
Foreword copyright © Nancy Vogon 2010
Afterword copyright © Sara Lochhead
Historical notes by K.V. Johansen, copyright © Sybertooth 2010
Cover design copyright © Sybertooth 2010

The letters and photographs (except otherwise noted) are from the Mount Allison University Archives, Lochhead Fonds, 8701.
Diaries and additional materials courtesy of the Lochhead family.

VanWart, Helen, 1893-
     Letters from Helen : a Canadian student in Germany on the
eve of the Great War / Helen VanWart ; edited by Douglas Lochhead.

Includes index.
ISBN 978-0-9810244-9-3

     1. VanWart, Helen, 1893- --Correspondence. 2. Germany--History--
1871-1918. 3. Canadian students--Germany--Correspondence.
I. Lochhead, Douglas, 1922- II. Title.

DD228.2.V35 2010   943.084092   C2010-903289-6

CONTENTS

To the memory of my mother,
Helen Louise VanWart Lochhead
1893-1983
~ D.L

Introduction

During the late nineteenth and early twentieth centuries, many private music teachers who operated their own studios in Canada had received European training; these included both European natives and North Americans who had studied abroad. One of these individuals was May McAdam, who opened a private studio in Fredericton in the early part of the twentieth century. She had been born in Boston and received her musical training in that city and in Montreal before travelling to Leipzig in 1905 to study piano with the noted teacher Robert Teichmuller.[1] In 1913 she made arrangements to return to Leipzig, taking some of her most talented students with her. Thus, in August 1913, Helen VanWart departed Fredericton with her teacher and a few fellow students for what was to be one of the most memorable years of their lives. The group of young women sailed to Liverpool on board the *SS Laurentic* and spent a week in London before travelling on to Germany. At Leipzig the girls settled into a strenuous routine of study and practice, renting pianos for their rooms in order to practise the nine hours per day they were allowed.

Letters from Helen tells the story of one of these young women's experiences as a student at the Leipzig Conservatory in Germany during 1913 – 1914. In this set of letters, carefully preserved by her family, we read details of what Helen VanWart experienced and her reactions to all her adventures from the time she left by ship in August 1913 until she arrived in Scotland ready to sail back to Canada in the late summer of 1914.

Helen VanWart was the youngest of three children and had received her schooling in Fredericton, including an arts degree from the University of New Brunswick (B.A. 1913). She was very close to her family and wrote home weekly describing her experiences in Germany. Her letters give a vivid picture of the musical and social life of Leipzig in the year prior to the outbreak of the First World War. She carefully documents details of food, people met, lodgings, places visited, etc., and includes comments on her thoughts and emotions as she spends a week in England and then a few days in Holland before proceeding to Leipzig. She then provides an almost daily account of her lessons, classes, practice sessions, concerts attended, as well as social events, and comments on the many people she met.

She describes numerous performances of pianists, including Wilhelm Backhaus, Edwin Fischer and Emil Sauer, several vocalists, the Gewandhaus Orchestra, chamber groups and services at the various churches, including concerts at the Thomaskirche where Bach had served. She attended many operas in Leipzig as well as in Halle and Dresden; she was particularly intrigued by this art form, which she had not experienced in New Brunswick. One of the first operas which the young ladies attended was Wagner's *Lohengrin*. "The music is just heavenly ... It only cost us 80 pfennings

---

[1] For information on Canada's connection with the Leipzig Conservatory see Nancy F. Vogan "The Maritime-Leipzig Connection" in *The Red Jeep and Other Landscapes; A Collection in Honour of Douglas Lochhead*, Goose Lane Editions, 1987.

apiece (20¢)." In March 1914 she attended a performance of Schoenberg's *Gurrelieder* conducted by the composer himself.

The experience of a young New Brunswick girl in one of the musical capitals of Europe was very exciting: "I am learning so many things each day that music seems only a small part of my stay here." The tremendous culture-shock proved to be overwhelming but stimulating. "When you get over here you certainly find out what a nobody you are along side the big geniuses that are all around you...Why, the people laugh when we say we have never heard the operas." However, she commented: "It gives you ambition to do something besides settle down ... I can't afford to waste a moment here, for I want to get the benefit of my stay in a foreign land. If the girls in Fredericton knew what a chance they were throwing away when they refuse a trip here, it would make some of them start a bit."

In addition to meeting several Canadians during her stay in Germany, Helen also made friends with students from many countries. Regarding her rooming house, she wrote: "We have Russian, Mexican, Jewish, English, at least eight Americans and lots of Germans and even a Roumanian ... We speak nothing but German at the table. My little that I got at college has helped me a lot." Besides private instrumental and vocal lessons, most students took classes in other aspects of music as well. In the spring of 1914, following a trip to Italy, Helen wrote to her family: "I have taken on all my extra subjects in German – Pedagogic (teaching), Form, History, Ear Training. It is going to be pretty hard but I am going to try it anyway."

Helen had made plans to stay for another term in order to take further lessons with Herr Teichmuller and pursue her vocal studies, which were progressing very well, but such was not to be the case. Her letter of August 2, 1914 reads: "Here is your little girl flying down the Rhine as quickly as possible to get away from the war." Even in the midst of this upheaval, she was able to comment on the scenery: "I couldn't begin to describe the Rhine trip to you. It has been simply grand – the old castles, and vineyards are fine."

Safely back in Canada, Helen VanWart rejoined her parents in Fredericton and began teaching music privately in their home. She had a large class of students who performed frequently in recitals held in the family parlour. Her thoughts of Leipzig did not fade, however, especially her memories of time spent with her "young Canadian friend, Mr. Lochhead". During a trip to Ottawa in the late 1970s I had the pleasure of spending an afternoon with Helen and her husband. The memories of her Leipzig experiences were very vivid in her mind and she recalled details with great pleasure and enthusiasm. She described the year in Leipzig as one of the most exciting of her life, one that she would never forget. The publication of these letters means that we can now share her excitement.

Nancy F. Vogan

Helen Louise VanWart
(Collection of the Lochhead Family)

Setting Out

From *The University Monthly*, Volume 32, No. 8, June 1913
Fredericton, N.B. University of New Brunswick

HELEN VanWART B.A. — Helen was our other town girl, being a graduate of Fredericton High School. She was the musical member of the class, and took a leading place in the college orchestra. When the piano was added to the reading room, Helen was greatly sought and Beethoven's Sonatas and Alexander's Rag Time Band alike flowed from her nimble fingers. She was always interested in football and football heroes were always interested in her. This tendency was discovered at her first Freshmen's reception and extended right through her whole course. Helen was a constant attendant at Y.W.C.A. and though not a regular member of Delta Rho, she was a clever debater. To see her in her element one should look into the Gym. when a college dance was in full swing. The centre of a clamorous throng, she showed to the disappointed youths a full programme and happy was the boy who secured a dance with her. Helen is going to Germany to study music.

From *The Daily Gleaner*
Thursday, Aug. 28, 1913

To Study Music

Misses Annie, Ida and May B. McAdam, Miss Helen VanWart and Miss Edna Baird of this city, Miss Grant of Southampton, and Miss Tabor of Lethbridge, Alberta will leave this evening for Montreal, where they will sail on the steamer *Laurentian* [sic], Saturday for Europe. With the exception of Misses Ida and Annie McAdam, all the party will study music in the Conservatory at Leipzig, Germany. This is the second term of Miss May B. McAdam at the Conservatory. Miss Grant of Southampton has been studying for some years at Woodstock and is an accomplished musician.

DIARY OF TRIP FROM FREDERICTON, N.B. TO LEIPZIG, GERMANY, AUGUST 28, 1913 TO SEPTEMBER 7, 1913

Aug. 28th

On August the 28th, 1913, Miss Ida, Annie, and May McAdam, Miss Edna Baird, Miss Gladys Grant, and myself started on the 5.50 train for Germany, via Montreal.[1]

After a very pleasant send-off, we settled down for our little journey to the Junction.[2] There, we met the Montreal and soon went flying on our way. As the party decided to sit up, we had rather a tiresome ride, but were very thankful to get started without any mishaps.

About five in the morning we arrived at Sherbrooke, where Harry Thaw was, after his escape from U.S.[3]

At nine-thirty we arrived in Montreal.

Aug. 29th

(Dr.) Wathen and his cousin met us, and after a much-needed wash Gladys, Edna and I had a cup of coffee. Jim [Wathen] then took us down to get our Traveller's cheques, after which we went through St. James Cathedral.

Goodwin's supplied a very neat lunch in their dining-room for Jim and I. Then we went up the mountain, and to the new theatre where they had a pipe-organ accompaniment for the moving pictures.

When we went back to the station, no other than Will Rising met us, having come up the night before, and missed me.

Jim took us up to the "Rose Tea Room", and we had *sour* lemonade.

Two cabs carried our weary bodies and somewhat heavy baggage to the Steamship, *Laurentic*, White Star Line Wharf.[4]

Jim and Will came on board, and after a very pleasant evening the good-byes were said, and we

---

[1] Sisters Ida and Annie (or Nan) McAdam were the aunts of May McAdam and her cousin Queen Tabor, accompanying the girls as chaperones. Ida had been in Leipzig with May previously.

[2] The village of Fredericton Junction.

[3] Harry K. Thaw, the millionaire murderer of architect Stanford White, escaped a lunatic asylum in Matteawan, New York on August 10th and crossed into Quebec, but was arrested on August 12th; he was held in custody in Canada until he was extradited to the US in February of 1914. The murder, Thaw's trial, conviction, and subsequent escape, made headline news around the world.

[4] The *SS Laurentic*, owned by the White Star Line, was launched in 1908; first used as troop transport in 1914 and then converted to an armed merchant cruiser, she sank on January 25, 1917, after striking two mines off of Ireland, with 354 dead.

Aug. 28, th.

On August the 28th
1913, Miss Ida, Annie,
and May McAdam,
Miss Edna Baird, Miss
Gladys Grant, and
myself started on
the 5.50 train for
Germany, via Mont-
-real.

After a very pleasant
send-off, we settled down
for our little journey
to the junction. There, we
met the Montreal and
soon went flying on
our way. As the party
decided to sit up, we
had rather a tiresome
ride, but were very
thankful to get started
without any mishaps.

About five in the
morning we arrived at
Sherbrooke, where Harry
Thaw was, after his
escape from U.S.

At nine-thirty we
arrived in Montreal.

First Page of Helen's Brief Travel Diary.

(Collection of the Lochhead Family)

went down to our dear little cabin which Edna, Gladys and myself shared.[1]

We had numerous parcels, of different shapes and forms, flowers, chocolates, and letters. It is very nice to be remembered when leaving. (Please remember, Helen!)

No cradle had to rock us that night. At five-thirty, we left Montreal, and passed up the St. Lawrence through a beautiful country.

Aug. 30th

At nine we had breakfast, and then wrote letters, till lunch at one. How many days will such frivolity last. Here's hoping it will be calm all the way.

At two-thirty we anchored at Quebec, and immediately our personally conducted tour disembarked, and decided, after considerable discussion and figuring up to hire two cabs for $5.00 to take us to "see Quebec".

It was my first glimpse of the dear old city, and I liked it very much. We visited the Plains, old fort, and Gates, the narrow streets of the old city, and the modern improvements in the upper part.

We saw a couple taking a baby to be christened, and heard the bell ringing in the Church. The man said, "It is only de people wit money who have de bells, more money, more bells." The old historical places were very interesting but appeared to be rather overdrawn to suit the American tourist.

All too soon our melodious bell rang for dinner, and when we came on deck in the evening, the lights of Quebec and Levis, were lighting our way down the river.

Aug. 31st

We wrote letters all evening to be put off at Father's Point.[2] I wrote mine, making about twenty for the day.

When we awoke next morning I was very disappointed that Rimouski had been passed and I had missed my last chance to send off mail to the home ones.

Service was held in the first class saloon, the orchestra accompanying the Church of England service. After a lovely hour there, I went to meet the doctor, but alas, he failed to appear.

After lunch May and I walked for a long time, and we read, talked, ate, christened several more of the passengers, having a good time altogether.[3]

Dinner was good as usual, and we did enjoy the concert given by the orchestra in the evening.

Still another great night was passed and we found a perfect morning, for our passage through the Strait of Belle Isle.

After a great smooth sail we began to approach the ice-bergs.

Sept. 1st

There were dozens of them, all around us. Soon we passed out of the Strait, past the Island of Belle Isle, where there are only two men living, the light-house keeper, and the signal man. What an existence!

---

[1] There are several men named Will in Helen's circle: her brother, William Alexander VanWart; a hopeful suitor, Will Skinner, and Will Rising. The publishers would like to thank Norma Paul for assistance with geneaological research.

[2] Pointe-au-Père, near Rimouski.

[3] Nicknamed.

After lunch the orchestra played some fine selections of the operas, and we then retired to our deck chairs to try to read or write. It seems impossible to do either, out here with so much to do and see.

Shuffle board is quite a pass-time but we are not experts by any means.

Sept. 2nd, 3rd, 4th

The doctor wished me to call to have my finger dressed, but I deemed it better not to go.

All these days, seem too much to put on one page, for I certainly did a lot during that time — mostly thinking, why? Warum?[1] Well Tuesday at noon this horrid old ship began to do anything from the tango to the Turkey Trot.[2] It seemed to get into my head, and stuck there for two days and a half.

Our Stewardess, Mrs. Geniss, was very attentive to us, and we had excellent meals, in our dear little cabin, (1st class).

Sept. 5th

I had a wireless from Will, and it certainly cheered me up.

On Friday morning we awoke to find just perfect sailing. Everyone made a desperate attempt, and at last reached deck.

Queenie, Gladys and I had ham sandwiches in our room for lunch but by dinner we were all sehr gut,[3] and began to enjoy our last night on board. We began to feel sorry at parting with such people as "Baron Herr von Schumberg", "Jerome K. Jerome", "Little Willie", "The Suffragette", "Huxley of America", "General", "Soldiers of the King", "Petticoats", and heaps of others.

We were also indebted to Mr. H. Pladdie, 5th Engineer, and our little deck sailor, for much information.

Thomas Watson, our steward, was of a very sarcastic disposition, but managed to keep our room fairly well.

We liked Mrs. Hodson, and her little girl, Nora, very much. Also Miss Moore, who dressed my finger so nicely for me, Dr. and Mrs. Hedblom, who were bound for China, and some other quite pleasant people.

Sept. 6th

We had a good farewell orchestra concert, and May and I played checkers for a while.

It was after twelve when we finished packing and settled down. We were glad to reach our last morning on board — Saturday.

At about eleven we passed the Isle of Man, which is an island, with Home Rule.

There were some pretty excited people on deck when we sighted New Brighton and the Liverpool Docks.

England at last! Our very first impression was good. First the trunks and baggage were taken off,

---

[1] German: "Why?"

[2] The Turkey Trot was a lively ragtime dance popular before the Great War and like the tango, regarded by some as indecent.

[3] German: "Very good".

The Telegram Home

(Collection of the Lochhead Family)

and soon we were being piloted down the gang-way by our first Cook's guide.[1]

After considerable searching we managed to get all the things together and then they were examined. No liquors or tobacco being found. Cook's took charge of our trunks and insured them through to Leipzig.

I cabled home, the extensive message, "Safe. Well".

Our first taxi ride was experienced on the way from the docks to the "Compton House". There we obtained three rooms, the one we had having room for three.

Immediately we took our shaky land-feet up to the Liverpool Gallery — the Wallace Collection.[2] There I saw my first great pictures. It was a very hurried tour, as we had to be back at dinner by seven.

---

[1] Thomas Cook and Son was a travel agency with origins in the mid-nineteenth century.

[2] The Walker Art Gallery in Liverpool contains a large collection of fourteen to early twentieth-century art and is probably the "Liverpool Gallery" to which she refers. The Wallace Collection contains paintings dating from the fifteenth to nineteenth centuries, as well as sculpture, arms and armour, porcelain, and goldwork. However, it is housed in Hertford House, London, and is not loaned out. Possibly this is a mistake or misunderstanding.

The waiter certainly served a record dinner in about fifteen minutes.

In ten more minutes seven dirty, tired looking specimens were seen in one of the back seats of St. George's Hall[1] listening to one of the finest organs in the world. I enjoyed the Berceuse from *Jocelyn*[2] most of all, but the semamatic runs on the pedals, in another piece, were wonderful.

Sept. 7th

Tired heads went down that night. At seven-thirty Sunday morning we crossed the river Mersey to Birkenhead, where we just caught the Great Western Railway for London. It was a great relief to get started, and think that we were really off in one of those stuffy little rooms of the English railway carriage.

Our companions in the compartments gave us much information about the different places passed. First, we came to Port Sunlight where our soap comes from. Everyone spoke of the kindness of the head of the Company to his employees.[3]

The next place of interest was Chester which is such a quaint old place, with its ancient wall, tower, and cathedral.

Every little station that we came to, seemed to be better than the last. The decorations, and cleanliness of the places seemed remarkable. We found out however that a prize was given to the best looking station, and it is very likely that keen competition has been the cause of such beautiful flowers etc.

We crossed a part of Wales and saw there beautiful Welsh hills in the distance. One little village built on a side hill, with a river flowing in the valley below, shall always remain in my memory.

The part of England that we went through was an immense garden. The hedges and small rivers impressed me, and the numerous bridges which surely must be hundreds of years old, and some may be were the Roman remains. The roads all through the country are just like marble — what a place to motor — stopping at the dear little wayside inns, such as "The Three Hounds", or any of the other picturesque little spots.

Birmingham was passed, and such an industrial centre it is, to be in the midst of such a garden. The children in the streets looked as if they needed the country air, and fields to play in.

Our lunch consisted of scenery, and a ham sandwich.

All the way down we kept passing varied scenes — there was no sameness, to any of the country. A castle or country home would appear, and then a church or a dear little garden, — till we came to Oxford. There we caught a glimpse of Trinity College and Christ Church and noticed that the suburbs of Oxford were very wonderful, — there being lovely houses, woods, and a river or lake.

At about five o'clock we saw Windsor Castle, from the distance, and as the sun was going down the castle showed up against such a background.

Soon we approached London, and began to get excited at the thought of being in the largest city in the world. We didn't know just what would become of us, only that we were to go to the "Pemboro House", 4 Pembridge Square.

Having had a taxi ride in Liverpool, there was nothing new in our trip to the boarding house

---

[1] St. George's Hall, Liverpool, is home to one of the largest pipe organs in Great Britain, built by Henry Willis and dating to 1855.

[2] Opera by Benjamin Godard, 1888.

[3] A model village built by William Lever, Lord Leverhulme, in the late nineteenth century to house workers employed by the Sunlight soap factory. It is notable for its Arts and Crafts Movement influenced architecture.

except, of course, the few streets we saw, and the gardens we passed. My first impression was good, and it continued so, all through my visit in London which was for a week, and a day.

Gladys, Edna and I had a lovely large room, facing the gardens, and the McA's had two other rooms.

"Front of the Institute Building" - Illustration from the Conservatory Prospectus
(Collection of the Lochhead Family)

LETTERS, 1913

I

On board S.S. "LAURENTIC"
Aug. 31, 1913

My dear People:-

I promised to write from Rimouski, and I fully intended to, but alas, we passed there this morning very early, and I had no idea of it. It seemed to me that we would pass there sometime to-day. There is no chance to send any more mail, until we do come to Liverpool, so I am beginning to-day to write a continued story of the trip, so that I won't have to relate it all when I get to Liverpool.

I wrote you last night, and after walking about the deck for some time we retired to our dear little cabin, and read, talked until about mid-night. I slept fine, and was up bright and early for breakfast. We had the loveliest pancakes. They had maple honey as good as Jackson's. The butter is good, but the cream would never suit mother.

We walked around deck for a while after breakfast, and looked through the sailor's spyglass. Then at half-past ten we went into the first class dining room for church. I never enjoyed anything better in my life. They had a great orchestra, and the hymns were perfect. The officers looked so nice in uniform. They had Church of England service, and a good sermon.

Tuesday morning — Hurrah! Still on deck. My but it is great to be able to keep up. Queenie and Gladys have been quite sick but have not reached the vomiting stage yet.

Yesterday we had a great day. We saw any number of ice-bergs, and went very close to some of them. They are certainly very beautiful. We hope we are past them all now, so we can speed ahead. To-day it is damp. Last night it rained and would you believe it a big splash came in on Edna in the night.

There is great fun here all day, watching the steerage, and playing shuffle board, and reading. We have two orchestra concerts every day, from 2.15 - 3.15, and from 8.15 to 9 p.m. The orchestra is certainly splendid. They play good stuff.

If all goes well, we shall likely land on Saturday. The sea is very calm, compared to what I expected, but likely we shall feel it rougher before long.

A nurse on board is looking after my finger. She says it is healing fine. The McA's did not like the doctor, and told me not to go near him. I received a wireless from Will last night, and was terrified for fear it was from you. He just wished me a good voyage. Foolish boy to spend his money so carelessly. More to-morrow. Well here it is Friday, and I have not written. It was very rough, or at least we thought so, all day Wednesday and Thursday. Gladys, Queenie, Annie McA. and I stayed in our cabins most of the time. Everyone that stayed out felt rotten so we stayed in and now we feel the better of it.

I vomited enough, mother, to take all the bile up, so I know I shall feel heaps better when I get off.

The stewardess was very nice to us and all we gave her was 25 cents a day. She brought all our meals, and was very good to us.

To-day everyone is packing up, and to-night we see the coast of Ireland. It will be nice to be on land tomorrow about noon. We are going to the Compton House, Mut,[1] and I expect to be going like Joe. I hope there will be more people in the place. We are going to take side trips to Chester, Stratford, and a few other places. I shall write you full particulars about them later. We get to all those places for $2.50. Pretty cheap, don't you think?

There are some very nice people on board. A doctor and his wife who are off to China. She is just crazy about going — an artist and wife and little boy who have been out West painting in some of the swell houses. Then there is a very cheap bunch, which we don't have anything to do with.

We have no trouble at all with Ida and Annie along. No one ever thinks of bothering us.

I have been thinking of you all so much. Since I went down to my berth, I'm not homesick you know, but I just love to think about home.

They have good meals but not like ours home. It is just as Mut said — I had no idea what a sameness there is to everything. We are all up and doing to-day. The sea is smooth as glass. I am going to cable from Liverpool, and I hope you get it real soon. We were going to send a wireless from mid-ocean, but decided it was best to wait. Don't worry about us for the Mc.A's are lovely. They never leave us, and always help us out.

I shall write the very next opportunity, when I land and tell you everything. Finger is coming fine. Lots of love to every one of you,

Helen.

II

On board "S.S. LAURENTIC"
Sept. 5, 1913.

My dear Ones:-

Here we are on the last day of our trip, if all goes well. We have had a great trip but we shall all be glad to get on land again. Tuesday, Wednesday and Thursday were rough and we stayed low most

[1] The VanWart family were very prone to giving nicknames. "Mut" is Helen's brother William.

of the time. To-day everyone is on deck, and feeling fine — only just a little tired. So far everything has gone fine in our party. The McA's aren't too bad, and we have nice times. There are some lovely people on board. It is a great place to study people. We nick-named most of them, and you should hear some.

I would certainly love to see everyone of you to-day. I know how to pity you, being away as long as I have been. It is not homesickness, but I just feel as if something might happen father and mother before I get back. Before I never understood when you said that.

We expect to have a great trip through England. We get in Liverpool tomorrow at 2 p.m. then see it, and take in a few places between there and London. Then we will be in London a week.

I shall write you from London sure — and tell you the new styles. Do write me Anna I would love to get a letter[1]. For fear Mother doesn't send my address, here it is:

7 Ferdinand Rhode Strasse

Leipzig

Germany

Lots of love to you all, and hoping you are all well.

Helen

III

Compton Hotel
Church Street
Liverpool, England
Sat. night, Sept. 6

My dear Ones:-

Here is your little girl sitting up in bed in this gorgeous big hotel, writing, chewing gum, and thinking about you.

Such a day! I shall never, never forget it. It is twelve p.m. now and I must not write long, for we start at 8.35 for Stratford-on-Avon and we want some sleep. We are as fresh as can be, though, considering we have been on board ship a week.

We landed, and I hailed a Cook's man and he saw every single thing about our trunks for 1 shilling. He insured them and we will never see them again till we get to Leipzig. You should have seen them look when I did things up so businesslike. Some traveller you bet! We came up to Compton House and left our things, and went straight to Liverpool. Galleries — they are swell. And I am crazy about pictures, and bought a few postcards of the ones I liked best. I will write heaps about them when I get to London. We came back, got a swell dinner, and went to St. George's Hall and heard the organ, supposed to be one of best in the world. I can't describe it, it was great. Here is programme.

Edna, Gladys and I are all in one room. We just divide everything evenly among us and it is very cheap — much cheaper than if there were only 2 or 3. We are all keeping an account of every cent.

---

[1] Anna was Helen's older sister, married to George Massie and living in Edmonton, Alberta. They had two children, Bruce and Helen.

Telegrams:-"COMPTON."

Telephone 3032 ROYAL 3 LINES.

Twenty New Commercial Show Rooms.
Replete with every convenience.
ELECTRIC LIGHT, TELEPHONES.
ELECTRIC PASSENGER LIFT, WAITING ROOMS,
&c &c
Rooms range
in size from
24 FT X 17 FT
to
74 FT X 17 FT.

COMPTON HOTEL
Church Street.
LIVERPOOL

W. RUSSELL, Proprietor.

Overlooking the
Pro. Cathedral
Gardens.

Sat. night Sept. 6.

My dear Ones:

Here is your little girl sitting up in bed in this gorgeous big hotel, writing, chewing gum, and thinking about you.

Such a day! I shall never, never forget it. It is twelve P.M. now and I must not write long, for we start at 8.35 for Stratford-on-avon and we want some sleep. We are as fresh as can be, though, considering

Sept. 6th - from the Compton Hotel, Liverpool

(Mount Allison Archives, Lochhead Fonds, 8701.)

I cabled and do hope you get it all right. The others paid 1/3 — Edna and Gladys. We shall likely be in London to-morrow night and I shall write from there, then. I am dying to hear from you, and hear if you are all well. We had a great trip and don't feel a bit tired. I never realised what a trip I was going to have. It is all wonderful and you shall hear it all when I get a chance to write.

Night - night, and lots of love

Helen

IV

The Pemboro Hotel
4, Pembridge Square,
W. London, England
Sept. 8, 1913.

My dear People:-

Here I am in the largest city in the world, and I don't feel a bit queer about it — seems the most ordinary thing in the world. For, we have not been around any yet.

Yesterday morning Sunday, we were up bright and early, had a lovely breakfast at the "Compton" and had our grips wheeled down to the ferry. We had to go over the River Mersey to Birkenhead to catch the 8.35 train, Great Western Railway, for London.

The "Compton" cost us about $2 apiece for dinner, all night and breakfast. We decided that it would be best not to spend any more there. We expected to go to Chester and Stratford on our way to London. Then we figured out that it would be cheaper to come straight to London, and then make side trips, for it costs so much to have what few grips we have, carried from place to place.

We were on the train from 8.35 a.m. to 6 p.m. and really I never had such a lovely day in all my life. I shall never forget my first impression of England in my life. It is the prettiest place I ever saw, just one continuous garden. We went so slowly that we had time to take in all the sights.

First we had three Scotch ladies to tell us all the places. Then there were several gentlemen and young girls who pointed out the places of interest. I never saw such polite people in all my life. They are so much ahead of us. Mother I wish you could have seen the Welsh Hills. I thought so much of how you and father would have enjoyed the trip down. At noon we got some sandwiches for 2d. apiece, and we each had one. We lived on scenery the rest of the day

We saw where Sunlight soap is made, and where the man who owns the place keeps his workmen. He builds their houses and takes off their wages - he also gives worthy ones trips etc. It is called Port Sunlight. Chester is a dear old place. We had glimpses of its tower, cathedral and old walls. I can't begin to describe the small places we went through. Birmingham was passed. It is a manufacturing place, and there is dirt and poverty.

We came via Oxford and saw some of the Colleges. If we get time we are going to go up some day. The castles along the way were great, and the dear old ivy-grown houses, and bridges. In the distance we saw Windsor Castle, and it was lovely. We expect to go there too. Tell Emilie we went through Reading, and I did want to get out to see her sister but we only had about ten minutes there. If I get a chance I shall go up to see her, but don't see where the time is coming from. We saw an aerodrome up there too — my first glimpse of one.

At six we arrived at Paddington Station and took two taxis for Pemboro House. Well, we were sure surprised on arriving here, to find such a lovely place. We dressed for dinner and I wish you could have seen the styles. They were fine. The dinner was the best we have had since leaving. I had been longing for good home-made cooking, and this is certainly lovely.

Monday Night

Well, at dinner they gave me the long-looked for letter from Germany, and our worry may be at an end for Frau Pastor Bergner has a room and perhaps two for me. Isn't it great. My I was relieved. I needn't keep them if I don't like them she said, so that will suit me fine.

Last night Annie, Queenie and I slept in one bed. I mean in two single beds, drawn together. I let Edna sleep with Gladys. We just have to baby her. They moved a bed in to-night, into our room for Edna, so Gladys and I shall be together, at last. I like her fine. We have a perfect understanding, and I expect we shall get along alright. Edna is not like the rest of us in many ways, and we pity her, and try to help her. Mrs. Dr. Jones told May, she had been spoiled at home. I don't care as long as Gladys and I get along so well together.

We had a great sleep and lovely breakfast. Then, we took an omnibus, and went away down to Cheapside shopping. I just saw that lovely scarf for you and simply had to buy it. Don't you like it for $5.65. I bought a lovely pair of chamois gloves (washable, yellow) for about 60 cents ($1.25 home). I had to get a pair that would stretch to go on my finger. It feels fine now, and I feel sure I shall be able to play with it when I get there.

We looked all around and came home in the underground railway (called the Tube). We had a lovely lunch. Everything is cooked fine, or else my appetite is extraordinary. After lunch, we went in an omnibus to the Tower, and saw a good part of it. I just wish I had had Mut with me, instead of six old women. They just tag around and I can't see half I would if there were only two or three. I loved the tower though. They won't let you even take a hand-bag in there now, or a camera — would it be on account of the suffragettes?[1]

We came out and took a "tube" for Madame Tussaud's waxworks. They are great. I just wish you could see Captain Scott, and Smith of *Titanic*. We rushed through for we did not have much time left. Then took a tube, and got off at the wrong place, and had to walk quite a way home. We were nearly famished when we arrived home, and I ate longer than anyone. It has been a wonderful day and we are all tired out to-night, and expect to go to bed soon. Tomorrow we go to the Galleries, and I am so glad. I love pictures.

Really this letter is terrible for someone keeps running in every second, and I can't do anything, let alone write. Everything is so new, and wonderful that I can't tell you half of it yet. I love it all so much, and I want mother and father to come over to come back with me, and I can show you around everywhere. Wouldn't we have a great time? They are talking so much, I can't write any more, will write a decent letter tomorrow. Lots of love to you all.

Helen

---

[1] A glass case in the Jewel House of the Tower of London was smashed by suffragette Leonora Cohen in February 1913, to protest the Asquith government's failure to introduce universal suffrage.

V

Pemboro House
London England
Friday night
September 12, 1913

Dear People:-

We are back again at the Pemboro, and oh what a change from an Earl's palace. We thought this place was pretty swell till we went to "Battle"[1] yesterday morning. At eight-thirty a.m. we were all on our way to Ashburnham Place to spend the day with them and all night if we liked.[2] We were all rather shaky about it on the way out but the very moment we got out of the train, it all left us, and we never felt the least bit embarrassed all the rest of the time we were there. None of us ever had such a good time, or ever expect to again. It was a chance of a lifetime.

Lady A.[3] met us at the train with an immense wagonette with her footman and coachman.

We expected to see some small place along the road, and found instead that it took 1/2 an hour to drive to it, 7/8 of which was on their land.

It is perfect, in their property. You go through 3 or 4 lodges before you get near the place. There is one there that was built in 1535. They have 800 acres for their 300 deer, as you drive along through the most beautiful woods I ever saw. When you go over an old stone bridge (very picturesque) Ashburnham Place comes into view. It is grand. In front are immense terraces, just covered with flowers, and walks. There is a beautiful lake with an island in it, right in front of the house with six or seven swans sailing up and down, with boats and steps to go down. Everything is very old but kept in perfect repair, around the house. The butler opened the door, and Lady A. called his Lordship who welcomed us in the freest manner possible to his house. We felt so relieved.

Lady A. ushered us up the grand staircase to our rooms — such rooms. I couldn't begin to tell you about them. They are just like those rooms in an old castle you read about. One of our rooms was the one slept in by Mary (Queen) before she was Queen.[4] It was gorgeous. We all had dressing rooms and a maid to wait on us, every moment we were there. Well, we were stumped at the four-poster bed, and the furniture, but when we went to lunch we all went dumb — no words left to express our thoughts.

They had everything that you could imagine. Oh yes, before lunch, the Earl and Lady A. took us all through the gardens and conservatories. They have roses as thick as weeds, and the rarest trees in the world — even the Cedar of Lebanon. They have every fruit growing you could name — the best grapes I ever ate — twice as big as our Tokios — and purple — also, pineapples, melons, peaches, figs and any amount of pears.

The butlers, footmen and everything else were just like you read about. I can't begin to tell you

---

[1] A town in Sussex, near the site of the Battle of Hastings.

[2] Ashburnham Place, near Battle, was the seat of the Earls of Ashburnham. The house Helen saw had been rebuilt in the eighteenth century; it was mostly torn down in 1959 following severe damage from the crash of an Allied bomber during the Second World War..

[3] Lady Ashburnham was a Fredericton woman, Maria Anderson, married to Thomas Ashburnham, who became the sixth (and last) Earl of Ashburnham in 1913 following the death of his older brother, the fifth earl. She is now best remembered for her sister Lucy's mustard pickle recipe ("Lady Ashburnham's pickles") and for being the heroine of a Wodehouse-like romance: telephone operator marries earl's heir.

[4] Possibly Mary of Teck, who as wife of George V was Queen Consort at the time of Helen's visit to Britain.

about them. After lunch we went to the drawing room and had tea — such silver — oh dear! All afternoon we walked just as far as we could go, along beautiful walks, everyone walked that day, almost. There were springs in old stone houses, and seats just like the finest park you could imagine. At five we came back, and had afternoon tea in the small drawing room.

May, Edna and I then sneaked out, without bothering them, & went around another way, by their dear old private church — it is wonderful, so old — they don't know when it was built.

Dinner at seven — well I can't describe it. We had place-cards and bouquets at each place. It was just sweet. The house was just loaded down with flowers. We had our tea to drink in the huge library before an immense open fire. Then we played duets on a big German Grand Piano — swell one. At eleven we retired. Oh what a bed. It was so large that Edna, Gladys and I slept together. The maid brought us tea, bread & butter & fruit before we got up in the morning. We had breakfast at nine — partridges, rabbit pudding and dozens of other things. I couldn't name them all. After breakfast the two of them showed us every single room in the house — their family jewels, nurseries, dairies, kitchens, strong rooms, and the immense tower. Lady A. showed us all her clothes and told us the price of everything. I never heard of such hospitality. She told us all the cheap stores in London, and everything she could to help us. Her bedroom is done in scarlet satin, or perhaps a little darker than that. It has everything in it. They insisted we should stay till the four train, and at three the wagonette came and we all got in except Earl A. who gave us a hearty send-off, before we got in.

We drove down to Battle and visited Battle Abbey, a very historic place, now owned by an American millionaire — Mr. Grace. We were shown through most of it, in the short time we had, and it was lovely, but could not be compared with the Ashburnham Place. Lady A. tipped everyone who looked at us, and she stayed till the train came, the footman put our grip in and she tipped the porter 60 cents to give us a compartment all to ourselves.

We arrived home at 7.30 — had dinner, and here I am writing. I am writing in pencil for I want my pen for letters I have to write in ink — please excuse paper — my other is in my trunk. Well, we all said we were never used as well in our lives. I could never write it all to you.

When we were on the top of the tower we couldn't see the end of the estate as far as the eye could see in all directions was his land. It extended to the sea. There are 1200 people living on it. Everyone worships her and she fills her place wonderfully. The woman before her was a beast, and Lady A. took them all by storm. The head steward or butler told us there were light feet and happy voices around there now. He was a great old chap who had been with the family all his life.

The curtains in their small drawing room were $750 per window. They have two ornaments on one mantel which were $5000 apiece. All their furniture is mahogany and Chippendale — their house is lined with oil paintings. I am tired writing but will try to write more soon about it. We are all too sleepy to stay up any longer.

Lots of love,
Helen

VI

London, England
Sept. 14, 1913.
Sunday night

My Dear Ones:-

To-morrow night we sail for Holland, and I must write to you to-night for we shall be so busy all day to-morrow. We have been hustling ever since we came back from Ashburnham's. Could you tell anything from my last letter, of the lovely time we had? I was so tired the night I wrote it that I don't know whether you could read it or not. I shall never forget it, though, and you shall hear full particulars when I come back.

Yesterday we shopped most of the morning and saw a lot more of London at its busy time. My but the sights are wonderful.

May and I both bought big heavy blue kimonos (blanket) for $2.48 each. Wasn't that cheap? They are swell too. We had to have them for the rooms are so cold in the evenings, and you can't rush down to a kitchen stove. My black one is great for travelling and I wear it a lot, but I had to have a good warm one for winter.

Yesterday afternoon we went to the Tate Gallery[1] and it was splendid. I wish you could see the pictures. You would love them. We also went to Westminster Cathedral[2] — the one Will raved about. What do you suppose we found on a stone there but the following inscription

"Pray for the soul of Evelyn Francis Van Wart
 who dedicated this station."

Did you know we had Catholic in us? My but I was interested, but did not like to ask about it, for there wasn't anyone around.

To-day we went to Westminster Abbey to service, and then for a short time to St. Margaret's, where the King goes to church.[3] This afternoon we went to St. Paul's[4] and heard a lovely organ & choir. Then Gladys and I walked all around Kensington Gardens and the palace.

To-night I am writing, talking, laughing, all at the same time. To-morrow night we sail, and by three or four more days we shall be in Leipzig. I want to get there to get your mail for I am anxious to hear how you all are. I hope you and Kath got your parcels. I am sending one to Anna to-morrow. We are getting along fine. Don't worry.

Lots of love,
Helen

---

[1] Founded in 1897; at the time of Helen's visit the collection focused primarily on contemporary British art.
[2] A Roman Catholic cathedral, not to be confused with the Anglican Westminster Abbey.
[3] Located on the grounds of Westminster Abbey.
[4] St. Paul's Cathedral.

VII

Hotel des Pays-Bas
Amsterdam, Holland
Sept. 16, 1913.

My Dear People:-

We are in dear old Holland, and have had the best day yet — (with the exception of the day at Ashburnham's).

Last night at 8.35 we left London, after having had a great taxi ride to the station on Liverpool St. We were on the train one hour to Harwich, and went right from the train to the boat, to sail to the Hook of Holland.

It was a perfect moonlight night, and the lights of the city made quite an illumination. It was lovely.

We went right to our bunks (included in the ticket), and I thought they were fine, but the others grumbled all night about them. They were perfectly clean and we were all in one room, with two other nice ladies. I didn't undress but just took off my skirt and shoes, hat, collar, etc. As usual I slept all night and did not feel the motion of the boat one bit. It was rough too they said.

At 4 o'clock this morning they woke us, and said we were in Holland. We got ready quick, and all rushed out to catch the early train for The Hague. We caught the train and saw, on our way, the sunrise through the mist of the low-lands. It was simply perfect. We arrived in the Hague at about seven o'clock, and after checking our baggage, ran across a guide, who offered to take us all over the place till our train went at 1.35 p.m. for 1 guilder (40 cents) apiece.

We went first and got a cup of coffee and a roll. Then he took us out to Scheveningen, the great summer resort (in a street car). We saw a lot of beautiful places on the way out, and I can't describe Scheveningen. It is just like one of the beaches in the States I suppose. They had those basket chairs, and wagons to go down to bathe, and great big restaurants etc. The sand was just like flour and almost white. They were riding bicycles and everything on it. We bought two or three cards and small china shoes (4 cents) for souvenirs. Then we came back to Hague and went to the place where they change money. There we met a lovely American couple, who were travelling, and they joined our party. We then started for a tour of the city. He took us to St. Jacob's Church, where the Queen goes to church (we sat in the Royal Box), and there they have an organ with 5000 pipes. There were many interesting things about the church, which it would take years to write.

Then we started for the gallery, and as luck would have it, it was closed for the morning. The reason was that the city was crowded, for it was the day of the opening of parliament. We struck it lucky for it is about the only day that the peasants come in to the city in their native dresses. Then, Mut, we are up to you, for we saw the Queen.[1] She opened the parliament, and she drove in her golden coach, through the streets. I never saw such a crowd in my life. They were perched in every conceivable nook and corner. It was a great sight.

Before this, though, we saw the Queen's winter palace, and then went out and saw where the Queen is living now. It is called the House in the Wood, where the first Peace Conference was held in 1899.[2] It was beautiful there — lovely avenues of trees, and a lovely canal. Then at about eleven

---

[1] Queen Wilhelmina of the Netherlands reigned from 1890-1948.

[2] The Hague Convention of 1899, signed at the First Peace Conference, was an attempt to reach agreement on the laws of war and to ban certain types of attacks, such as poison gas and aerial bombing.

we went to a restaurant which the guide had arranged about. We had a good lunch for 60 cents (you know The Hague is the most expensive city in Holland).

We went from there to see the Queen, and we saw her pass down between the two rows of mounted guards, or police. Not a soul was allowed to cross the street for hours before the time. On our way to the train we saw where the Queen was to enter, at the Parliament buildings, and the guide told us all about everything. We went on a street car to the station & the guide went away for the afternoon with the American couple. They were lovely.

We caught the 1.30 express, and came to Amsterdam, and came up in the bus to Mut's hotel "Des Pays-Bas". It is very good. We have great rooms. McA's in one, and we three in another. All but Gladys and Annie McA. then started to see Amsterdam. They were tired and stayed here — don't catch me doing that — we took a street car to the celebrated Gallery, and saw all the lovely pictures — Rembrandt's 'Night Watch' and Maes' 'Silent Prayer', and heaps of other celebrated ones. On the way we saw a lot of the city. We don't leave till to-morrow at 11 a.m. so we expect to see a lot more. To-night we ate from 6.30 to 9 o'clock. I never ate as much in all my life. My but I love their grub — I guess the change is doing us good. We can't get enough to eat, and we had 8 courses to-night.

Tomorrow we go to Hilversum to meet May's friend. Then tomorrow night we go to Leipzig, getting there Thursday morning. We have rooms in several places, so we can decide when we get there just which one we want. To-night we have been settling up our accounts, and it is great fun. We get puzzled sometimes over the money, but figure it all out when we get to our rooms. Everything goes along fair and square and above board.

We all loved London and hated to leave Pemboro House. I could go there on my way back, alone, if I had to, for it is lovely and quiet. It is only $1.25 a day and it is a great place.

Now my dear ones, I am so tired, as you can imagine that I must drop into this lovely bed. I think about you all so much, and wish you were here with me to enjoy the lovely sights. I am going to try to improve my opportunity and give you the benefit of it when I get back.

Am so anxious to hear from you.

> Lots of love,
> Helen

VIII

> 4 Sophien Platz
> Leipzig, Germany
> Sept. 18, 1913.
> (Thursday night)

My Dear Ones:-

At last we have reached our destination, and are all settled as to our board, and now only have our music to see about. Let me go back and tell you all that I have been doing since I wrote you last, in Amsterdam. We were there Tuesday night. Wednesday morning we went shopping for a while and at 11.30 we took the carriage from the station to go to Hilversum. We loved Amsterdam but saw more of The Hague, for we had a good guide there. I like Scheveningen great.

Amsterdam is a very expensive place. It cost each of us $3.20 for hotel, and bus bill. The Pays-Bas is a good place though. Well it only took us about twenty minutes to get to Hilversum. It is the sweetest place we have seen. The people are a good deal like they are at Markem I guess. They go around in wooden shoes and their regular costumes, and we saw a regular "messa" (place where they sell everything, in the street).[1]

I saw a boat going up the canal at Amsterdam, just full of chambers, and not one covered up — my it was funny.

We wandered around Hilversum and had a hot time getting a little lunch but managed finally to get a good one for 15 cents. After that it started to rain and all but May and Ida started for the station. They went to see their friend. We didn't want to go for she was sick, and could not be excited. They only paid a very formal call. At four we left for Amersfoort where we went to get the express for Leipzig. We were all pretty tired, but when we got to Amersfoort, May, Ida and I started to see the place for we didn't leave the place till nine that night. The others don't care about anything else but eating, and writing letters. May & I get disgusted with them. They don't realise what they miss. I never missed one excursion in the whole trip, only the day I was in my bunk most of the time. I could stand any amount of going, and I have seen a lot.

Amersfoort is a quaint old place. We saw a boy delivering ice there, father, in a wicker basket, on a bicycle (everyone rides bicycles in Holland). The cakes were about a foot long and two inches wide, and two thick. It couldn't touch Earn and Fletch.

We left Amersfoort at nine and spent a pretty poor night. The customs officer came in at twelve and didn't open a thing. Then we found out we had to change cars at Hanover for here, at four in the morning. That meant not much time for sleeping, but I curled up like I always do and had a little snooze. We arrived in dear old Leipzig at about nine this morning. The McA's took a cab to their place, and we took one to the pension that I heard from. We had translated the German letter wrong, and she had said she had only one room, and that would be only till the first of October. Her flat was away up in the sky anyway. I hated it. There was a nice little girl there who spoke English and she told me about this pension on Sophien Platz. We thought we would take a look at it anyway, so came around, and asked for rooms. We were certainly lucky, and then Providence must have been with us, for it is a lovely place. She had several rooms but the cheap ones were mostly all gone. She speaks English and gave us all particulars. We have two other rooms for to-night, and to-morrow Gladys and I go to our dear little room with two beds, and Edna is right across the hall, in a much smaller room by herself.

It is much cheaper for Gladys and I to room together, and have our piano together. It costs us $26.40 per month including everything — light, fuel, and all except washing. If we were alone it would cost us over thirty apiece. We are scheming like everything to make the most of our money. We went down to McA's, and our trunks were there. They were just sent up here a little while ago, and everything is o.k. Weren't we lucky? We haven't paid the freight yet, but it was very reasonable.

McA's place is not nearly as nice as ours. They can't even have one piano in the house. They have to go out to practise in some shop or some such place. Their rooms are not half as nice as ours, and they expect to pay as much. They haven't heard yet.

We had a lovely dinner at 1.15 p.m. and then May, Ida, Queen and I went down to get some

---

[1] Probably her rendition of a Dutch word similar to *Messe*, German for a fair.

money to pay our board in advance, and our first term of music. They showed me how to find my way around and then came up, and approved of our rooms. They were very nice about it, and told us that they thought we can practise nine hours a day here, and it is a very quiet place. There are other conservatory girls here, or at least they are coming. We met a dear little girl who is to room next to us, and she is going to the Con. It opens next week some time, so we expect to get all settled and down to work in a day or two.

May and Gladys were both completely "all in" when they got here. Edna was tired but I am fine. I eat everything that comes along. They served afternoon tea and had a lovely supper to-night. I can't write you it all in one letter for there is so much to tell you. It will have to come out by degrees. We just want you to know we are very comfortable, and have good rooms (they are very scarce now).

To-morrow we are going to get our piano and get to work! I would love to see you all to-night, but I just make myself stop thinking about you, for I know what I have ahead of me, to accomplish.

I haven't had any letter from you yet, but expect to any day now. Did I give you my address? Jim wrote me and Brown, but that is all so far. I expect more to-morrow and would rather have a line from you than anyone else in the world.

Lots of love, Guten nacht![1]

Helen

P.S. These are some stamps I had left over and they will do for my letters. More Love Helen.

IX

c/o Fraulein Schröter
4 Sophien Platz
Leipzig, Germany.
Sept. 21, 1913.

My Dear Ones:-

If you could only step into our dear little room and see us this afternoon (Sunday), that is all that would be required. You would be so delighted that you would never think twice about us again. Since you can't step in, I shall have to tell you what you would see. Gladys and I have a room together and we have just measured the room with my tape line. It is approximately 20 by 12. Now isn't that some size? It has two large windows in it (as big as four of ours). The room is papered in a soft shade of old blue, and is very pretty. Then we each have a bed, which are like our cosy ones home, only much more comfortable. They have springs like Kath's cosy corner. At night (while we have supper at about 7 o'clock) the maid comes in and makes up the bed for the night. In the day time it is all fixed like a cosy corner, with a lovely blue cover to match the paper.

The floor is hard wood, (polished oak) inlaid like this (I am no artist). In the centre of the room is a lovely blue rug. We have two little tables in two corners of the room, with a large mirror over each. These we use for dressing tables. In front of the windows, stands our writing desk, and alongside of it a lovely upholstered arm chair (very comfy). Along one side of the room is a bureau with three

[1] Correctly *Gute Nacht*: German, "Good night".

drawers in it, then comes one bed, and our large washstand (marble topped, and we each have a commode set). It is curtained off with a curtain like yours in your bedroom Mother. Then comes our stove — a huge thing in the corner of the room, made of pale green tiles. It is a great ornament, to the room.

On the other side of the room, is our clothes cabinet (a large one, for two), a bed, and our dear little piano. Before I go further let me make a sketch to see if you can understand. Some artist! I couldn't draw how nice it is, for really it is too sweet for anything.

Now for prices — Gladys and I pay 110 marks apiece for this room ($26.40) per month. That includes fire, light (two lamps and candles) and our meals. Rooming alone it would cost us 120 marks apiece or 130. They have rooms at 150. 90 marks is the cheapest price allowed anywhere.

Edna has a little room, facing a dirty old yard, and she has to pay 105. You see she is alone.

Now for our pianos. We expected to make one do us, but we have decided that in order to get the most out of the year we had better each have one. Last night we settled about them. The fraulein (Fraulein Schröter) is going to allow us to use her piano in one of her rooms, for the nine hours we are allowed to practise each day, for 10 marks a month ($2.40) a month more. Then she is renting us her piano for 8 marks ($1.92) while we have to pay 10 marks ($2.40) for the one in this room. Our whole expenses apiece for one month, including all the above is $28.56. Isn't that great? We have figured till we are sick, and we think we have reached a pretty good price. The McAdams have to pay $28 apiece, and I wish you could see where they are. That does not include their pianos. They can't practise in their house at all. They have to go out to a shop or somewhere. We can play from 7 till 1 o'clock in the morning, and 3 till 7 at night. Then we can play pieces till ten at night.

It was the most wonderful thing I ever heard of that we got this place. Even the people are all lovely. We speak nothing but German at the table. My little that I got at college has helped me a lot. The other two girls do not know anything about the language.

We get up at any time from 7 till 10 in the morning. Our breakfast consists of rolls, marmalade, and fairly good coffee (not like Mother's, but as good as we have had since starting). We may have cocoa or tea.

At 1.15 we have dinner. I can't describe the lovely things we have to eat. Really everything is just like a first class hotel — soup, fish, two or three kinds of meat, riced potatoes, cabbage, cucumbers, cauliflower, and always some lovely dessert. To-day we had apples, peeled and cooked, soft just like apple sauce. Then a little hole was put in the top and a bit of jelly put in. They were lovely. We had small ducks (one apiece), with lovely dressing. There is lovely stuff to eat and plenty of it. The fraulein is lovely to us all. She kissed me yesterday and said she wanted to make us as comfortable as possible. Yesterday we practised most of the day. We are getting ready to play at the Con.[1] My finger is coming fine but I don't know whether I shall be able to play for a week for the professors. Everyone says they always give anyone time if they have a sore finger.

To-day we have had a glorious time. This morning we went to Eng. church — the McA's, we girls and Marjorie Woods (a girl from U.S.). She is a lovely girl and is going to study vocal at the Con. She is also an authoress. She has a girl friend Miss Moore, from the U.S. who gets her meals here and rooms somewhere else. They room separate so they will not speak English.

I will tell you about all the lovely people I meet in every letter. We liked the church of Eng. pretty well but think we will look up the Congregational church next Sunday.

This afternoon I have been trying to write this letter chiefly, but we have been having so many

[1] The Conservatory of Music in Leipzig was founded by Felix Mendelssohn in 1843. At the time Helen was studying there, it was the Royal Conservatory or *Königliches Konservatorium der Musik zu Leipzig*.

interruptions that I haven't accomplished it yet. We have just had a lovely afternoon tea out in the garden — tea, coffee and cake. It was lovely. Every afternoon they serve us afternoon tea in our rooms at 4 o'clock — nothing extra for it either. They give us tea buns, and 'zwieback' (a kind of toast). On our way home from church we saw 7 balloons in a race. They looked wonderful to me, but I refrained from displaying my ignorance on the subject. They were silver and gold in colour and would often disappear behind the clouds. It was a great sight. Every window was up and some old German stuck out gaping at them. We have seen the wonderful Zeppelin. It is a sight, and is the most wonderful thing I ever saw. It goes around here all the time. They have dining rooms and everything in them. It only costs 100 marks $24 an hour to sail around Leipzig in one of them. We expect to go every day or so, Ha! Ha! We have seen aeroplanes too, but the Zeppelin has got me.

I must not write any more now for you will be tired reading it, but everything is so wonderful, I can't stop telling you about it.

Leipzig is a beautiful city — lovely gardens, and the stores are as good as London. We merely look in the windows. There is only one thing I want to get before I come home and that is some of the Saxon lace for mother — it is terribly cheap and beautiful. I shall send you a small sample some day when I get time to go to the stores.

Oh yes I forgot to tell you that I may accompany Marjorie Woods 1/2 a day in her vocal work. That will give me some change for little things & be excellent practice. She wants me to but I haven't decided yet.

I go every day to see if there is any mail for me at McAdams' and I have only received one letter since I got here and that was from Jim Wathen. I can't imagine what is the matter, but suppose it will come soon. I know you have written but perhaps it has gone astray. Write to this address now and I shall get it in the morning at breakfast. (I would rather get a letter from home any time than eat). I know I shall get all my mail soon for I am going to the post-office to tell them to send all mine here. I must close. Hope you are all well, I can only pray for that.

Lots of love,
Helen

P.S. All my letters can't be as long as this or I will be up all night. Golden Rod out of the garden.

X

4 Sophien Platz
Leipzig, Germany
Sept. 25, 1913.
Thursday night.

My Dearest Mother:-

Just a short note to you before I go to bed. I never get one moment to write for there is something doing all the time. It is now ten o'clock, and we must be getting to bed, but I was bound to write you a note, so you would not have to go so long without a letter.

I wrote you last on Sunday, now I must tell you all the news since then. Monday night about six o'clock or after, May rushed up to tell us that the Con. pupils had to be registered that night before seven. Well we rushed down right off, and thought that we had to play the next morning, but we didn't have to till Wednesday morning.

Tuesday we practised a lot, and got all nerved up for the ordeal. At nine-thirty next morning we went down, shaking in our shoes and all the McA's were there at the door to listen to us. We all went up the winding stairs and sat at the big piano and played for four fat old Germans, and Teichmüller[1] who is a dear. He was very nice to us, and talked about our studies etc. He wants us to take some finishing touches with his head assistant for about a month, but we don't know anything definite yet.

I can take voice, Italian, Harmony, Theory, History and anything I like. It is going to be fine, and we are all tickled to death about it. Everyone says we are so fortunate to get the promise of going to Teich.

On Tuesday we go to get our time-table and find out full particulars. Till then we are preparing for our studies — at least I am. To-day I practised technique most of the morning. Then after dinner we always have a game of croquette in the garden at the back of the house, or rather in the courtyard, and then I did two solid hours of harmony, with a short break for afternoon tea. Then Marjorie Woods (a dear little U.S. girl who was in Paris all last year) and I went for a long walk, and my but it was lovely. The air was great and we did enjoy it so much. I have been working harmony and have accomplished a lot.

Now let me tell you about my appetite. I can't begin to get enough to eat. I am quite starving from morning till night, and yet I eat everything in sight almost, and not deprive anyone else. The girls say I am getting fat, and I can believe it for my corsets are getting too small. We have lovely things to eat, but my appetite is beyond everything. The cake and candy stores are very attractive here, but I haven't given in yet. If I started on those, I wouldn't have a cent, so I am not going to. When I see some good fruit (apples) I am going to buy two or three, but we are very economical, and are doing our best to get along cheaply.

We see the McA's every day or so, and they are very nice. I think Annie will be contented. May and Queen may take privately I guess, for they can't stay till the end of the year (only till April or May, I guess).

I wouldn't take private for then I wouldn't get any harmony or singing.

I am just dying to hear from you, and it will surely be time for a letter soon. I have only had my London letters so far, and one from Jim Wathen. I can't imagine why it takes so long. Perhaps you haven't received all of mine, but I have written quite a few, and you will get them in time.

I will write you full particulars as soon as I know them, and tell you more also about Leipzig. It is a great place and we like it fine. We are having a chance of a lifetime and I am learning German (the others say I am learning very quickly).

Lots of love, and hoping you are well.

Good Night
Helen

My finger is coming fine.

---

[1] Robert Teichmüller (1863-1939), one of the foremost piano teachers of the day, who had himself been a student of Carl Reinecke.

XI

4 Sophien Platz
Leipzig Germany
Sept. 29, 1913.

My Dearest People:-

How perfectly delighted I was to get your letter (mother) on Thursday and I was so sorry to hear about poor dear old Mut being sick. I was so worried about him, and am anxiously waiting for the next letter to come with the news. I do hope to hear from home, and I read the letters over and over, to be sure and not miss anything. I do hope you got all my letters, for they were rather lengthy and I wouldn't like you to miss any part of the trip. I didn't write yesterday for I wanted to wait till I had been to the Roadmans' so I could tell you all the news, and now how shall I begin.

I wrote Mrs. R. when I came (after I had played at the Con.) and she answered right off and asked me out to Halle on Sunday.[1]

She said Mr. R. would call for me in time to take the 3.10 p.m. train for Halle. I wrote back, and accepted with much pleasure, and so I was ready waiting at about two. He came clear in here from Halle, for me, and it is about an hour's ride (costs about 60 cents return). He is just great, and so young — simply a boy. I was taken so by surprise. We took a tram to the station and he was bound to pay even my ticket to Halle, but I refused to let him and bought my own ticket.

When we arrived in Halle Mrs. Roadman, Mr. Heber Harper, Mr. Tom Middleton, Baby Erline were all there to meet us. You can imagine how I felt meeting so many but it only lasted a second for they made me right at home in no time. Mrs. R. is young and I think she is beautiful — black hair and a lovely complexion. She can't be more than 25 at the most. The two boys are university students and are studying the same as Mr. Roadman, to be 'Methodist' ministers. I can't describe them to you — for they were so nice to me. I haven't words enough to express my opinion of them. We immediately started for a walk, and we saw the loveliest places — Halle has a population of about 172,000, and is a good deal like Leipzig. The river Salle is lovely — it is like our Nashwaaksis, only dirty. The trees are lovely along the banks though. Well, we walked on and saw the greatest old castle — in ruin — Moritzburg. I took a picture of it.

After a while we went back, and went up to their rooms — about four stories up — the top floor. They have four rooms and do their own light housekeeping. We had a lovely supper of ham (cold) some kind of a potato thing (hot). It was great. They had radishes, apple-sauce (home-made) and some kind of a jam and cake. Everything was lovely, and they were so free and easy. We had great fun.

In the evening we played the piano and sang and at 9.45 my train went, and what do you think — Mr. Harper came clear down here with me — and came almost to the door. I simply made him not come clear here, for I was so afraid he would miss his train and have to wait till morning. I arrived home at eleven, and I was very tired after such a lovely day. They are the best people I think I ever met, and they are so good. They are not a bit like Methodists, and are so fond of sport. They are having the time of their lives.

I am going to write Uncle Will all about them, for they will mean so much to me if I should want anyone. They want me to go over all the time but of course I can't spare the time. They are coming

---

[1] A city close to Leipzig. Mr. R. became Dr. Roadman, president of Dakota Wesleyan University and Morningside College.

in to Leipzig though for the day sometimes and I shall see them lots.

They are going to take a walking trip through the Thuringian forest next week, and Mrs. R. is going to Eisenach in the train to meet them, and she wants me to go too. Imagine! it would be a gorgeous trip and I shall go if I can arrange my lessons, at the Con. I won't neglect them for anything but it would certainly be a chance of a lifetime to go with them. That is where the Wartburg[1] is and we could go to Weimar (very near), and see the shrines of Goethe and Schiller[2]— I can't think about it because it all seems like a dream.

I learn so much every day, that it is hard to remember it all. These trips over in Germany are so full of interest. Every house has some historical interest. I read, and study, and try to know about everything and I feel myself broadening every day — you simply can't help it — the rough corners soon disappear, if you keep wide awake. Now let me tell you about going to church yesterday morning.

You know last Sunday we went to Church of England, so this time we thought we would look up the American church[3] (all churches which are protestant). It is held in a school building some distance from here and it is a lovely place. We went in and enjoyed the service but afterwards was the nice part. Everyone in the place came up and introduced themselves. All the Americans and Canadians go up there. We met a dear lady — Mrs. Frink and her two daughters from Montreal, who are keeping house here — they asked us to come see them. Then I met a girl who knew a Mrs. Malcolm from Moncton whom I have met. Then everyone was so nice that we are going there. It is just like the Presbyterian service and the man is a good speaker.

Saturday we had a great treat in hearing the Boy Choir at the Thomas Kirche (Bach's church).[4] They sing every Saturday at 1.30 — no admission. The place is packed. Just think how much the Germans appreciate music. All the businessmen and everyone were there. The boys were from four to twelve years old. They beat the St. James Cathedral choir even.

Oh this is a great place — we like it fine. We play croquette all quiet hours 1-- 3 and have heaps of fun. I am going to do some work after to-morrow, when we get our time-table. I shall write you all about it. Oh I forgot to tell you there are two couples here from Edmonton — one of them has heard of George[5]— more particulars when I get a moment.

Lots of love,
Helen

---

[1] An eleventh-century castle; in 1521-1522 Martin Luther found refuge there after his excommunication by Leo X, and during that time completed his German translation of the New Testament, thus making the Wartburg an important site in Protestant history.

[2] Johann Wolfgang von Goethe (1749-1832), German writer and thinker, author of *The Sorrows of Young Werther* and *Faust*; Johann Christoph Friedrich von Schiller (1759-1805), German poet, playwright, and philosopher.

[3] American-British Evangelical Union Church.

[4] Johann Sebastian Bach (1685-1750) was choir director at the Thomaskirche from 1723 to 1750, and is buried there; the famous boys' choir, the *Thomanerchor*, was founded in 1212.

[5] Helen's brother-in-law, George Massie of Edmonton.

XII

4 Sophien Platz
Leipzig, Germany
Oct. 2, 1913.

My Dear Ones:-

Here it is Friday night, and I have not written your mid-week letter yet. I have been waiting till I got my work planned out, before I wrote, so that I would have some idea of what to tell you.

This week we were given our time-tables from the Con. They had me down for two lessons a week in each of the following — piano, voice, harmony, and Italian. I was tickled to death about it, and was so glad that I could take so much. Gladys and I had about the same time-table. Edna wasn't going to take voice.

Our first lessons were on Wednesday — singing — from 5-6 in afternoon. Gladys and I went down and took our songs to sing, and an old man wobbled into the room, and couldn't speak one word of English. He heard us sing but could not say a word about it, but smiled very sweetly. He called the secretary in, and they jabbered away for ever so long, and then the secretary told us that we must learn German before we could take from this man, and that the other voice teacher (the best they have) who could speak English, had not a place left, especially for beginners.

We were pretty sore about it, and went out and walked off our feelings before supper. Next day, Thursday, I went to my piano teacher, Fraulein Lutz Huzögh, Tiech's head lady (she told me May was her pupil and May never told us she had to go to her first, did she?). She was lovely to me, and said I had lots of feeling and temperament. She didn't tell the other two girls one thing. She said one could get technique by practice, but never the temperament. She asked me all about my name — whether I was Dutch or not, and was lovely to me. I was tickled to death about it all. Then in the afternoon we three went to our harmony lessons to Herr Prof. Schreck[1] and he was also great. Both he and the piano teacher speak perfect English. The piano teacher's mother was an American and her father a Swede, so she speaks English. The harmony man's wife is English so he speaks well.

We are well settled about that part of the work, and I have started in well by practising 4 1/2 hours to-day, besides being out twice, away over the town.

Really I have so much to write that I can't scratch fast enough. Now about the voice — I have been enquiring ever since we couldn't go to the Conservatory about teachers. They said we could enter the Con. at Christmas but we didn't want to do that, for you couldn't get anything in one term, and then we would have to conquer German, and then it is hard to study when you might not understand what the man was talking about.

We have met the loveliest Americans here,— a family — mother, father & daughter — Paull is their name. Anyway the father is a composer.[2] He wrote "Ben Hur's Chariot Race", and such pieces. They made great hits in their day. He has written a piece which is to be played at the great celebration here on Oct. 8th at the unveiling of the great monument in memory of the battle of Leipzig 1813. They are great authorities on music, and they have told me of a great vocal teacher here whom Miss Paull took from — Mrs. Alves. She is a New York lady, and is a concert singer. She

---

[1] Gustav Ernst Schreck (1849-1918), composer and choir director of the Thomaskirche Boys' Choir from 1893-1918.
[2] E.T. Paull (1858-1924), American composer and music publisher.

is wonderful, and I wish you could hear Miss Paull sing.

I have met two or three other Americans who take from her and Canadians. A Mrs. Hawkins told me she was the best they could find. She and her daughter have been in Paris and everywhere so they ought to know. Fraulein Schröter has been in our room all evening and she says she is splendid. Well to-day Miss Paull took me up to sing for her, and see if I had a voice. She was very plain spoken (is that a word) about it, and said I had a very sweet voice, and if it was trained properly it would be wonderful, she thought. Of course she said it was impossible to tell just at once but by a month's time she would be able to tell me for sure. She said I was very musical, and enunciated as well as any trained singer. She said I wouldn't have to learn that. I told her I would take for a month and write home to you and ask your opinion, and if you wanted me to, I would keep on. You see in the meantime I can look around. She is worth trying anyway, and I am sure my voice will turn out alright for I am not one bit nervous about singing.

Mrs. Alves has beautiful apartments, and just looks after every one of the pupils. Her daughter is beautiful and I heard her sing this morning. She has a great voice. Then her son teaches her method in New York, and if I wanted it, I could go there when I come back. She expects to go back herself in a year or two. Now for prices — which is the main thing — she charges about $7 an hour lesson. Now I planned on taking a half hour lesson, which we figured out, would cost me $3.25 — the other is not quite seven, and then I would only take one lesson a week. That is only $12.75 a month, and they say that in 6 months you would never know your voice. She was so delighted with my voice that I do want to have it trained. Now I am going to deny myself everything to do it, and come home steerage to do it if you think we can afford.

Now I want you to sit right down and write me, for I shall stop immediately if you think it too much, and not be a bit disappointed. It will mean the addition of $100 to my year, at the most, and I shall do it on the least possible price, and economise in any other way. I haven't bought one cent's worth of candies or cake since I have been here, and I am conquering my appetite. We get good wholesome food and everyone says I am getting fat — the McA's especially say so. They come up to see us often, and are very nice. They are advising us all to take vocal, if we can. Gladys does not think she can afford it, but I think Edna will take when she gets around to it, but she has no voice. My but I'm glad I had musical ancestors. You see both teachers have told me the same thing. Now I am not going to give up my piano for anything till I see how my voice pans out, but it is a way ahead of piano. The girls here just rave over this teacher and they all sing well. She said I could stop any time, and she always gives her pupils over half an hour if she is interested in them. Miss Paull says the Germans as a people have no voices. They are so mechanical. They tell me that the teachers at the Con. ruin voices, for they don't have time to put on them. Everyone takes privately in voice and piano at the Con. We are going to get after Teich. and we are almost sure to get him soon. His assistant is splendid though and we all love her.

I am so anxious to hear from you. I have only had one letter since I left home and I am sure I have written dozens. It is five to eleven now, and we must get to bed. I am always the first down to breakfast now. It is served at seven — earliest, and any time after between then and ten. I go down about 7.15 or 7.30, and then we are ready for practice at 8, which is the earliest we can play. I have an account sheet all made out for you of my trip, but this letter is too big to send it in. Next time I shall! I am speaking German fine they say.

Guten Nacht,
Helen

View from the Wartburg

(Mount Allison Archives, Lochhead Fonds, 8701.)

XIII

c/o Pension Schröter
4 Sophien Platz
Leipzig, Germany
Oct. 5, 1913.

My dearest Anna and George:-

    You must think I am a very careless creature not to have written to you before, but really I have never had a chance. By the time I write home, my hands are tired for I write regular Mumsey Magazines to them, and I told mother to send them all on to you so that the letters were as much for you as for anyone. I hope she has done so, and I also hope that you have received the box I sent from London. Such a time as I had getting that box ready. It just got off and that was all, for we were on the go all the time, and I didn't have time to choose a thing. The blue smock dress and Baby Bonnet came from Peter Robinson's. That is the swell store, but everything is so expensive there. Those were the only two things I bought and I thought they were sweet, if you only get them and in good condition. I racked my brains for something for Bruce, the last day I had to get the box off, and we had to go home before I could get anything. I was so disappointed, and I am sure he would be, but under the circumstances I did not have a chance to get him a thing. But just the same I bought him something in Amsterdam which will arrive in time for Santa I hope, and you tell him, I waited to let Santa take it to him.

    Well we did have a great trip over, and had various experiences, which I could never write in years. Our trip to Ashburnham was wonderful and you have no doubt read about it in my letter. Then in Holland we rushed things terribly to see all we could, and in the shortest time. It was a great disappointment to me not to be with a party who were true sports. Someone was always tired or didn't want to do this or that, or could not afford to. We did not see half as much or quarter as if there had been only two and one of those had been some of your own.

The McA's were very nice, and always treated us squarely, but they were afraid to do this, or go there, and the rest had to abide by the consequences. Imagine! we were in London a week and not out one night. They were also afraid to go on the tops of the buses, and you know that is the only way to see London. We did have an excellent opportunity in being with them though, for the trip for me was perfectly safe and never had to worry about that. Now I would not be afraid to travel anywhere alone, no matter if I didn't know the language. It is very simple to what I expected. If George could only have seen us when we were "seeing London" and seen Ida running away from the vehicles, he would have died. Whenever a car would honk a block away, she would start to run. Honestly I never shall forget it as long as I live. The other girls noticed it too. We three are thanking Providence though that we are here together in this lovely pension, together, and we don't have to bother about them at all. They are very nice to us and we are so much better friends than if we were with them. I couldn't stand it a day. Queen Tabor is just another McA.

We have lovely people here in this pension, and they are from every country. It gives one a great insight into the different nationalities of the world. We have Russian, Mexican, Jew, English, at least eight Americans, and lots of Germans and even a Roumanian. They are all nice. Our Fraulein is the sweetest woman. She is very educated, and is giving me German lessons. She speaks French and English just as well as German. I am learning German very quickly they say for I had a foundation in it at College. Gladys and I have a dear room. I wish you could see it. In front of me on that desk is that little silver frame which Louise Neales gave me with May's little picture in it. You know the one with the over-alls on. Everyone just raves about it, and I simply put it in that frame. One person said it certainly should be enlarged. Now I want you to either have a family group taken or else a separate picture of each, for I just long for a look at you all. It is very hard for me to be away from you all, and I do think about you, and talk so much about our good times together. It all seems a dream that I am over here, and so much to enjoy, and see and the wonderful privilege it is. Every moment I learn something new, and I can't seem to take it all in. The days aren't half long enough, and we work or go sight-seeing all the time.

We are pretty well settled as to our music — 2 lessons a week in piano and harmony and one a week in voice. I am so encouraged about the latter — for she (my teacher) said I had a wonderful chance if I only knew it. Everyone raves about her here, and I am so elated about her opinion. Would you drop your piano or make it secondary for your voice, if it turns out to be good? Please write me and give me your opinion for I am being perplexed about it.

I shall not tell you about my trip to Halle and the Roadmans, for it would take years. I know mother will send you the letter. We are going to Eisenach and Weimar[1] next week though, and I am just wild about them and it all. They can't do enough for me, and they are so kind. The two young men who are with them, all the time, are so nice too. They were in Leipzig yesterday, and came to see me. The men are going to start earlier for Eisenach and walk through the Thuringian Vald.[2] Mrs. R. and I are to go in the train and meet them at Eisenach. That is where the Wartburg is and in

---

[1] The small city of Weimar was, in the nineteenth century, a great cultural centre of Germany.

[2] Correctly, the *Thüringer Wald*, or Thuringian Forest, a region of low mountains. Helen's German is sometimes phonetic: "vald" for *Wald*, etc.

Weimar are the shrines of Goethe and Schiller and lots of other interesting things.

Really Anna & George this is the most uninteresting letter I ever wrote. I have been interrupted I am sure a dozen times. We have been down to afternoon tea and then everyone comes in whenever they wish. We visit each other's rooms all the time. It is a dull afternoon and everyone is playing and singing, so you can imagine how much I can think.

I do want you to write me. I have only had one letter from home, and have been gone so long, and Mut sick and Kath receiving,[1] and that you were well, is all the news I have. I can't imagine why I haven't heard. I just watch the mails and would give anything to hear from you, even a short note. You know how one feels away from their relations. I shall try to write as often as I can and I know you will get mother's letters. I want to send you so many things, they are so cheap but I want to know if you got the other box first.

Lots of love to you all,

Old Gum Chewer

P.S. Be sure and put 5 cent stamp on. I have done nothing but pay excess postage and am almost bankrupt. Ha! Ha!

XIV

4 Sophien Platz
Leipzig, Germany
Thursday night,
Oct. 7, 1913.

My Dear Ones:-

I am sitting here in my blue (heavy) bath-robe at 10.30 o'clock writing to you. I simply must write now for dear knows when I shall get a chance to write for a few days. There is so much to do & see that we can't begin to do it all in one day, and have to sit up later than I like.

To-night we heard our first great pianist — Wilhelm Backhaus.[2] He is supposed to have the best technique in the world. Oh I can't describe him to you. He played wonderfully. We all sat enraptured. Our seats were in the gallery and four rows back. There was not a very big crowd so we moved up and Gladys and I were in the very front seat and could see him fine. Mind you our seats only cost us a quarter. Did you ever hear of such a thing? In America we would pay $5 a seat.

We are all inspired by his technique and expect to get to work at our poor little fingers. He played Liszt's Second Rhapsody, and it was fine — May and I have played it so often. They were with us and liked it great.

The people were wild about him. They rushed up and clapped after it was all over, and stood around the stage till he simply had to come back again. He is going to America soon, to tour, and I

---

[3] Receiving visitors as a new bride. Kathleen Hatt had married Helen's brother William (Mut) on Aug. 6, 1913.

[4] Wilhelm Backhaus (1884-1969), known particularly for his interpretations of Beethoven and Brahms. An admirer of Hitler, he was appointed *Reichskultursenator*, or Reich cultural senator, in 1938.

Wilhelm Backhaus (souvenir postcard)
(Collection of the Lochhead Family)

bet they will pay to hear him. We can't realise our opportunities here and it is all so cheap (except voice).

Well to-day I had my first voice lesson. Mrs. Alves was great. She told me how to stand, breathe and walk, and gave me almost an hour lesson, for a half hour. I am sure I can do something with my voice, and it will be so nice to have. I am not going to drop piano — don't worry. After tonight I made up my mind about that, but I do want my voice trained.

(Note) I made a mistake and wrote on the other paper & hope you can read it all.

I never spend on anything that isn't of some profit to me so don't worry. I am going to try to find a cheaper pension if I can get good food. That is the main thing here. I never ate as much in my life — Mother — not even in Edmonton. I simply eat everything on the table, and nothing between times.

I am taking two or three German lessons from Fraulein Schröter. They are 25 cents and I am getting along famously. Everyone must have German here in order to live, and then I must have it for voice. After I get my German I can do Italian easily. My French helps me a lot.

Gladys and Edna are not taking lessons and they are making the mistake of their lives — everyone says so here — but they know best.

There is so little time for one to get all there is to be had here in Germany that one can't waste a second. The girls stay downstairs and play silly games but I dig right up here, and am going to do it too, all winter, unless I find it too much.

Edna and I expect to take advanced harmony. We are going to-morrow to take a lesson & see if it is too hard for us. We have a great teacher and just get along fine — He is in the Con. you know. We will get then four lessons a week in harmony and two in piano. That is enough for that place — we get our money's worth. The voice is different, one must have the best for it.

I have reckoned and I can't see how my expenses will be more than $600 for the year. I do

Wartburg Castle: Earl & Irma Roadman, Heber Harper, Helen, Tom Middleton.
(Mount Allison Archives, Lochhead Fonds, 8701.)

nothing but figure all the time for I won't waste a cent. I want to go to the best concerts and operas and certainly won't deny myself of the things I need, but I just want you to know that I am doing my best to get all I can.

I had a letter from Mrs. Roadman about going to Eisenach. The men have started on their walk through the Thuringian vald (forest). We are to meet them Thursday night or rather Friday morning and spend Friday and Saturday in Eisenach and Weimar. They are two of the wonders of Germany, so I must see them. The Roadmans are so nice to go with — and the other boys are great — real good boys.

Mother, dear, I got your letter yesterday. I was never so glad about anything as I was to get it. It is the second I have had from you. I also had a corker from Earle — and Jim, and I hear from all the others but they are not you. I am so glad you enjoyed Mrs. C. and Gladys and that you are having people in to see you, and keep you from being lonesome. Really, mother, it is such an opportunity for me, that you must not worry. I am situated perfectly and everything is running smoothly. The girls here are lovely — especially Mrs. Paull. She has invited me to her home in New York and they have a small cottage in Maine. I think they are very wealthy but she never brags. She has opened my eyes to lots of things and it is great to know about things and not have to find out by experience.

Now my clothes are fine. I wear them till they are simply black, and I have never had one white waist[1] on since I came here. My suits are fine and my sailor-suit is so sweet. It is getting tight for me, but all my clothes are. I am much fatter.

Tell Kath I got her letter and tell her to put 5 cents on next time or I shall get after her. I have had to pay so much extra postage that I am nearly broke. I am so glad she had so many callers. I hope Mut is all well again, and that his little house is sweeter than ever. Mut I would drop in a faint if you wrote me a letter. Please do, and tell me about Celia (poor thing!) and how is my boy Micy-Mic? I get so lonesome to see him, and the cat.

I met a swell engineer on the *Laurentic*. He was 5th engineer of the boat, and he has written to me. I am going to send him some snaps I took on board, and he is going to send me some of the West Indies. It is funny who you meet over here. He was very nice.

Now I must get to bed for it is after eleven, and I am sleepy. I could write to you for hours more, but must get some sleep. I hope you get the scarf. If not let me know and I think I can get it by getting the man at the Pemboro to see about it.

Please remember me to everyone. I haven't a moment to write. Tell them all I am so busy.

Heaps of love to everyone of you,

Helen

XV

4 Sophien Platz
Leipzig, Germany
Oct. 12, 1913.
Sunday afternoon

My Dearest Mother, Father, Anna, George, Mut, and Kath, and any other members of my family who may be interested, such as Baby Doll or Mic:-

I shall guarantee to interest every one of you with my tale.

It is Sunday afternoon and I am back in Leipzig after having had the most enjoyable trip of my life. It is all a dream to me yet, and I hardly know how to write you about it, but shall do my best to remember at least the principal things we saw.

I was very loth to leave my lessons to go on a pleasure trip but I arranged them perfectly and only missed one harmony lesson, which was an extra one I am taking besides my regular course. Edna took my exercise, and she is going to give me all the notes, so I haven't missed one thing, and have learned more than I could write you in a year.

On Thursday night at 6 I went all by myself to the station, bought my ticket and started for Halle. I didn't tell Mrs. R. (Irma) that I was coming for the boys were not home, and she would have had to have left her baby to come meet me. I asked people (in German) anything I wanted to know, and arrived there at about seven. Then I found a cab and drove up to their home. Irma was tickled to death to see me, and we started right away to get ready to start early next morning to meet the boys in Eisenach. I went to Halle that night so we would be sure to connect in the morning. That night

---

[1] "shirtwaist", i.e. blouse.

we were out walking and I saw a lot more of Halle. At eight the next morning we two started out for Eisenach, and had a great time getting there. We did not know we had to change at Naumburg and when we got out of the car we didn't get right on the other car, and before we knew it was our car, it went off. We had to wait a half hour, and then go on. We felt so foolish about it, but mind you the boys had missed their train then when they went through. At twelve we arrived in Eisenach and were met by the three boys, whom I must call by their first names, Earle, Heber (Harper), & Tom (Middleton). We were very glad to see them I can tell you.

They took us to the best hotel I was ever at for the money. It was very cheap, but just now let me tell you that Mr. R. paid everything for me, and I am to pay him, so you won't be able to know till I hear from him. I never knew such kindness. They won't let me pay for hardly anything I know, and I am going to insist.

Well we went up and had our dinner, which only cost us about 35 cents, and we had everything you could name for that. We started right away for the Wartburg castle, and really, I can't begin in any way to describe it to you. It is an old castle built in 1070, and was where Luther was confined for 10 months and where he translated the Bible. We saw his room and all the relics of his time. The view from every window in the castle was superb. The surrounding hills were in autumn colours, and we could see for hundreds of miles.

There are beautiful paintings and the stories of them are very interesting. I have the cards of them and a little book in German, which I am going to read telling all the stories. There is much about it concerning Wagner's opera, *Tannhauser*, and you can imagine how interested I was. Earle & Tom are making a special study of Luther, and we have learned so much about the great reformer. After we had spent about an hour or so in this most delightful of places we left for a walk around the forests surrounding the mountain. It started to rain but the boys put their coats on us, and we never felt the wet. I had my old summer hat on, and could not have hurt it anyway.

We climbed over rocks and every old place, and had heaps of fun, then as we were trying to find a certain good view-point we lost our way and wandered considerably through the loveliest woods you ever saw. Finally we struck a street and went down to get pictures of what we saw. I have some beautiful cards but think I had better keep them to show you when I get home so that they won't get broken. Irma and I are going to write on the back of each one, what we saw and all about it so you shall hear it all when I come back.

On our way home we saw the house where Bach lived, and his monument. Then we went to the old Luther house where he stayed with Frau Cotta for so many years. It is a dear old place, and we heard that lovely hymn that Luther wrote 'A safe strong-hold our God is still' played on a beautiful instrument something like a piano with bells. We enjoyed that place so much, then we went back to the hotel at about eight, and the man gave us a room all by ourselves for the evening and we had our supper and a piano to play on. I played and Irma and the boys sang. Irma had bought a box of home-made fudge and some dear little cakes. We never had such an evening in our lives, and could hardly go to bed, tired as we were. Next morning we were up bright and early, had a light breakfast, and caught the eight train for Erfurt & the boys planned every single thing for us (Oh, by the way, I forgot to say that the night before that Mrs. R. and I had a room together, and the boys had two rooms between them). Well, I thought that pretty nice of them, don't you, for Irma had not seen Earle for a week. You know the boys walked through the Thuringian Forest, and they said it was perfect.

Well before we came to Erfurt[1] the boys had planned everything, and we just felt so easy, and

---

[1] Now the capital city of the German state of Thuringia.

enjoyed it all. We went from the station to see the oldest church in Erfurt. There we saw a communion set worth $7000 and solid gold. It was very fine. They were getting ready for a wedding and they had so many preparations to get ready. Well yesterday in our travels we saw where there were five weddings, and we wondered why we saw so many. It seems that Sat. is the day for weddings here.

Then we went to the great cathedral which is very noted. We climbed away up to the tower and such a view — we saw the immense bell that it takes ten men to ring.[1] It is very old, about a dozen of us stood under it. The inside of the cathedral is great. The altar is made of wood, but you would swear it was marble. The windows and paintings were great.

We saw the immense market and I do wish father could have seen it. It was in an open square, and there were only women — poor and with such heavy loads on their backs. Really we Americans have no idea of work and hardship.

We then visited an old picturesque inn where Luther, Gustavus Adolphus, & numerous others stayed.[2] They were having an auction there, and stared at us some, I can tell you.

We had a good cheap dinner, and then went to the Augustinian monastery where Luther stayed for so long. It was very interesting. I am going to work up Luther's life well for it is so nice to know, after seeing all the places.

We just caught our train to Weimar by two minutes, and arrived there at three o'clock. We were all getting tired and just fooled along for a while, and had great fun. We saw, while walking around, a big monoplane. It was the most wonderful thing imaginable, and was just like a bug in shape and the sound made you all the more certain. It had two wings, a tail and a thing like a head and it just flew, and buzzed. Anyone who had never heard of a monoplane would swear it was a bug.

We strolled through the dear old city, and loved it more all the time. The roses were still in bloom, and the finest pansies I ever saw — whole beds of pure white ones — just as good as if it was July. We went on, and went up to the house where Liszt lived for so long, and I said I didn't care about going in for I didn't like to take the others in for it cost 50 pfgs (12¢) to go in. I took a picture of it, and said I didn't mind about going in. Anyway, we went on down to the Goethe house and saw it, and when we came out Heber said that I simply had to go back to the Liszt house and go in.[3] He said he knew I wanted to go in. I said I didn't mind but they all said I must go. People, I shall never forget that place as long as I live. It was the best treat we have had. We went to his work room, and there was his piano. Heber asked if I might play and the lady said "yes", so I played. It was wonderful to think of it but sacrilegious of me to play on his piano. We saw all his gifts from all the kings, etc., and the old lady who keeps the house was his young servant when he was alive. She told us all about him, and we felt so nice and easy in his dear room, in comparison with the grand cathedral. Heber was so thoughtful I thought to think of taking me back. We went then to see the Schiller house and then to the Grand Palace, where we met the others. We could not go in it, for we were too late, but we all walked around the place, and saw the park, and river and everything was one mass of colour. I don't wonder what Goethe and Schiller and Liszt became wonders there.

We strolled around till I was simply struck dumb with Weimar. In fact we all were. About six o'clock we discovered a dear little restaurant and ate a hurried meal of omelette and coffee. We

[2] The cathedral in Erfurt is famous for its bells; the largest is the Maria Gloriosa, cast in 1497 and weighing 11,450 kilograms.

[3] Martin Luther (1483-1546) sparked the Protestant Reformation with his writings. Gustavus Aldolphus, King Gustav II of Sweden (1594-1632), was one of the leading generals of the Thirty Years' War and a champion of Lutheranism.

[4] Franz Liszt (1811-1886) lived and composed in Weimar from 1848 to 1861.

rushed like everything and got the train. When we arrived in the train we were nearly dead, and could hardly keep awake. In about an hour we were in Halle, and they wanted me to stay all night, but I would not for I knew it would bother them.

I simply fought to go alone to Leipzig for it was about nine o'clock. I was not a bit afraid for I only had a short distance to go before I got my car, and I knew just how to go. Well, just as it was time to go Heber insisted on coming for he said it wasn't safe for me to go alone — and mind you he came clear over here to my very door with me. Poor man he must have been very tired when he arrived back in Halle, sometime the next morning.

We all said it was the most perfect day of our lives, and to-day I am simply dazed with it all. I can't describe it to you for it is beyond words. When I arrived home simply in the seventh heaven (except for being tired), I found six letters awaiting me from Mother, Mut, Myrtle, Art Taylor, Jim and Will. I was simply exhausted with so many nice things, and did not get through them all for hours. I loved both of your letters so much — please write it is so nice to get letters.

Now don't think I am going to keep up this excitement for I am settled down now for a hard fight to do something in music. I heard a girl sing in church this morning (one of Mrs. Alves's pupils) and it was splendid. I am sure my voice will be good when trained.

The Roadmans and the two boys were so nice to me that I shall never forget them. They have done everything that any human being could do for another person. They are very educated and refined, and I have learned so many good things from them. We may go other places together in the holidays and I shall go if possible. We travelled 4th class when possible and went as cheaply as possible. I shall send you the accounts later. I have every cent paid out for something worth while. I

Liszt's House in Weimar, photographed by Helen on her trip with the Roadmans.
(She was allowed to play on Liszt's own piano.)
(Mount Allison Archives, Lochhead Fonds, 8701.)

have had a terrible time writing this letter & it has taken all afternoon for someone has been rushing in to see me every moment. Please excuse mistakes and I shall tell you everything when I see you for I am going to write it all down before I forget.

Lots of love to every one of you, hope you are all well.

Helen

XVI

4 Sophien Platz
Leipzig, Germany
Sunday afternoon
Oct. 19, 1913.

My Dearest Home Ones:-

Here is another Sunday and I haven't a letter written to you for a whole week. Well I really think it has been the busiest week of my whole life. I haven't written a line to a soul since Tuesday except to Irma Roadman. Now I have to condense my news as much as possible for I have hundreds of letters to write, and cards to send, to those I haven't time to write to. I have an hour and a half now till four o'clock when we are all going out to see the wonderful denkmal, which was officially opened yesterday. Now for my busy week.

Monday I worked like everything. Had my two lessons as usual, and in the evening worked also at Harmony, and German. By the way, they all say I am going to speak very quickly.

Tuesday I had a singing lesson, and made out fine. She encouraged me very much, and I can feel my chest expanding so much and my tones are much better. That was only my second lesson.

That night we heard Frederick Lamond, the great Beethoven player, in the Kaufhaus (concert hall). It only cost 35 cents (ground floor). He was Scotch, and played with much interpretation.

Wednesday, the dreams of my life were fulfilled. I saw my first opera. It was *La Tosca* by Puccini.[1] I just can't describe it to you. The best tenor in Germany took the leading role, and the best lady singer in Leipzig took the part of Tosca. The orchestra was wonderful. My but we were in our seventh heaven, which was almost true for we were in the fourth gallery, and right next the ceiling. Gladys, Edna, Miss Paull, and I went to it, and sat in the cheapest seats (80 pfennigs — 20 cents)— just what we pay for a moving picture show. I am going in those seats always so that I can hear all the operas.

I am writing all the stories of the operas I see, in a book, and will be able to tell you about them when I come back.

Thursday night Gladys, Edna and I were invited to Mrs. Flint's apartments for the evening. She is a Canadian lady from Montreal. She has two daughters and they have been here for five years, and expect to go home next year. There we met the minister Mr. MacHatton again, and also a Miss McKenzie, who is Mrs. Alves' pupil, and sings nicely. They gave us lovely cocoa, sandwiches, "home" made brown bread, and lovely cakes. We were just delighted to get into a Canadian home. Oh yes, I

[1] *Tosca*, Giacomo Puccini, 1900.

forgot to say that the night before, Miss Woods had a chafing dish party in her room, after the opera. We had great fun, it is just like boarding school here.

Anyway Friday was the big day. Now early in the week Irma wrote that she wanted me to come out to Halle Friday night and go to *Tannhauser* with them,[1] and then we could all come in for the big celebration next day. Well, I thought it all over, and wrote her that I really could not come. Fraulein Schröter and I decided it was too soon for me to go out again. After I wrote the letter the girls all got after me and said that it was wonderful to have such friends over here, and that if I really thought they wanted me, by all means to go, for they would not ask me again.

I thought & worried and wished I had mother to ask, but finally decided it would be better to go, and then I would not have to promise to go later on. Then we saw the Wartburg together, and it is closely connected in every way with *Tannhauser*, so it would have been a great mistake not to have gone. Then the money question was alright, for I earned 3 marks (75 cents) which was the price of the return ticket by accompanying for Miss Woods, so I really felt I could go.

They were tickled to death to see me, and Mr. Harper and Middleton met me — in other words, Heber and Tom. Irma had made the greatest time getting supper ready, and she had the boys there too. She had baked beans, baked potatoes and apple pie. Well Mother, dear, you can't imagine your daughter that night. I was in a state of bliss, not capable of being expressed on paper. We then went to the opera *Tannhauser* and such a time as we had. We were also in the highest row, there, but heard the music perfectly. I studied it all up beforehand and was able to tell the others all about it. I knew the music, of course, and it made it all the nicer. You can't imagine what "Evening Star" was like, and the Pilgrims' Chorus.

After the opera they took me to a lovely café, and we had strawberry ice-cream with whipped cream. Wasn't that some day? They were all so nice to me that I can't get over it.

I paid Mr. Roadman that night for my trip to Erfurt, Weimar and Eisenach and would you believe it, it did not come to five dollars for the whole thing — board, railway fare, sight-seeing, and everything for two solid days travel. It is great to go with people who really know how to travel. We saw everything and think of the small cost.

Next morning early we left Halle for Leipzig, and there were eight of us. The other three were Mrs. James and her daughter, and Mr. Campbell. The former two are Americans and are in Halle, where the daughter is studying. They are very nice and so good, true and kind. The latter is a Yale grad. '08, and is at the university in Halle. He travelled all over Europe this summer with Yale boys.

We all came in to the wonderful celebration, and now let me tell you about it, if you don't know. There is a big monument here of which I am sending you a picture (card cost 1 cent). The monument cost 2 1/2 millions and is supposed to be an altar in memory of the battle of Leipzig which was on Oct. 18, 1813, when the French were defeated. (They never say with the aid of the English, here). It is the largest monument in Germany and is wonderful they say. We are all going out to see it this afternoon for yesterday you could not get within miles of the place. There were hundreds of thousands of people in the city yesterday and every second man was a detective or policeman. They were afraid of anarchists, when so many crowned heads were here.[2]

We brought our parcels up to my room and then started out to see the Kaiser, who was going to drive out to the Denkmal at a certain time. Most of the people here in the pension went to some window in a house and paid ten marks ($2.50) to see the parade. Gladys did it, and Edna did not, and

[1] *Tannhäuser*, Richard Wagner, 1845.
[1] The *Völkerschlachtdenkmal*, or Memorial of the Battle of the Nations, commemorates a significant defeat for Napoleon in 1813 at the Battle of the Nations, also called the Battle of Leipzig.

LEIPZIG. VÖLKERSCHLACHT-DENKMAL.

The Denkmal, Leipzig (Memorial of the Battle of the Nations).
Postcard sent home by Helen.

(Mount Allison Archives, Lochhead Fonds, 8701.)

I rag on her. Gladys can't seem to say "no" and I don't know what will become of her, if she keeps on.

We (the Roadmans and our crowd of Halle Americans) went to a side street, where the Kaiser was to pass and we got in a big crowd, and waited for him to come. After a long wait he did drive by, and we saw him. He is a grand looking man and looked so nice, but we were very disappointed because the people did not applaud. They don't dare do it here, you know, but we were certainly disappointed. The boys got desperate and when we saw any-one later on they took their hats off and jumped up in the air, and said "Hey, there Bill, old boy". I was terrified for a woman was arrested in Berlin one time for just speaking about the Kaiser one time in a street car, in rather a disrespectful way. Anyway we had one grand time.

The Roadmans and Mrs. James brought a gorgeous lunch for we couldn't get anything here yesterday. We ate it up in my room here, and had potato salad, egg sandwiches and ham sandwiches, lovely cake, fudge, and fruit. Imagine them providing all that. I sure ate some potato salad.

I got hot water from the kitchen and Irma brought her tea-ball. It was the best treat I have been since I left home, except Ashburnham Place, and it was a different kind of a treat.

In the afternoon we went out again, and saw the crowds. None of us could go to the Denkmal for the seats were $30 apiece. We saw lots of students though, for all the students in Germany were there. We stood nearly two hours in a big crowd to see the Kaiser again. The people made much more of a time over the Crown Prince of Saxony,[1] than they did over Kaiser Bill.[2] He is young and handsome. I was nearly dead after such a stand, as 2 hours, but we all were bound to stand till he came and it didn't cost us one cent, when the others paid $2.50.

Well, we went from that right to the university church, and heard the loveliest quartets, solos, and organ pieces that you ever heard (4 cents admission which included a programme). It was wonderful. The music just made me fall over, for I was so tired but I enjoyed it just the same.

Then we all came up here, and had our supper. They made me take the pay for it but I did everything I could to prevent it. They can't do enough for me. They said I provided the room, and that was enough. I will do something for them when I get a chance, though, so don't worry.

In the afternoon I took Edna with us for she was alone all morning. Poor little thing. I pity her, and she is a good little girl too. She was tickled to death about it all and in the evening she went too. Gladys was out with another bunch, who spend more than we do, and are not half as nice. She is alright, now, don't think I mean anything but she just takes her own head, and goes and comes as she pleases. I advise when I can, and we get along famously, but she likes different things from me, so we each go with whom we like, and where we like.

I care nothing for cafés, and ice-cream and she is wild over them, so I do as I please, and she does too, but we have great times together and I just wanted to tell you this so you would know. Don't breathe it to a soul. Everyone likes her, but she does not do much work. She is too young to be here, you know, but it will do her worlds of good. I am off my subject but now I must finish.

We went out in the evening to see the illumination. It was fine. Every house had hundreds of tiny candles in the windows and there were large monuments made of wood and painted and had big

---

[2] Saxony was still a kingdom, although part of the German Empire ruled by the Kaiser. Crown Prince Georg of Saxony (1893-1943) was never king, as the monarchies of Germany were abolished at the end of the First World War. He became a Jesuit priest in 1923. Father Georg von Sachsen, as he was then called, was an opponent of the Nazi party, speaking out against the persecution of Jews. He apparently drowned while swimming in 1943, and since he had been under the observation of the Gestapo, and his body was not found for three weeks, some believe that he was murdered.

[3] Kaiser Wilhelm II reigned over the German Empire from 1888 to 1918.

fires going on the top of them. There was a Platz[1] where all the main buildings are, and there were thousands of people there, hundreds of thousands I might say. It was wonderful.

The Roadmans left earlier on account of the baby being home. All the others but Mr. Campbell went home at 9.45. He is staying over to-day, and so he, Edna and I went around all evening. It was a sight of a life-time. He took a picture of the lights, with his big camera and is going to give me one of them. We got home at about 10.30, and wasn't I glad to get to bed. We had breakfast at ten this morning and went to church. The sermon was fine and there was an American girl there who played three pieces on the cello. They were grand.

May and Ida met us and walked up a ways with us. Ida was up last week, and she is very homesick, and cried to me about it. Imagine! I really pitied her. They are nice to us when we are in another pension but I would never board with them.

Mother, your letters have all come, and I just love them. You tell me so much. About the bed at Ashburnham's, yes May and Ida had it. I thought I said that but in the rush, evidently I didn't.

Now I must stop for it is four. I shall finish when I come back from the Denkmal.

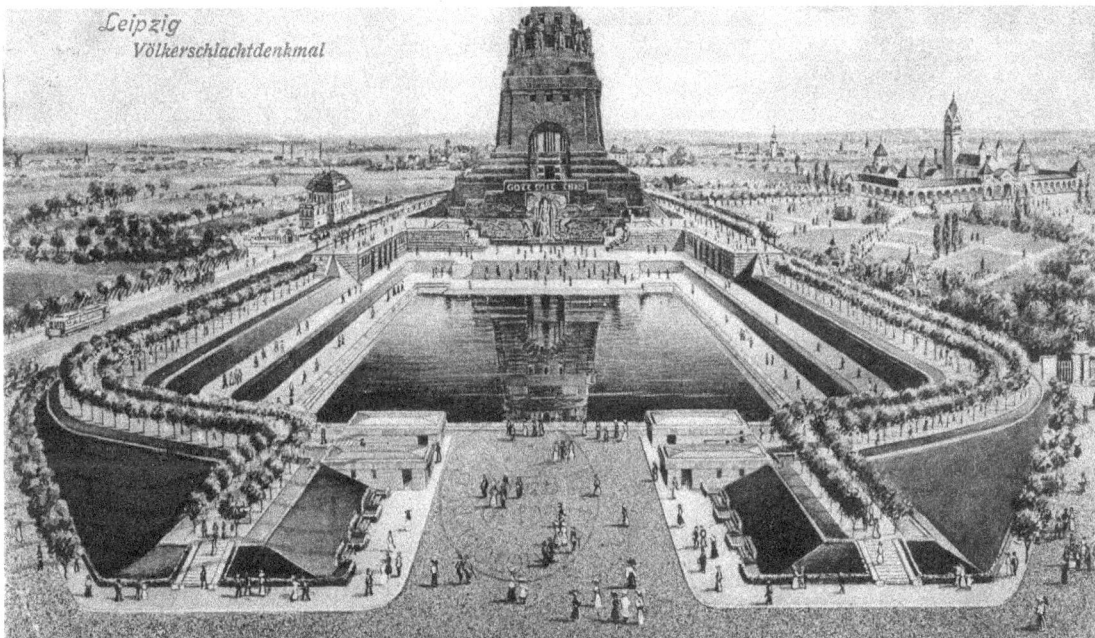

The Denkmal, or Memorial of the Battle of the Nations, Leipzig.
Postcard sent home by Helen.

(Mount Allison Archives, Lochhead Fonds, 8701.)

Sunday Night.
Well dear ones, we have seen the Denkmal and it is the most wonderful thing I have ever seen of its kind. Really it is beyond my feeble description. I am sure it will make Leipzig famous for tourists in years to come.

---

[1] *Platz*: literally "place", here, a public square.

A crowd of us went out with Fraulein Schröter's two nephews. They are very nice, but we keep them that way from a distance. No Germans for Helen —

I am sitting here thinking about every one of you dear ones to-night. The others are all having a high old time except Edna and I. We have been singing hymns and do enjoy it so much. We make our Sunday that way. Here the people don't treat Sunday the way we do, and we are going to keep it ourselves. Don't worry about me. I am so fat that I can hardly walk, and am working like sin, when I get at it. No more trips to Halle till Xmas. It was really necessary for me to go this week. Now I am going to dig for fair. Really I see so much and learn so much that I can't tell you a thing. I hope I am better for you to enjoy when I get all this knowledge.

Lots of love,
Helen

XVII

4 Sophien Platz
Leipzig, Germany
It is Fraulein Schröter instead
of Frau. I made the mistake in
telling you Frau.
Wednesday, Oct. 22.

Well, my Dear Ones:-

I am going to try and get a mid-week letter off to you to-day, for I know you like to hear how I am getting along, and I am going to write you, and let the other people go.

This week (as I said I was going to do) I have worked, and have accomplished so much, that I am encouraged. Monday I always have two lessons you know, piano and harmony, that takes most of the time. Fraulein Lutz told me I was doing fine and gave me a lot of new stuff — Bach and Beethoven. I have worked like everything on it since then and have it up for to-morrow. Then I go to the Kindergarten Harmony, that's the first class, and also an advanced class, so that makes four lessons a week in Harmony.

On Tuesdays and Fridays I have a lesson in German. It only costs 25 cents a lesson and I have to learn to speak in order to live here at all. They don't notice anyone who can't speak German. That makes ten lessons a week, with my singing. Soon I shall only have eight, for the primary harmony won't last long. Yesterday I practised four hours piano and one on voice.

To-day I have accomplished a lot, I tell you. 3 1/2 hours piano, one hour, more or less, on voice, and have been to a harmony lesson and a Gewandhaus concert,[1] which was three hours long.

Now let me tell you about the latter. It was the most wonderful thing I have ever heard - an orchestra of about 100 men, conducted by perhaps the greatest conductor in the world — Nikisch.[2]

---

[1] The Gewandhaus concert hall Helen knew was the second of that name, in use from 1884 until it was destroyed by Allied bombing during the Second World War. Its replacement opened in 1981.

[2] Hungarian conductor Arthur Nikisch (1855-1922).

Besides the lovely numbers by the orchestra, Julia Culp the world-famous singer, sang a lot of pieces.[1] She is the most wonderful singer I have ever heard. She has Mrs. Alves' method too.

Why let me tell you about my voice? Everyone is raving about it. There was a woman and her daughter here to-night to supper with Mrs. Paull, and she heard me sing at my lesson the other day, when she was waiting for her daughter to take her lesson. She was so anxious to know whose voice it was that she asked Mrs. Alves and Mrs. A. started to tell her how pleased she was with my voice. They say it will be very large, and sweet. I love to sing, and have a dear German song now, which they all say I sing well. Now don't think that I am listening to flattery for I am not. I know I have to work like everything but already I feel how my voice is growing. It increases every day.

If you would rather I should not take or think it is a lot to pay, I just wish you would say for I do want to please you all. I could stay here for ever as far as staying goes, but I don't think I shall stay more than one year for I am so afraid that poor father and mother are so lonesome. I want you to hear what I expect to have done by that time, for fear something might happen to you and you would not see the fruits of your labours. However that is a long way off, and I shan't worry about it now, but just dig in and do something.

What do you suppose? A Canadian woman, Mrs. King, (from Edmonton) has asked us over to her house to-morrow morning to breakfast for porridge, toast and eggs (regular Canadian breakfast) Isn't it great? She and her husband were here for a while and they were such nice people. Her husband used to be an Alberta College (professor, I think). There is another professor and his wife here, Mr. & Mrs. Luck. The poor woman has been gradually dying for a month. She has liver trouble or something like that — they say from eating too many pills. I have never seen her, for she is above us (next floor), and is always in her room.

Mother, dear, your two letters came Monday. I got six letters that day — one from Bob Shrives, Harry, Will, Mr. Jackson sent a picture of the house, (our house) and I was tickled to death to get it, for I didn't have one of the house.

Yes, Mother, I wish you would send me the *Monthly*,[2] and if they send in a bill for it please pay it, for I do long to see it. Be sure to send the graduation number for I have looked forward to that for so long. If it didn't come, Harry will send me one, he said.

The Roadmans were terribly taken with two of my pieces 'My Task', and a 'Perfect Day', for I sent to McMurray's for some copies to give them and the boys. So if they send a bill it would be best for you to pay it, instead of sending it to me, it is all the same anyway. They paid for so much for me that I simply must do some little things like that for them.

I wrote to Mr. Gerard the prop. of the Hotel where we were in London, and asked him to see about your scarf and I feel sure you will get it now. Did Anna ever get hers? Anna I got your letter but did you know dear, that you did not write my name on it — only the address. It went from McAdams' pension to ours, a few times, and then I located it and was right glad to get it, I tell you. I know how much you think of home letters, now, Papa you must write a line, now and then, for I would love to hear from you all. I am sure Mut will, and Kath said she would write soon.

I can't write to you all separately for I spend all my spare time writing just the one home, and I do love to tell you all about what I am doing etc. I can't begin to tell you quarter that goes on. I just touch the high spots.

I would give anything if you could see how fat I am. Really my clothes are uncomfortable. I can't

---

[3] Dutch mezzo-soprano Julia Culp (1880-1970); of Jewish background, she survived the Second World War in hiding in the Netherlands.

[4] A University of New Brunswick publication.

wear my old suit at all. I can't sit down in it, even. When I get working it will all go I bet.

Gladys gets the *Telegraph*, and I saw where Edith is engaged. Well, all I can say is that I don't envy her, one bit. I wouldn't be in her shoes for anything, with her chance to travel and improve herself. When you get over here you certainly find out what a nobody you are along side of the big geniuses that are all around you. It gives you ambition to do something besides settle down. There is lots of time for that later.

I am going to write Irma a note, and thank her for all she has done for me, and the lovely time she has given me. You needn't worry over me, when she is within a half hour's ride from here. We are great friends. The boys would do anything for me too. It is a wonderful thing to have such friends here.

Well I must run along to the other letter, and then fix up my things, and get to bed, so as to be on hand bright and early in the morning.

I am thinking about you all to-night and hope you are all as well and happy and busy as I am.

With all my love,
Hun

XVIII

4 Sophien Platz
Leipzig, Germany
Sunday night
Oct. 26, 1913.

My Dearest Ones:-

I must write you in lead pencil to-night for I must write fast in order to write a lot before I get asleep. It is now nearly half past ten and I must go to bed at eleven so as to be up bright and early for work to-morrow.

Now let me tell you what I have been doing since Wednesday when I wrote last. Thursday I had two lessons as usual, and was very busy all day. At night there was an affair in the American Church. Sort of a concert and social. We went and met some very nice people. I met a very nice Mr. Lochhead from Montreal. He is just a student and knows lots of my friends, and Gladys' friends too. We went with a Mr. Mills from America. He is a theolog, who is studying here and is one fine fellow. He takes us all everyplace. I just want to get to know a few people, and find out who is who. I am not going to go out much for I have too much work to do.

I had a singing lesson Friday morning, and Mrs. Alves said for sure that I was very talented and had a beautiful voice. You would never know it even now. I am sure you will be pleased with it, and I am going to work like everything to make it the best I can. I practised four hours piano also that day and worked Harmony in the evening. I am coming on well in that too. Then Saturday was yesterday. I worked all morning and took a lesson from 2-3 in Harmony, and at night Gladys, Edna, two Miss Shearers, Miss Hunt and I went to *Carmen*.[1] Now I can't describe it to you, for it would take years

---

[1] *Carmen*, Georges Bizet, 1875.

really. The music was grand, and a whole education in itself. After the opera the Miss Shearers took us to Café Français for an ice. It was the second I have had since I have been here, and Miss Paull gave me that. I tell everyone I can't spend the money. Well the Paulls went away on Friday to America. I was sorry to see them go for they did everything for me. They both invited me to make their house my home if I ever go to New York and Miss Paull gave me the piece her father composed for the unveiling of the Denkmal. It is something to have. She wrote me a card from Bremen before she sailed & I was the only one who got one. She told me she liked me best of anyone in the pension, and she certainly was good to me.

We had a great breakfast with Mrs. King the other morning. They are so plain and nice, and ask us around whenever we can go.

Yesterday mother dear, I received your two lovely letters, and poor darling old Nan's. I wish you could see me when I get them. I am dead to the world till I have almost memorised them. Mother I am so glad you are reading, and keeping your mind occupied. We will have so much to talk about when I get back, and enjoy ourselves so much. My books are all good, and you will enjoy them. I just long to read but don't get much time here. I do what I can though. My German takes most of the time, for I am bound to talk it. Fraulein Schröter put me between her two nephews at the table, and I learn much from them. She would just do anything for me, and I am going to try to keep her good graces.

I got eight letters yesterday and one to-day. Besides yours I got one from Mrs. McNutt, Wallie, Dane, Will, and Irma Roadman. To-day I got one swell letter from Tim O'Brien (the boy who sent the wire the day I left). It keeps me busy sending cards and a few letters but you people come first always and always will. To-day has been perfect. We all went to Bach's church at half past nine this morning. Then we went to our own church at 11:30. Dinner at 1.15 and this afternoon we went walking after our afternoon tea. The Kings were in to call on us awhile too. To-night has been perfect. Edna, Gladys, Mr. Hills and I played and sang all evening. He has a great voice and is a minister of the nice kind. We all like him, and think he will be such a help to us in this pension, where most of the people don't care about Sunday. We all stick together and they can't harm us. I am learning so many things each day that music seems only a small part of my stay here. Our progress in piano must be slow for awhile for the technique is so necessary. Still I never give in, and dig away until I accomplish it. Gladys and I are doing fine together now and I am sure we shall. It is much cheaper to room together and then we never get lonesome.

Mother dear, I thank you for your kind advice in all your letters. It spurs me on, to try to do my best for your sake as well as my own. I think I should not be much if I didn't try with such parents as I have.

My motto is that song which I sing so much, and which I have given to so many people. It is such a favourite of dear old Mut's and Kath's. They must get it, and play it often for it is so sweet.

"To love someone more dearly every day
To help some wandering child to find his way
To ponder o'er a noble thought and pray,
and smile when evening falls."

"To follow truth as blind men long for light,
To do my best from dawn of day till night,

To keep my heart fit for this holy sight,
and answer when He calls.
This is my Task"[1]

Don't worry about me with this for a motto, I never feel afraid, for there is always One who is near, and I know He is watching us all, and will not allow any harm to come to you or to me. That is why I am never what you would call home-sick. I just long for you all some-times, but it is pleasant to think of you all, and what you are doing.

The time just flies here, and we are going to see through a year in no time. Miss Woods is going to give a Hallowe'en party on Friday. We are all planning on it, and expect to have great fun.

About the money part, I keep an account of every cent in my little book, but never get a chance to copy it out to send you. It will come as soon as I can send it. I am saving in every way I can. I have never had a white waist washed yet, and have never bought but ten cents worth of fruit & 5 cents worth of chocolate. Isn't that pretty good? I am still fat and feel fine.

I hope you are all well and not working too hard. I am so glad you sent Louise the cup & saucer. I must send Stell something — a little lace or something. Mrs. King is going with me to get Anna's Christmas box, and I can get her sweet aprons like Lou's very cheap. So glad you got the box, Anna. Mother dear, I am sure yours will come. I haven't heard from Mr. Gerard yet but will write you what he says. It was a beauty and I hope it gets to you.

Go out mother, and see your friends and try to content yourself and father till I come back, and then you can retire and just listen to me sing.

A good-night kiss to everyone of you and two for my little "Sunny" in Edmonton,

Aunty Hun

XIX

4 Sophien Platz
Leipzig, Germany
Oct. 30, 1913.

My Dearest Home Ones and Western Ones:-

Mother's lovely letter here to-day, and wasn't I glad to get it. I think she is so good to write so often, and just to think you have been lonesome. I am sorry, for it is a horrid feeling to be left alone in the house all day. You should have some of your relations all the time, Aunt Isa, Jeanie or Mary for it is not right for you to be alone.

You can almost begin to look forward to my coming back, though now, for next summer is not so far away, when it is Nov. 1st, almost now. I expect to come back then, and earn enough to come back on. Then you will have a chance to see what I can do, and judge what is best to do with my voice. I am sure now that it will be something and I do want to have the best training. I had a splendid lesson on Tuesday. She always gives me an hour, and takes every interest in me. She has

---

[1] "My Task", tune by E.L. Ashford, these two verses by Maude Louise Ray, 1903.

a pupil who has been touring the States all summer, and he has done wonders. He is coming back again this winter to take from her.

Now for this week's doings. I have worked very hard and my technique is coming fine. Wednesday, that was yesterday, I went to a Gewandhaus concert, for 50 pfennigs (10 cents). I got the ticket at the conservatory. Everyone else has to pay 50 cents. But listen! I heard Liszt's pupil play. His name was Friedberg and really I never heard anything like him.[1] He was the best I have ever heard. He played with the whole orchestra of one hundred men conducted by Nikisch. When I hear that orchestra I just leave the world and go to some other region. It is so grand that you just can't imagine how it is done. We go at 10.30 and hear that music till 1. Did you ever hear of such a concert for 10 cents. You would never hear it in America for $5 a seat.

Yesterday a new man arrived in the pension. His name is Mr. Haeberlin. He is a German, born in America and has been over here for years studying. He is very well read and seems nice to talk with.

Everyday we all take a walk, and it is great for us for the weather is great now. The roses in the parks are still blooming. The leaves are beautiful, for here, but have not our gorgeous colourings. We went to-day for a half hour's walk by the river, and I wish you could see it. Really it is not more than ten feet across, or perhaps twenty. We would call it a small brook. The people walk along its banks, and think it is wonderful. They swim in it too and have dear little boats on it. One has to go up the shore, and hold on till the other one gets by. It is funny to me after the Saint John.

Tomorrow is a fete day — Reformation day. We are not allowed to practise at all. I have heaps to do just the same in German, Harmony and reading — also my hair to wash. It is funny here — everybody's hair gets oily. Mine never was, you know, but it is a little over here. I think it is the food. Mother, I eat all kinds of vegetables — in fact anything that comes along. It is as Mut said — when I got away from home I should not be so particular.

The other people expect to go to a suburb of Leipzig for the day and walk about half of the day, but I am not going to do that on my holiday for they are few and far between, and I must rest and get up in everything for the coming week. I can't afford to waste a moment here, for I want to get the benefit of my stay in a foreign land.

To-morrow night we have our big Hallowe'en affair. There will be about thirty of us all together, and we expect to have some time — all Americans and English.

I meet dear girls all the time. They are all so different from any I have ever met before. They all have aims and ambitions, and we all compare notes. I know two lovely English girls, and we were out for a walk after our Harmony lesson to-day. They are nicer than the Americans, I think. In our easy Harmony class there are about a dozen of us, all English or American, or at least they all speak English.

Irma Roadman wrote me to come out for last night to a good supper and then to go to *Carmen* with them. She said they were lonesome to see me. I wrote back that I could not possibly go on account of my work, and she will understand I know. When I go so often it costs too much, and I must go to the operas and not so much to their place. They are nice to ask me though, don't you think?

Saturday night I am to have the treat of my life in hearing Wagner's *Tristan and Isolde.*[2] Urlus

---

[1] Possibly Carl Friedberg (1872-1955), a German pianist who was a student of Clara Schumann, not Liszt, but who was teaching at the Cologne Conservatory from 1904 to 1914. Ignaz Friedman, Polish pianist and composer, 1882-1948, (and not a pupil of Liszt) also played in Leipzig in 1913-1914. Saved programmes show that Helen attended concerts by both Friedberg and Friedman in 1914, and a postcard of Ignaz Friedman was among her papers. .

[2] *Tristan und Isolde*, Wagner, 1865.

Ignaz Friedman (souvenir postcard)
(Collection of the Lochhead Family)

(Germany's greatest tenor) is going to sing for his last time this winter in Germany.[1] He goes to America now. I got the last cheap seat there was to-day and am so glad I could get one. It only cost about 60 cents in our money, and that is on the ground floor of the opera house. I expect to sit alone but don't mind that for the others from the pension will be there to come home with. Gladys is not going. She expects to have to pay $50 on her teeth and so she has to save. Don't tell her people for fear she doesn't. We get along fine now and I like her great. Fraulein Schröter may give us a larger room for the same price if anyone will take this room. It will be nicer to have a larger room, especially for my voice which is now too large for this room.

Now dear ones I must go to bed and not sit up too late and lose my beauty sleep. Oh yes, could you possibly send my boots and skates and ankle supports? We are all going to skate here and I should like to have my skates, if it wouldn't cost too much to send them. Gladys brought hers, I never dreamed there would be skating. Do as you like, or rather think best. I could buy a pair here, if it costs much to send them. Ask McNutt. He would know mother. I am so glad you are reading. It is wonderful to have the time to read. We will read together when I get back. Love to you all,

Helen

XX

4 Sophien Platz
Leipzig, Germany
Nov. 2, 1913.
Sunday night

Dearest Ones:-

Another busy day has passed even if it has been Sunday. We have not been doing anything we shouldn't have but the days go so quickly here, that I never get half written to you that I should like. We did not get up till after eight for we were tired. Then we went to church and "Mephi" (short for Mephistopheles) our little 14 year old English boy and I went in the Museum for a short time before dinner. Then we stayed around for a while, and took a lovely walk out to the Denkmal. It was a grand day to walk, and although we were tired after we got back, still it was a grand autumn day. I have written two very long letters — one to Mrs. McNutt and one to Myrtle. Mrs. McN. wrote me a lovely letter, and I wrote to her and Earle. Then Myrtle's parcels have been sweet. I never saw such thoughtful things in my life — pictures, books, a little <<Kewpie>> for my mascot,[2] a dust-rag, a pen wiper, and heaps of things. I simply had to write to her and thank her. She is sweet to have gone to so much trouble.

Friday night we had our big shine in Miss Woods' room. It was a grand success, and we bobbed for apples, had pumpkin pie, tea, salad, cakes and candy. It was a fine evening for Hallowe'en.

---

[1] Jacques Urlus (1867-1935) was actually a Dutch *Heldentenor* or heroic tenor; he was the lead tenor at the Leipzig Opera from 1900 to 1914.

[2] Baby-like Kewpie dolls, based on the American *Kewpie* cartoons by Rose O'Neill (1874-1944), began being manufactured in Germany in 1912.

Postcard, Leipzig Museum of Fine Arts
Opened in 1858, it was destroyed by Allied bombing in 1943; much of the artwork had been removed.
(Mount Allison Archives, Lochhead Fonds, 8701.)

Saturday, yesterday, I worked hard — took a singing lesson, and got two new German songs. She said my voice was coming fine — that I would not have much trouble with it at all. It is so encouraging. I love to sing and you will enjoy it. Last night I went to *Tristan and Isolde* alone. The others could not get seats together and they would not go, so I said I would go and it is perfectly safe to go alone, and I wouldn't have missed it for the world. I went at six o'clock and got out at half past ten. Arlus, Germany's greatest tenor sang for the last time before he leaves for America. It was grand mother you must read the story of it in my book, called *Wagner Operas*. It was wonderful really. The part where the shepherd plays on the reed pipe while they are watching for the ship to come in bringing Isolde, was beautiful. The scenery was grand. You can tell by reading the story of it what it was like. I studied it all before I went, and appreciated it so much more. *Lohengrin*[1] comes next week — next Saturday night. Also read *Carmen*, and *Tannhauser*, and *La Tosca*, if they are there. You will find two green books, one called *Famous Operas*, the other *Wagner Operas*. You will enjoy them both I know.

To-night we sang hymns, for ever so long. You know they don't have church at night so we have our own. Then I tore myself away to write, and I am afraid my writing is so bad you can't read it. Tomorrow I expect to do a whole lot of work, for I have no lessons, except a little German to study. I shall sing and play all day, and try not to waste a moment.

We are getting along fine, and like the place and people fine. We are all going to Dresden at Christmas I guess — for a day or two to see the Galleries, etc. It would be a great trip.

---

[1] *Lohengrin*, Wagner, 1850.

The Roadmans have invited me out again in a week or two but I don't know whether I shall spare the time or not. They are so kind to me. Please write Uncle Will about them. It is late and I must get up bright and early like mother and father and get my work done. I think of you all the time and wonder how you are. Please don't get lonesome and never worry about me. I am doing fine and saving as much as possible.

Helen

XXI

4 Sophien Platz
Leipzig, Germany
Monday morning.

You Dear People:-

I just received at breakfast mother's letter, which was grand, saying nothing of dear old Mut's, which I assure you will get a long answer very soon.

And Anna's paper about George![1] Well that was the climax. I danced the tango and all the German hops all around the dining room and even had to translate what I could of it to the German Fraulein. Oh it is so good. I am so proud of you George, that I don't know what to say. Anna, you are some lucky girl to have that "brute and beast" now I tell you.

Here's hoping I get such a "brute and beast". It makes me want to work my hands off to do something. Mother dear, and poor Grampie, you must not cry about me, for if you could see me you would be so happy, you wouldn't know what to do. I expect to take privately with Teich after Xmas, but where I am now is good enough for my technique, and then I shall get a start on voice by then.

I am sending you some pictures. I can't send them all for I only had a few printed. Be careful of them and when you are through with them, send them back, for everyone is so interested in seeing the Earl and Countess. They are a good looking couple don't you think? I just had to write this morning, so you would know I got your letters. I also had two lovely ones from Earle and Jim.

Mut, I only got one letter from you, before. I am afraid some of my letters don't come. I will write you some epistle soon. You kiss Kath for me, and Anna you give Daddy[2] a bunny hug for me, and mother don't let Grampie worry. When he sees me he will faint — I am so fat. Am so glad about your clothes. Must get to work.

Helen

---

[1] Most likely a reference to George Massie's having been appointed a judge.
[2] A nickname for her brother-in-law, Anna's husband.

XXII

4 Sophien Platz
Leipzig, Germany
[November 9, 1913]

My Dear People:-

Here I am sitting by our little desk at ten o'clock trying to collect my scattered thoughts enough to tell you what I have been doing. There has been so much going on that I can't begin to tell it all to you but I shall do my best to remember the most important things. If I omit any particulars, please tell me, and I shall explain anything you want to know.

I have received two lovely letters from mother this week, Mut's account of the game, which I was so glad to get — and would you believe it, two letters from Anna — who is so busy with the kiddies. You can't imagine how pleased I was to get them all and you are all good to think of me so much. When we get letters here it means something, and gives you something to think about when you are tired of work. It is the greatest recreation I have, and I read your letters over and over again. I was so glad to get Aunt Fannie's letter telling about Irma's opinion of me. She has been good to me and Friday if all goes well I am going out to have goose dinner with them. It is Mr. Roadman's birthday, and I have the pieces of music to give him — the ones I ordered at McMurray's, and you see I won't have to pay out any money to buy a present. They put off the dinner because I wouldn't go out before, so I feel I must go when they are so kind. I shall go 4th class if possible.

Now this week has been grand. I work every moment that I can, and never sit idle at all. My lessons take so much time, that it keeps me going to get practice in between times. My piano is coming along good. I feel my technique is improving every day. Then my voice is the surprise of the house. It is coming fine and I am enjoying it already. It makes me appreciate the operas so much more when I know about singing. Still, Anna, I am taking your advice and have no intention of giving up my piano for voice. I am keeping piano first, this year, and if I want to change them, it will be time enough. I want to have something to earn the good old dollars with, and I shall be able to do that in piano if all goes well, by the end of the year. After Xmas I may take private from Teich, but am asking and enquiring in the meantime about everything, and am not going to rush into anything.

You know this trip is doing me worlds of good just planning and scheming. It is a wonderful trip in every way. I realise it now every day. Now I must tell you about this week's affairs. Tuesday night I heard a cellist play in Albert Hall. He was great. An orchestra accompanied him, and you can imagine what it must have been like. One of the German girls here in the pension gave us the tickets and we went. It was much nicer to go free than to have to pay. You know I am a regular miser now.

Wednesday night Miss Woods had a party in her room. She made fudge in her chafing dish, and it was fine. I left quite early and came to bed for I don't believe in sitting up so late when one is studying. Everynight we have a little fun but have to stop at ten o'clock for the Fraulein won't allow it after that — that is a big racket. The other nights I worked and last night Gladys, Edna, and Miss Hunt (Eng. girl in my piano class) and I went to hear *Lohengrin*.

Well it was beyond everything. The music is just heavenly. We sat in Nigger Heaven.[1] It only cost us 80 pfennigs apiece, 20 cents. I was in the very middle seat and could see the stage perfectly and look down on the big orchestra. The Wedding March was beautiful. Mother, you must read about

---

[1] The balcony; a reference to the segregated seating in most American and some Canadian theatres at that time.

the story in my book entitled "Lohengrin". It gives good pictures and the story is well told. You read it now, and then I shall read it with you when I come back.

Yesterday noon we went to the motette in Bach's church — the boy choir. Their voices seem like the angels ought to sound, the tone is perfect.

Now about to-day. It has been so perfect. This morning we started early to church, and went over to the big art Gallery for a short time. It is only free on Sunday from 11-1. Church is from 11.30-12.30, so we are planning on spending a half hour both before and after church each Sunday till we see the wonderful things. There is a museum here too that is very noted. It has all kinds of oriental stuff, and students are here from everywhere studying about the things. They have a room for North American stuff and they have all kinds of Indian dresses, feathers, beads, etc. and Alaskan and Laplund stuff. It is very interesting. I am going to study it up and read a lot on it. Students study it for the development of civilisation. We had so much at college that it has interested me more than the others. This afternoon we tried to answer a few letters, but alas, it was in vain — too many interruptions — people running out and in. Then we played and sang. Mut — imagine Gladys playing the piano and singing alto, me playing the mandolin and singing soprano, on "A Perfect Day". We drew the crowd I tell you.

Tonight, I shall not forget. We went to Thomas Kirche to hear "Ein deutsches Requiem" by Brahms. There were about 150 men and women — an orchestra (including a harp) and Bach's organ. Gladys, Mr. Haeberlin (very fine chap who boards here, and goes to the university), Mr. Hills (the methodist minister who gets his meals here) and I went to it. The two boys got us tickets cheap at the university. We only had to pay 1 mark — 25 cents. The other seats were 4 and 5 marks. It was the most perfect thing I ever heard, of its kind. It is like an oratorio — Handel's *Messiah* for example. There were two soloists from Berlin, and such voices. It was so heavenly that you just wanted to fly up in the air. The words were all Bible texts and the German is so beautiful in songs. I am learning all German songs now.

There goes eleven o'clock, so I must get to bed to be up at seven tomorrow morning. I could write to you people all night but must sleep to keep my health. I am sitting here with my velvet dress unbuttoned — it is so tight. My chin is double now, and I am not getting fat all in one place either.

Daddy Massie, or rather Judge Massie — I am going to write you a letter of congratulation when I get time. Love to you all and write when you can. Don't work too hard.

Helen

P.S. We all expect to go to Dresden at Xmas and Rome at Easter. More particulars later. There will be a big party going on.

XXIII

4 Sophien Platz
Leipzig, Germany
Sunday, Nov. 16

My Dear Home Ones:-

It is a whole week since I wrote you, and I am so ashamed that I don't know what to say — really I did not have the time to write, although I have thought about you all just as much as ever, and tried to get a moment to write.

This week has been the busiest yet, I really think. Mother's letter came Friday morning and wasn't I glad to get it! I got a lot of others too and it is so good to hear from even New Brunswick — Helen Morrison wrote me a lovely long letter and told me all about her teas, Edgecombe wedding etc. She is a true friend to me, I think — not E. McMurray style. Mother, you are branching out great — it is so nice for you to have the delegates, if you don't go to too much trouble for them. It will keep you from getting into a rut, like most of N.B. people are. Really it is wonderful when a person comes over here, and finds out that they know absolutely nothing. I have felt that way till just lately, when I begin to find my bearings a little. Why, the people laugh when we say we have never heard the operas, and read about the great men, etc. They can't understand it here, that we know so little. The Americans know much more for they are generally about to hear some operas — but you know how few we ever get in F'ton. One person said to me "I am surprised you are civilised, at all, coming from such an atmosphere". If the girls in Fredericton knew what a chance they were throwing away when they refuse a trip here, it would make some of them start a bit. Every time we turn around here we learn something new. We are running up against famous people every day, and it certainly must have a broadening effect. I want you all to know how much I am appreciating this trip, and hope I can hand it on to you all when I come back.

Now I must get down to news before the others come in to bother me.

The first of the week I worked very hard, every day, with the exception of Wednesday when I went around to have afternoon tea with Mrs. Shearer and her three daughters, at their pension. They are such lovely English people, and are very kind to me. They have treated me three or four time to coffee etc. The youngest daughter is in this pension studying music. The others are just here for a month or so to see her. They are very wealthy I think and all have new sets of furs that they bought here. They are simply grand, and if I have one cent when I get through this year, mother, you shall have a set when I come back.

Well I was simply delighted with this other pension. It is very refined and they have very few boarders — only doctors, lawyers, etc. and it is not a musical pension. I enquired about rooms and they showed me a real nice room on the first floor, for 120 marks a month, which is what we have to pay for a room here (rooming alone). There is a mother and two daughters who run this pension, and the latter are about 35 or 40, and are just dear girls. They liked the Shearers so much, that they said they would take me and let me practise what I wanted to, and I am wondering whether to change or not. The food is better than here, and there is an air of refinement about the place that I am sure is what I want. They teach you German for nothing, and I help them with English. I asked Miss McA. about it and she approved very strongly of it and said "Helen, I know you are perfectly capable of knowing what to do, and I don't feel any more capable than you to decide. You are no chicken!!" Hurrah! at last they have found out that I am not as soft as they thought.

I can't leave here for a month anyway, so there is lots of time to hear from you, and find out more particulars. Gladys can get a room too the 1st of January if she wants it, so perhaps she will take it too. She does not notice the lack of refinement here, but I do, for we are all students and don't know much yet. At the other place, there are finished artists and people who can teach us something. It is in a beautiful part of the city — the very best and quiet, not expensive, and very home-like.

This place, Pension Schröter, has a name but the Fraulein is more after the almighty dollar than our comfort. She is sweet to us, but we are not in a home, merely a boarding house.

Don't you worry as to what to tell me, for I am [not] about to decide what to do, and I have lots of time to do it in. I just thought I would tell you I was thinking about it.

Wednesday night the Shearers, Edna and I went to *Der Freischütz*.[1] Gladys didn't want to go. It was a great opera — much lighter though than Wagner — but the choruses were fine.

Then Friday afternoon I went to Halle for the birthday party. It was simply great. I went at 4.10 in the afternoon and came back next morning at 12.25.

Now about the dinner. It was a surprise to Mr. R. and Mr. Middleton. Harper & Irma and I were the three who knew.

Irma had lovely goose, mashed potatoes, real gravy, creamed onions, lovely dressing, apple sauce with almonds in it, fruit salad, American cakes, coffee, bread and three birthday cakes for Baby Erline, Mr. R. and Mr. Middleton! Their birthdays were November 12, 14 and 18 (I guess that is correct). All the decorations were yellow and green, and most of the cakes etc. were carried out that way. She had dear little place cards, and under each plate was a present for each of us, all rolled in yellow paper and tied with ribbon. It was a picture of the baby; mine was one of she and the baby too. It is too sweet for anything. When I can spare it, I shall send you one.

After dinner we played and sang all evening. They insisted on my staying all night for Harper was coming into Leipzig next day, so I had company. Mr. R. is simply wonderful. He has a great brain and is so broad in his views. I had great discussions with him. They are all such perfectly good people and so gentlemanly and lady-like. It is a treat to hear them talk. Harper and I went to the motette in Thomas Kirche when we came back to Leipzig. Then we had dinner in the large restaurant here, "Panorama". It is a swell place. Then we went out to the Denkmal, and went in it. It is the most wonderful thing of its kind I ever saw. The figures inside are hundreds of feet high. I haven't time to describe it to you now, but will later.

We came back and had an early supper and went to the *Flying Dutchman*.[2] We had grand seats — the best I have had yet. They cost 3 marks 30 pfennigs (60 cents) apiece. They were box seats, only not the most expensive ones. The opera was grand — and the scenery was beyond anything I ever saw. It is sea scenery and the ships just fly around. They had everything, waves, and the boats rocked just as naturally as they would in the Bay of Fundy. When you read the story you will realise what the effect must have been.

Harper decided to stay over Sunday to see the Art Gallery and Museum, and also to hear a grand concert in Thomas Kirche this morning.

It poured when we all went to the concert this morning but we enjoyed it immensely when we got there. After the concert Harper and I went to the Art Gallery for another hour, and it is a wonderful place. It will take the whole year to see it properly.

---

[1] *Der Freischütz*, Carl Maria von Weber, 1821.
[2] *Der Fliegende Holländer*, Wagner, 1843.

The Bohemian String Quartet (souvenir postcard)

(Collection of the Lochhead Family)

I came home then at 11.30 to write this letter to you, and the others all went to American church. I was afraid I would not get a chance to write to you again to-day for there is always such a crowd around. (Dinner gong, will finish later).

2.30 p.m.

Here I am again and the others have gone for a walk. It is so cold that I decided to stay in and write. Sunday is my only day for that you know. Tonight we are going to hear the Bohemian String Quartet. They say it is grand.[1] Harper expects to go home this afternoon, and won't be able to hear it. He is an awfully nice chap — so straight forward. He has insisted on paying everything since we have been going to the Denkmal and all the other places, but last night I slipped ten marks ($2.50) in his hand before he knew it. He has fought all day to-day about it, but I am not going to take it back, for I don't want to be under any obligation to him. He is over here on a fellowship and I don't imagine he is a millionaire. I want to be independent of men for some time yet — believe me. They are just kind of handy when you want to go places, but that is all.

I wish I could see all you dear ones to-day. I know Sunday is your long day but you really must not worry about me, for I am doing the best I know how with my work, and having a great time besides. Mrs. Alves told me again last day that I was doing wonderfully. She gives me over an hour lessons nearly always, and I only pay for 1/2 hr. Fraulein Lutz told me that my technique was coming fine.

She confided in me about Edna. She said she could not seem to get the method, but that Gladys and I were doing fine. I thought it was nice of her to say this to me, and she told me not to tell the others. It showed that she took a special interest in me. I have a dear little friend in my piano class

---

[1] A Czech string quartet founded in 1891.

— Miss Hunt. She is English, we have great times together.

Now I have a dozen letters to write yet, so I must get busy to be through when the others return. I shall write twice this week, sure, and tell you more particulars. Anything that I forget to tell you that you want to know please ask me.

I hope you are all well, and not lonesome. The time goes so quickly here that I don't get time to think much about how I feel. It is better to be busy. A great big kiss and hug for everyone of you.

Love,
Helen

XXIV

4 Sophien Platz
Leipzig, Germany
Wednesday night
Supper Time
(just a little time for a few lines to you all)
Wednesday, November 19, 1913

Dearest Ones:-

This week, thank goodness, I am going to have a few moments to write to you. To-day has been a holiday, and we have not been allowed to practise at all, so we have had just a little more time for fun, and resting. It is great to have these breaks in our work once in a while for our life here is very strenuous.

Monday I started in to work in earnest. In the morning I got considerable mail — and mother's and father's letters. Well I was just tickled all to pieces to get them both, and father, you must write often for I do love to hear from you, and mother too. It cheers my whole day, and makes me dig in for certain. We all look for mail here and I am so pleased when some comes.

I got the *Monthly* and I am reading it when I get a spare moment. Wasn't it a good write-up on me. Muriel Steeves was responsible for it, I know. I must write to her. She is such a dear girl. Monday night I stayed in and rested. Tuesday, that was yesterday, I did one long day's work — four hours piano, and one hour voice, and was interrupted considerably so think I did pretty well. Then we all had supper early and went to hear Josef Pembaur play.[1] He is one of the teachers in the 'Con', and played very well. May and Queen were there and I sat with them for I got my seat late and couldn't sit with Gladys. May and Queen were very very nice and I did enjoy the evening.

I was very tired, however, after the long day's work and we did not get up till about 8.30 this morning.

Gladys and I took the camera, and went away out to the beautiful park and took some lovely pictures, for you home ones. I do hope they are good.

This afternoon, Gladys, Mr. Haeberlin, Mr. Hills and myself walked to Connewitz (just a suburb of Leipzig) and came back on the car. It has been a beautiful day and we have enjoyed every moment

---

[1] Joseph Pembaur (1875-1950), an Austrian-born pianist and composer.

of it. We saw a large deer park and all kinds of interesting sights. I wore my red coat, sailor suit, my black fur hat, and carried my muff. I was really quite in style.

Gladys and Edna are up at Mrs. Flint's calling, now, but I was tired, and wanted to write to you, so I sent my regrets. To-night we have an early supper, and then go to Thomas Kirche to hear an Oratorio of Bach's. You see we are kept busy all the time and it is grand for then we don't get time to think of ourselves.

To-morrow night we expect to go to hear a Symphony sung by 1000 voices. It will be grand I know, then the rest of the week I am going to rest if possible, and not lose all my lovely fat.

The boys are very nice to us, and buy our tickets cheap, at the university. We gain considerably by it, and they are very sensible quiet fellows, and help us out of many difficulties, such as standing in line for hours before a ticket office.

I must write Irma and thank her for the lovely time she gave me, and also Mr. Harper. By the way, he returned the ten marks and laid it on the table before he left, Sunday afternoon. He has been very kind to me.

Isn't this one grand picture taken at the Wartburg [see photo, page 42]. A German minister took it, who was with us. You may keep this copy for I have another. Hasn't Irma a lovely face? Mr. Middleton is fine looking, but you would never know it here. Mut, I still have the smile on. It simply won't come off. Mr. Roadman is the best of the lot. He is great fun.

Anna! Do you see Brown's bag? Some class! I have my blue suit on, Irma's was her old one, and she does not look as nice as she generally does.

Must run, Heaps and Heaps of Love now,

Helen

XXV

4 Sophien Platz
Leipzig, Germany
Sunday night
Nov. 23, 1913.

Dearest Ones, in New Brunswick and Edmonton:-

Thought I would get two letters off to you to-day, one to Anna and one home, but one will have to do, for it is very late (10 o'clock), and I want to write you all the news, and it would take years to write it all twice. I know you won't mind.

I wrote you Wednesday, the holiday. Well Thursday I had my piano lesson in the morning, and did not expect to do much for I could not practise the day before it being a holiday. I went feeling pretty nervous, but what a surprise I got. She gave me a fine lesson, and said "I see you have a very warm musical feeling. It shows even when you are playing technically". Now I just want you to know that that is something for Fraulein Lutz to say. I was so glad to hear it. We have been kind of nervous before her, for she is a very independent creature, but I was glad to hear that, I can tell you.

Helen "im Wald" - In the Woods, Leipzig, Autumn 1913.
(Mount Allison Archives, Lochhead Fonds, 8701.)

It made me want to work, and I have been doing my best to get my technique up.

You know it is just what May said "You never know how little you really know, till you get over here." I have found that out long ago, and am struggling hard to get a footing on the ladder, so that I will at least get a start towards the heights. Well, to go on with my story — Thursday night Mr. Hills and I went to hear a Symphony given in a large hall here. It was the grandest thing I ever heard — 1000 voices — male and female. An orchestra of over 150 — including about 75 violins, 4 harps, all kinds of wind instruments, drums, bass viols, a piano, organ, and three conductors. Just imagine! We paid 50 cents (2 marks) just to get standing room in the highest gallery. We stood two hours but it was well worth it. It was written by Mahler, a German conductor who died a short time ago.[1]

Friday morning I had my singing lesson. Well, I can't begin to tell you about it. Why she simply went into raptures over my voice. I was never so taken in my life. I sang my little song once, and she called her daughter (who is a great singer) in to hear me, and she said she couldn't believe it was me that was singing. She said I had done as much in two months as other pupils did in a year. She told me to write you that I had every chance of having a wonderful voice. She said you must not think of the money, for she will guarantee that I will reap three-fold the moment I begin to sing. She said she would take me to New York with her if she went next year, to study with her.

Now don't think I am conceited, for I am not in the least. It is all such a revelation to me, that I can't realise it. I never dreamed I had a voice. I just love it though and sing as much as I can. It helps me in every way. Mrs. Alves is an artist in every way. She has one pupil, perhaps more, who comes clear from Dresden to take from her.

I think there must be some little encouragement in what she says anyway, and I am going to work at it like everything to try and sing, for I love it so. You would enjoy hearing me sing now and I am getting much more tone. However I am not going to drop my piano till I am positively sure about it all, and that will take a year anyway. I love my harmony, and for that reason I am wondering if I had not better stay on at the Con. I can stay till Easter anyway, and then perhaps take a few lessons privately. I have met lovely girls at the Con. through my harmony classes.

Well, so much for my progress — don't think I am a whirl-wind yet, please, for I am just getting a start. It will take years to be developed perhaps.

Last night I went to hear a pianist — Edwin Fischer.[2] A girl here in the pension gave me a free ticket, so I went alone and enjoyed it fine. Gladys and I had a little feast in our room afterward — lemonade, cake, etc. it was grand.

To-day we went to church — had a great sermon, and this afternoon we went to Mrs. King's to afternoon tea. Miss Shearer, Gladys, Edna, Tattersal (our 14 yr. kid we call "Mephi") Mr. Hills, Mr. Haeberlin, Mr. Siegel, Mr. Sterne, and Mr. McLeary were all there. It was just lovely. We had tea and doughnuts.

She is a college grad. M.A., and sings beautifully. She is the Edmonton lady. Her house is over by the university. She is just lovely to us, and will do anything for us. They are good Christian people too, and it is so nice to know them. The other men are all theologs or university men and it is nice to meet them. We didn't get home till supper time, so I didn't have time to write you before. I have written to Aunt Jeanie, Isa, and Min to-day so am tired to-night.

Herr Schröter (Fraulein's nephew) asked me to go out with him to-night but I refused. He is an officer now and wearing a uniform. Couldn't you imagine me going out with him? Don't worry. I

---

[1] Gustav Mahler (1860-1911), Bohemian-born Austrian composer and conductor. The work referred to is his *Symphony No. 8.*

[2] Swiss pianist Edwin Fischer (1886-1960).

Helen again: another pose "im Wald", Autumn 1913.
(Mount Allison Archives, Lochhead Fonds, 8701.)

know perfectly well who to go with. Gladys and I are going to have our Sunday School lesson out of the *Quarterly* now, so I must close, and get to bed as soon as possible.

Mother dear, I got two letters from you yesterday, and they were grand. You write such interesting letters. It encourages me so much to get them. Don't work too hard. Take care of yourselves till I come back. Love to you all,

from old Sunny in Germany.

XXVI

Pension Schröter
Leipzig, Germany
Nov. 23, 1913.

Dear Aunt Isa,[1] Annie, Uncle James, Ken, Emilie, Ralph, Jennie, and Pinchty:-

Have I included everybody? I know Mother and Aunt Isa keep the Springhill line hot most of the time talking about letters from Montreal, Winnipeg and Leipzig but I just thought you would rather have a little line from me, myself, instead of getting it second hand. Was I right? I could never write to you all, so I am going to ask you all to read this. Anyway I don't know Emilie's address. I am hoping by this time that she is her dear old self again, and that she is settled down for the winter. It takes so long for news to come over here, that it is stale by the time I get it.

Mother has told you all about my work, I know, so I shan't repeat it all.

Germany is a wonderful country and very different from Canada. Every inch of ground is used for something and all the trees are clipped and kept in perfect shape. Imagine one doing that in Canada! The leaves are very beautiful here in the fall, but not as brilliant in colour as in Canada. They stay on the leaves very late in the fall, and when they fall they are more brown than red. We have had some beautiful walks here and the fall has been very delightful — so warm. We begin to think we are not going to have any winter, but I suppose it will come.

I should love to drop in and tell you all about my trip and work, but shall have to wait till later I guess. I think about you all so much, and mother tells me how you all are, and I am so interested.

Aunt Isa, I think about you whenever I go to the grand operas, for I have your bag with me always. It is so handy and pretty. Gladys takes it when I am not going, for we both love it so.

My love to you all, and hoping you are all well,

Sincerely,
Helen

---

[1] Helen's mother's sister, Isabella Mitchell Campbell.

Helen (r.) and Edna Baird, November 1913
(Collection of the Lochhead Family)

XXVII

4 Sophien Platz
Leipzig, Germany
Sunday, Nov. 30, 1913.

Dearest Ones:-

You are going to get a long letter to-day for I could not get a letter off in the middle of the week. It seemed as if there was not a moment to write a letter, and I haven't written one all week.

First of all let me tell you that I received the skates O.K. and there was only 5 cents to pay on them. Wasn't that fine? I was so glad to get them, for everyone says this is a great place for skating. Mother's letter came yesterday, and don't you worry about your letters not being interesting. They are grand and I tell you they sound good to me.

Gladys K. wrote me and thanked me for the lovely chocolates and you must have sent them in my name. It was lovely of you to do it. She wrote me all about their home etc. They like it fine. I would not exchange places with her I tell you, and be out there not seeing anything, but merely being a social butterfly. I have something else to think about now.

Now for my busy week. It has been work, work, work, all day and at night some concerts or opera. Tuesday night we went to hear Emil Sauer, a pianist play.[1] He was simply grand - the best I have heard yet. He was Liszt's pupil.

Wednesday morning I went to the Gewandhaus and heard a wonderful elocutionist. One of the best in Germany. He was accompanied by the orchestra, of 100 men, and Nikisch conducted. Wednesday night Fraulein Wit and I had a German lesson. She gives me German and I give her English. Then it does not cost anything. It is grand and she is a university girl and is very clever. Thursday was the big day. I had two lessons as usual, and then at night was the big American affair. It was a concert, dinner and dance given by the American church to get money. It cost 2 marks (50 cents) for tickets. Then if you wanted dinner you paid more. We only went to the concert and the dance, for I didn't want to eat at 9 at night. The concert was grand. Two of Mrs. Alves' pupils sang, and they did splendidly. It certainly inspired me to work.

We all went together from this pension. Gladys and Mr. Haeberlin, and Mr. Hills and I and Edna, and two Scotch girls, the Misses Beatty, from here. May, Ida and Queen were there, and we were together a lot.

Mr. Hills did not dance, but he waited till I was ready to go home and watched us dance. He reminds me of Carpenter more every day, so please don't think I take him seriously. He is just an overgrown boy. Gladys and I don't care a rap about either of the boys, but we all have a good time together, and they are such good boys.

I had some great dances. Mr. Lochhead a Canadian, was there.[2] He knows Jean Hodge and Mildred Carvel, having met them at MacDonald. I had four or five dances with him and they were grand. Then I met a lot of people, and we had a good time all around. I didn't stay till the end. We all left early (2 o'clock or after). Mr. and Mrs. King were there and they were so nice, they are just like a father and mother to us.

---

[1] Emil von Sauer (1862-1942).

[2] Allan Grant Lochhead graduated from McGill with an MSc in Chemistry and was at this time working on his doctorate at the University of Leipzig.

ERNST EULENBURG
LEIPZIG : KÖNIGSTR. 8

Städtisches Kaufhaus zu Leipzig

Dienstag, den 25. November 1913, abends ½ 8 Uhr

KONZERT

von

EMIL SAUER

⊶⊷

PROGRAMM

1. Gavotte und Variationen . . . . **J. P. Rameau**

2. Caprice über Ballettszenen a. „Alceste" **Gluck—Saint-Saëns**

3. Sonate Fis moll, op. 11 . . . . **Robert Schumann**
     Un poco adagio — Allegro vivace.
     Aria. Scherzo e Intermezzo. Finale.

4. a. Nocturne, op. 27, No. 1 . . . . . .
   b. Polonaise Fis moll, op. 44 . . . . **Frédéric Chopin**
   c. Impromptu, op. 29 . . . .
   d. Etude . . . .

5. a. „Clair de Lune" . . . . **Claude Debussy**
   b. „Quand vient l'été" (Sérénade) .
   c. „Spieldose" . . . . **Emil Sauer**
   d. Moto perpetuo in Oktaven . . .
      (Edition Peters)

6. Tarantelle „Venezia e Napoli" . . . . **Franz Liszt**

Grotrian, Steinweg-Konzertflügel
Vertreter: Hug & Co., Augustusplatz Nr. 1

Karten zu 5, 4, 3, 2, 1.50 M. bei C. A. KLEMM und FRANZ JOST

A programme from one of the many concerts attended by Helen

(Collection of the Lochhead Family)

Next day we were tired but I did a lot of work, and had a grand singing lesson. Mrs. Alves gave me tickets for a concert on the 10th of December. Wasn't it nice of her? She can't do enough for me, and she told Mr. Hills a lot of stuff about how proud she was of me etc. Then yesterday, Saturday, I practised a while, and then went down to Fraulein Lutz's apartments and had a private lesson. I am to have one every two weeks, besides my lessons in the Con. It costs 10 marks a lesson ($2.50, almost) but I assure you it is worth it. I had a great lesson, and she told me more stuff than I could tell you in a year.

She said I had the Teichmuller method all right now, but she said I certainly didn't when I came over. She said Gladys had had a better teacher than I. She said she was so surprised to think that a pupil of Teich's could not teach his method better than that. I have worked hard, though, and she says I see the method now, and that I am very musical. I told her I wanted to earn my own living, and she said she thought I was so wise.

At first when I came over here, I was frightened to death of her, but now I like her fine. She told me all about Edna again yesterday. She says she can't seem to make her learn. I do feel so sorry and tried to tell Fraulein Lutz that she was handicapped with her deformity and a lot like that. She said Gladys would come allright but she didn't know what work was yet. She is such a kiddie. Now perhaps you think I should not take so many lessons but I am trying my best to get every single thing out of this year that I can, and I felt that I was not getting half enough in the Con. and so I wanted a few extra lessons to get a good start. You see she doesn't get time to give us more than 15 minutes in the Con. and when you take privately she takes much more interest in you. If I find it too much for me I shall stop. It means $5 extra a month. I am going to save by not moving till February, anyway. Fraulein Schröter is going to give me this room all to myself for the same price as her small rooms. Gladys is going to have a smaller room, and she will have to pay the same as I do, and mine is much nicer. F. Schröter would do anything to keep me. I decided that if I ever got sick that I would be all alone with Germans and you would feel much safer if I was with the girls. However I may go the first of February. Soon I am going to stop my singing to one a week, then I won't have so much to do. I have made so much progress with my voice that really I can't believe it is myself singing. This afternoon I went down to see my dear little friend Miss Hunt. You know she is English, from Portsmouth. She is very small but told me to-day she is twenty-five. She says she knows all about singing and thinks my voice marvellous. She plays my accompaniments so well, and she takes a great interest in me. She is very refined and cultured. I am sure she will ask me to visit her on the way home. Wouldn't that be grand?

Well last night I went to hear Wagner's *Valküre*.[1] It was so wonderful that I can't describe it to you. I went alone and came back with the German girls of the pension. It was over four hours long — went in at six o'clock.

My but it was wonderful. Mother you must read it in the Wagner book. It is one of a series of operas which are called the *Ring*.[2] You must read them all. The scenery was wonderful — real fire burning on the stage, and the sky effects were grand. Oh I can't begin to describe it.

This morning we went to church and heard a great sermon by an Englishman. Mrs. King and I walked home together. I just love her, you will see her in the picture I am enclosing. She had us three to breakfast, and here we are. Don't I look as if I had lost all my money, or friends. I was quieter than the others, you see and did not have a blurred picture. The other is a picture taken at Kings'

[1] *Die Walküre* or *The Valkyrie*, Wagner, 1870.

[2] *Der Ring des Nibelungen* or *The Ring of the Nibelung*, a cycle of four operas by Wagner: *Das Reingold*, *Die Walküre*, *Siegfried*, and *Götterdämmerung*.

the afternoon we were there to tea. It was a flashlight and you see I shut my eyes. It is part of a big picture we took. I haven't a copy of it yet. See how fat I am.

All kinds of love,

Helen

XXVIII

4 Sophien Platz
Leipzig, Germany
Thursday, Dec. 4, 1913.

Dearest Ones:-

Although late, you are going to get a mid-week letter. I know how much you look for the letters from Germany. It is terrible when posty goes by isn't it? Well, every week gets busier, and I don't know what will come next. I honestly don't have time to go to the bathroom (I never thought I would reach that stage).[1] Monday — two lessons as usual. That night there was a concert by one of the teachers here. I didn't go for I wanted to converse in German. I had one grand lesson with Fraulein Vide and she is bringing me along fine. Tuesday, my singing lesson was good. She is giving me an aria now, so you can imagine my speed. She says I learn very quickly.

Friday noon.

I had to leave this last night, for supper and then afterwards I didn't have one moment to write you, for Gladys and I were listening to Mr. Farley, a blind boy, all evening. He is so wonderful and has composed some beautiful things. He wants me to sing them for him, and I am going to learn them. It is such a pity he is blind, but he is very educated and refined and is nice to talk to.

Well to go on with my story — Tuesday night we heard Beethoven's one opera *Fidelio*. It was very typical of Beethoven, and the music and scenery were fine. You must read it Mother in the book you have read the others out of. We sat in zweite rang (next to the top gallery), and I saw the funniest sight there — a man learning to conduct an orchestra. He had his book, and baton, and was standing alongside of a little red light that was left on, beating away and nodding his head to an imaginary audience, as the conductor was doing down in the orchestra below. It was certainly funny.

You see very funny sights here anyway. There are so many students and they all must practise and get the most out of their stay here, as possible.

Wednesday was one busy day. Irma came in at nine in the morning to spend the day, and to hear Elman play in the evening. I met her and took her up to the Art Gallery and left her there for the morning. I came home then and worked hard at my piano and singing all morning, so that I could go out with her in the afternoon. From 2-3 I had a harmony lesson so Gladys stayed with her till I came out. We then (Irma & I) went out to the Denkmal, and then came back and bought a few Xmas presents. Believe me, mine must be few and far between. I simply can't afford many. Now I had to get something for Stell Jewett, so I got her a little lace doilie for 3 marks, 75 pfg — about 80 cents in

---

[1] To take a bath.

our money. Was that too much? I must send her something for Anna's sake as well as my own, and it is a sweet thing. You go see her presents and likely she will show it to you.

Well Wednesday night was a treat. Mischa Elman is certainly grand.[1] He is only 23 and can bring anything out of his violin. Sometimes you could hardly believe it wasn't a voice. It was so late that Irma could not go home, so Gladys and I pulled our beds together and we slept fine. She left at 7.45 the next morning and I had an early start at my work. I had two lessons as usual and then Gladys and I went shopping again.

I would give anything if I could send you people all I want to. The stores are gorgeous here but I am not going to run any risks like the scarf, for fear you don't get what I send. I hope you see the scarf in the end.

You will all know I wanted to send you more but could not take the risk, or spare the money. When I come home I shall bring you a host of things for you can take anything after living here a year. Don't you think this wiser?

Now about Muddies toys for the kiddies. I can't promise that they will be there for Xmas for it takes so long to choose them. Then I am not sure whether I can send them without an enormous duty. If I have to pay double price for duty, it won't pay, but if not they will come sooner or later. However, as I said before you will all get heaps when I come back. I am so afraid the parcels get smashed, or stolen or something and you would not get them.

Then I am so busy that I haven't much time. I am dropping one lesson in singing a week till I get my shopping done.

Mother, if you and Anna could only see the shops here, you would go wild. They are so beautiful.

I am going to the dentist here to get two or three holes filled, and imagine it will cost me something. Gladys must have had $100 already on hers here. But I am only having the bad ones patched up till I get home.

I worry all the time about the money I am paying for singing, but dear ones, I honestly feel that it is worth it. Everyone who has heard me says that I must make it my special but I am going to do both if my health permits.

I am so well, and as happy as can be, only for the money problem. If it costs a lot this year I won't stay another year so it is as broad as it is long. I sure am improving my moments. I never have an idle second and can hardly take time to sleep.

By Dec. 20th I will have this room all to myself for 120 marks per month. It will give me much more room and I will get along faster. Gladys and I are such friends and we hate to part but feel it is for the best. I just love her and we will always be great friends, I know.

Irma may go to Italy and Switzerland in the holidays and if they go they say I must go too. I can't decide for I spend so much on voice. Mr. and Mrs. King may go to the Harz Mountains and if they do we may go there.[2] Then we had planned to go to Dresden for a day or two. I don't know which of the three I shall do, yet.

Mother, you and Father must come over to go back with me if I go in September. We will travel home by France, England, Scotland and Ireland. I wish you would come for we would have such a good time, and I could travel anywhere alone now.

---

[1] Ukrainian-born violinist Mischa Elman (1891-1967).
[2] The Harz Mountains are a low range in the region where the states of Saxony, Thuringia, and Saxony-Anhalt come together.

Mischa Elman (souvenir postcard)
(Collection of the Lochhead Family)

Will expects to come over to Europe in January I think, so will likely call on me.[1] If he is in F'ton he will be around I am sure, to see if you want to send any messages, and also to tell me how you all look. He has business to do in England and France, and will likely make a side trip over here, if he has time.

It would be mighty good to see anyone from the other side, I can tell you. I get lovely letters from everyone, and Mother dear, I sent Hib a card when I got over here, just to let him know I held no ill-will against him, and he wrote me the loveliest letter you ever read — and asked if we might not be friends, and apologised for all he had done etc. and said he called while in F'ton, and you were out. That is about a week ago, and I haven't answered it. Later I shall probably write him but I never think of him now at all. He has completely gone out of my life. I could never be bothered with him, I am sure, I want someone that I can depend on, and not be frightened for fear they are going to do this or that.

Now have you seen this picture of the judge?[2] You see that he is so noted that his photos even reach Germany. I thought I would have a fit when I saw this at Mrs. King's. They cut it out and gave it to me. Some Class! Ha! Ha! Daddy! Some man to have his cartoons out already. Must away — I am so busy. I will write a better letter Sunday, telling you the things I have forgotten in this.

Love! Love! Love! and then some,

Helen

XXIX

4 Sophien Platz
Leipzig, Germany
Monday, Dec. 8, 1913.

Dearest Mother, and all the other members of my large family:-

Your letter arrived this morning, and I was so glad to get it. Now dear ones, when you don't hear from me, please know that I am all right, for I would let you know the moment anything goes wrong. Really I am so busy that I never get a moment to write hardly. We have so many lessons and concerts to go to, and then our practise. I am perfectly all right, only don't get time to sleep, hardly.

When I get my room alone, on the twentieth, it will be much easier to get more sleep, so by the time you get this I shall be in my room alone, and you know I shall be perfectly happy. I do hate for Gladys to go, but we both realise that we will be better alone.

Yesterday I wrote letters to all my friends, almost, and wished them a merry Xmas. Then I put some snaps of myself in, and they serve as presents. You will get yours in the next letter for I had to have more printed. Now I have bought you some presents, but may wait and send them with Will when he goes back, for I don't want my good money lost. I have a dear remembrance for Mother from Holland, and won't trust it to the mail, so please don't be disappointed. It will arrive later.

I sent Mut one of my favorite pictures that is in the London Gallery, I am sure he must have seen

---

[1] William Skinner, apparently, like "Hib", an unsuccessful suitor.
[2] Her brother-in-law George Massie.

it, and hope he likes it. I did not have a card to send in it when I was at the store, so please excuse it going without any. I had to pay a quarter to send it, so I don't think it pays very well to send much do you? If he does not get it, write me, for I registered it, and he must get it. Perhaps it will be delayed in the customs. Give it three weeks anyway.

Well I have a present for Kath too, and it will arrive, sooner or later.

Now dear old Muddie, yours will come too if I ever get time to take it down to the mail. I have it most ready, but am waiting for my snaps and a few other things to put in. Perhaps I may send some of your things in Mother's box, and let her send them to you. Keep up courage, you will get all sooner or later. I have two dear aprons for May and Betty but may save them for Will to take back, if you would let the kiddies wear them after he had carried them home, Ha! Ha!

To-day I got another grand letter from Earle, telling all about the law dinner, and enclosed a menu. He is sure some boy.

Mother, dear, don't you worry about me, for I never look at a boy here. Why I am as sedate & prim as any old maid. I expect to be like Ida McAdam soon.

Now about white-slavers — why we never hear tell of such a thing here, and never feel afraid. Fraulein Schröter says it is perfectly safe, no one ever says a word to us, and we never feel afraid when out. Don't let Mrs. Grant make you afraid, for I feel safer here than I did at home as far as that is concerned. Gladys and I just roar at you and Mrs. Grant for being so anxious about us.

If you could only see how comfortable & happy we are you would never give us a second thought. Of course we are always careful and never go where we think there is danger. I appreciate your care, and thought, but don't worry for we are all very model children. Yesterday we heard a great sermon at church, and in the evening we heard the Bohemian String Quartet again. It was grand. They only play on Sunday night, and it is great to sit there and enjoy their wonderful music. It is as inspiring as church, almost. We don't have church here at night.

I was so sorry to hear about papa's potatoes, but hope he has got rid of them by now. He would worry so much about them I know.

Now I had to draw a lot of money as you will notice for my singing lessons for two months. It just broke my heart to do it, but then when I sing it all seems perfectly right for me to spend it. Really my voice is coming wonderfully.

This week I am only having one lesson, but am afraid that I must have more after a while. She says she will take the responsibility of saying that I must have two a week. I am seeing how much I can do this week with one, and will act accordingly. Gladys started singing from Mrs. Alves to-day — two a week. She is also going to take privately with Fraulein Lutz in piano, the way I am doing. At Easter we expect to leave the Con. and go with Teich. There is no sense in being with him till our technique is good, and Lutz is splendid for that.

She gave me a great lesson this morning and is very nice to me.

Wasn't it nice of Dave to give you the meat.

[remainder missing]

XXX

4 Sophien Platz
Leipzig, Germany
Sunday night.
December 14, 1913.

My Dearest Ones:-

Two weeks from to-day Xmas will be over, and we will soon be on our New Year's work. The time has just flown since we have been here, and oh we have been so busy that I can't realise it all. It all seems like a dream to me.

This week I have done nothing but write letters and cards for Xmas. I sent you a handkerchief Mother, and yesterday I sent Father a tie. Then I sent Anna a picture which I am so fond of <<Hope>>.[1] It is in the London Gallery and is very wonderful. The other one of September morning, is perhaps the most noted picture of the day.[2] That is for Daddy. It is beautiful don't you think? I do hope you like them for it was so hard to choose.

I sent a box to Sunny with a toy. Then I sent Kath an opera bonnet, which you cross in the back and fasten at the sides. I also sent the kiddies some pictures for their nursery. I just loved them and know you will.

I took a big box of kiddies rubber clothes down to the mail to send to Anna last night, and they said it wasn't packed hard enough to send. I am going to try it again tomorrow, and if they won't send it I shall save it for Will to take back. It contained the Dutch pins too, and I don't want to lose those. They wanted to charge me 6 marks $1.50 for sending it the way it was and I would not satisfy them by paying it. Anyway the things were not worth it.

I had my pictures taken with my camera, and put them in dear little cards, with calendars on them to send all my special friends. They were very cute, but I have worked terribly to get them off. It has been quite a worry, but I have about everything off now.

Oh yes I had a lovely long letter from Minnie Smith so I sent her one of my pictures, and also a letter from Mrs. McNutt, containing a beautiful hand-made handkerchief. Greta also wrote me a lovely letter. Earle writes a lot too. He is doing wonders at Dal. and is working some hard.

Now about the news of the week. It has been mostly work and made calendars for Christmas. We went to *Falstaff* [3] Wednesday night. It is a grand opera taken from Shakespeare's *Merry Wives of Windsor*. The scenery was the best I have seen here.

This week there are going to be two good operas to go to — *Martha*[4] and *Romeo & Juliet*.[5] We shall likely go. The music is always heavenly — with the big orchestra.

---

[1] Probably George Frederic Watts' "Hope" in the Tate Gallery, London, although he painted several versions of the composition.

[2] There are a several landscape paintings and etchings with the title "September Morning", as well as "September Morn", a nude woman bathing in a misty lake, by Paul Chabas, which was very famous and much-reproduced at the time.

[3] There are two operas with this title, one by Guiseppe Verdi (1893) and one by Antonio Salieri (1799).

[4] *Martha, oder Der Markt zu Richmond*, Friedrich von Flotow, 1847.

[5] *Roméo et Juliette*, Charles Gounod, 1867.

Then I have been to the dentist's a lot. Every one of us has been there and have found hundreds of holes. It must be the change of food I guess.

Well, Saturday, yesterday, I had a grand lesson in piano — private — with Fraulein Lutz. She was so nice to me and said many times that I was very musical and that I have the method now.

Don't worry about Teich, for I shall go to him before I come home. At Easter I shall probably leave the Con. and take privately with him. I could take from him now if I wanted to but there is no need of paying $7 a lesson when you can get the same grounding with Fraulein Lutz, much cheaper. I am getting the method, and that is the chief thing first. She can give it to me just as well as he, and then he gives the finishing touches. Don't you worry about it, for everyone says we are doing the right thing.

Now to-day has been so busy. We went to church, then after dinner we wrote letters till four — had afternoon tea here at four. Then we were invited out to Miss Daly's to afternoon tea in her room. She is a music student here and is very nice. She is quite old, and plays and teaches both. Her professor was there too, Herr Prof. Lembrino. He is Madame Carrerro's best pupil (she is the greatest lady pianist in the world).[1] She had a lot of others and it was so nice to meet them all. Then we had supper home here, and now we are waiting for the MacAdam's to come up. They said they would come up to see us to-night. I wanted to get your letter started before they came for it will be late afterwards, and I won't feel like writing you such a long letter.

I must go now and help get our little cup of tea that we are going to give them ready. More later!

Monday morning.

It was after eleven when we came to our room last night, and so late that I went right to bed. Now I am sitting at the dining table waiting for my coffee, and writing to you.

Well it was such a wet cold night that the McA's did not come up. We had a cup of tea ready for them, and some little cakes and Gladys' fruit that she brought from home.

Mr. Luck[2] (the man from Edmonton, whose wife has been so ill for the last three months) came down, to talk Canada to us. He plays the banjo, guitar and mandolin and he taught Irene Harbottle the guitar. He knows lots of Edmonton people — Fifes included. Anyway he played fine for us, and I think perhaps he will help me with my mandolin. He gets very lonesome when his wife is under morphine. They have to keep her that way most of the time, for the pain is so great. It is her liver.

Well I have a lesson this morning, and must get my technique up for it. I have to practise Beringer a lot, and it is great for the fingers.

We have our last piano lessons this week before Xmas. Then we are going to have a rest, and go to Dresden for a day or two, perhaps.

We are going to have a grand Xmas. Everyone says that Fraulein Schröter gives us such a good time. We sing and have a Xmas tree. Then Xmas night we are invited out to Mrs. Doering's to a Xmas tree. She is a lovely American lady, and a great friend of our singing teacher, Mrs. Alves.

It is impossible to write here at the table. They are talking all kinds of languages around me, and it is hard to write.

I got your lovely letter Saturday Mother. I love to hear from you all so much, and I watch the

---

[1] Probably Télémaque Lambrino, pupil of the famous Venezuelan pianist Teresa Carreño.
[2] Elmer Luck.

Arthur Nikisch (souvenir postcard)
(Collection of the Lochhead Family)

post every four hours for a letter.

I will write some every day now till after Xmas so you will hear all that we do.

Bye-Bye for now,

Helen

Love, & Merry Xmas.

XXXI

4 Sophien Platz
Leipzig, Germany
December 16, 1913

Dearest Ones:-

As I promised to write every day, from now on, I am going to make a good beginning and write a note tonight. We have just returned from hearing *Martha*. It was splendid, only the singers were not as good as usual. Oh! if you could only have heard "The Last Rose of Summer". I thought of you all when it was sung, especially of Mother, for she always sang it so much. The music of it is wonderful, and it was all so familiar to me. Gladys, Edna, Mr. Farley (the blind boy) and I went. We take him to the operas sometimes and he is so grateful to us for doing it. He goes just for the music.

Well we are having very dark weather here. It is regular Leipzig weather, they say. We work away though, rain or shine.

To-day I had a grand singing lesson, and she gave me all kinds of encouragement. Now don't think that she is all blarney for the last lesson was not nearly so good and I worked very hard for this one, and she knew it.

I was at the dentist's this afternoon and he said that he had heard, from Mrs. Alves, that the quality of my voice was grand. That is encouraging don't you think? I have only to go to the dentist's once more and then I am done. It is great to get them all fixed up. If I am going to sing I must preserve my teeth.

I must away to bed now — more to-morrow! Night! Night!

Thursday night.

Well, here I am again sitting up in bed, writing you this little note, before I go to sleep. Yesterday I just could not get one moment to write to you for I was more than busy.

I had a lesson and then I heard a grand Gewandhaus concert in the morning. Well I just can't describe it to you. There were two numbers with the orchestra and, then the Thomas Choir (all boys under 20) sang Xmas music. It was divine. Nikisch conducted the orchestra pieces and Dr. Shreck (my harmony teacher) conducted the boy choir. He is the dearest old man I ever saw. They sang one of his own compositions. He is world-renowned and we are certainly lucky to have such a teacher. I have four lessons every week with him, and it keeps me working to get up my work. Oh yes, the choir also sang "Winken, Blinken and Nod". You know it is a poem by Eugene Field.[1] Of

---

[1] American children's poet (1850-1895).

course they sang it in German. It was the prettiest thing imaginable.

Well Fraulein Lutz said it was better for me to have a grand piano so Miss Moore was going away, and I have hers. It is not here yet but is coming to-morrow, I hope. It is a beauty, right from the factory (20 marks per month — $5). That is what they all cost but this is an extra good one.

I had a piano lesson to-day and she told me my tone was very fine. She is giving me a very difficult Beethoven Sonata, and she gave me a whole movement to do in the holidays. I had my last lesson before Xmas — to-day.

How I wish you could see the shops. They are grand. The streets are full of people, and there are all kinds of pedlars selling paper flowers, toys, etc.— all the poor people try to get a little money selling odds and ends at Xmas. It is a wonderful sight. More to-morrow. The window is open, & I am cold so must cover up.

                                                         Helen

Sunday afternoon.

Here it is Sunday and I have not written for two days. I shall tell you why — Gladys and I have been fixing up our rooms. Now we are all settled in our separate rooms, and are as happy and contented as anyone could want. My piano came and I can progress much faster with it. It is also much better for my voice. I am saving five marks on light by only having a lamp. Gladys uses gas for her eyes are killing her almost. Now Mother dear, you must not tell Mrs. Grant one personal thing that I tell you about Gladys, for it gets me into trouble. I always tell you everything and evidently she does not, for her mother wrote her a terrible letter about Mr. Haeberlin, for Gladys never mentioned his name to her. Just be careful, first, and feel around before you tell her anything. For goodness sake don't mention the watch to her for Gladys doesn't want her to know about it, for fear it worries her. She couldn't help losing it.

I received about twenty letters and cards this morning, and I couldn't read half of them before lunch. Mother dear, your three handkerchiefs arrived. They are just lovely and we girls appreciate them so much. They are beauties. I do hope you get the one I sent you.

I got cards from Robertson, Dimpy Walker, Minnie Smith, Doc. Smith, Carpenter, Miss Thorne, John Page, and heaps of letters including one from Pug Russel, the girl in my class. It will take me months to answer them all.

If you only knew how hard it is for us to get one moment to write here, you would be glad to get what poor letters I do write. I am always so worn out when night comes, that I am too nervous to write generally. I always have to hustle when I write, for there is always something waiting for my hands to do.

I am sitting here thinking of you dear ones, to-day. You are all getting ready for Xmas, and how busy you are. We are to have our holidays now, and we will be busy too, I can tell you. I am not going to stop my singing one bit more than I can help for I don't want to go back any.

Mrs. Alves told me Friday that she expected much more from me than any of her other pupils (on account of my talent, I suppose). She says she doesn't know my voice from one day to the next. It grows so much bigger each week. I am so encouraged about all my work, and am really going to do my best to make a success of my piano and voice. I have the talent and it will only take time. I shall stay as long as you say, and as for getting married, it is out of the question, so please don't worry your brains about that. I must make my voice heard in many halls before it starts cradle songs. Kath, I shall sing for you, if you like, but not for mine for some years yet.

The Conservatory Concert Hall - from the Prospectus
(Collection of the Lochhead Family)

Friday night, Miss McKenzie, Miss Barnett and one of her girl friends and I all went to hear *Königskinder*[1] at the Theatre. We went in 85 pfennig seats — about 20 cents. It was the most beautiful fairy story imaginable. Humperdinck wrote the opera. He is living now and I have one of his songs. He conducted the opera in New York some time ago.[2] It was so beautiful. There was a snow scene, which made me think so much of home. Edna & Gladys did not go for they don't care as much as I do about operas and concerts. They couldn't be bothered running the chance of having to stand up for two hours. I never care as long as I hear the music, and we had great seats. Miss McKenzie is studying vocal, and is a pupil of Mrs. Alves. She has invited Gladys and I up to afternoon tea to-day, and we are going soon. I shall tell you about it when I come back. Gladys is here, so Good Bye for now!

Well, here I am again. It is after supper and I am ready to write to you.

We were out to tea with Miss McKenzie. It was so nice. She has lovely tea, toast, cake and popcorn. Mr. Hills was there and Mr. Lochhead, who was at the American dance. He is a McGill grad. and knows all the Macdonald College girls — Jean Hodge, Mildred Carvell, Marion Estabrooks and a host of others. He is over here studying and is a very fine fellow. He walked down with me, and a whole crowd of us expect to go skating on the tennis courts to-morrow if it is cold enough.

Last night Gladys and I went with some of the girls and had a grand skate. It was not like N.B. ice

[1] *Königskinder* (*The King's Children*), Engelbert Humperdinck, 1910.
[2] 1910.

Inside the Conservatory - from the Prospectus

(Collection of the Lochhead Family)

but we had a pretty good skate. We only stayed till half past eight. I was so glad to have my skates. I would have been so disappointed if they hadn't come. I can skate so much better on them and didn't have to pay one cent on them.

Now about the cake — I think it is mighty nice of you to send it to me — and I hope it arrives safely. We will have one grand feast when it arrives.

I am going to buy a little tea pot and have tea in my room when people come in. That will be what you give me for Xmas. With the money Anna sends I should like to buy a pair of opera glasses for I must have a pair. I would always have them to remember her by. Don't you think it is a good idea?

Those are the only two things that I want, and so I shall buy them as Xmas presents.

We are invited out to a Mrs. Doering's for Xmas night and also to Mrs. King's but we think that we shall stay here in the pension for Fraulein Schröter always makes a lovely Xmas for the people in the pension. She has a tree, and everyone has to buy a present for one person in the pension. It is not to exceed 25 cents and make up a piece of poetry about the person. We drew lots to-day, and I have to buy something for Gladys. I will write you all the particulars later. Now Saturday the Kings are going to Dresden — that is the 27th. We expect to go with them. We found out that Mrs. King is the daughter of one of Toronto's wealthiest millionaires, Mr. Luck told us. He knows them all very well. Her father is giving them all the money they want, for this man to go through the university. You would never know to look at them that they had ever smelled a million. They are so plain and have so much common sense. I like her almost as well as Irma. They have two lovely Toronto people with them, who are also going to Dresden. A Mrs. Parlow and her daughter Maida. They are over here to see about the girl's eyes. They think she will be stone blind in a very short time. It is so sad, and the mother is so nice and the daughter is beautiful. They are cousins of Kathleen Parlow — the wonderful violinist.[1] This girl is an artist and does wonderful work in her studio they say. It will be such a pity if she goes blind. It is just some little thing that comes in the eye, and no one knows how. It is not a disease exactly, but it just seems to happen, and sometimes it goes away. Mrs. Parlow is a dear, and reminds me so much of Aunt Min. They are all college people, and care a lot about education. Mrs. King is an M.A. and sings beautifully. I want to keep in with them all so I can go to see them when I go back. Imagine visiting the millionaires in Toronto! We are great friends, and I drop in to see them often.

I don't expect we shall be in Dresden more than a day or two. We all need a little change for we have worked very hard. We have to be very careful here for there are so many nervous wrecks in Leipzig. The climate is very hard on anyone here, and when you work hard you give out.

I am very careful and Edna says I look as if I was four months gone — my stomach is so fat. Little Miss Hunt has the same trouble. My skirts won't go around me, hardly. Then I am developing a double chin from singing. I shall be a peach when I come back.

I am afraid I can't put more than this in the envelope, but I shall write very often now.

All kinds of love,

Helen

XXXII

4 Sophien Platz
Leipzig, Germany
Tuesday evening
Dec. 23, 1913.

My Dearest Mother and Father:-

Perhaps we shall be too busy to-morrow night to write, so I must get a letter off to you to-night.

I do wish I could have one good old talk with you instead of writing. It is so stupid. I always forget the important things when I start in to write.

We have been busy getting our Xmas things off, and getting our work fixed up for the holidays. We are not giving anyone anything but the McAdams. We all clubbed together and bought them some nice pictures and handkerchiefs and a few such things.

Everyone over here understands that we don't have much money, and they don't expect any presents. Irma and all the others are in Italy. I think I told you about them going, didn't I? Well anyway they wanted me to go but I would not leave my work to go for such a long time. Italy is nothing in the winter anyway. Everyone advised me not to go.

We leave for Dresden Saturday, if all goes well, and will be back Monday.

---

[1] Kathleen Parlow (1890-1963) was a Canadian-born violinist. Maida Parlow French became an artist and author.

Yesterday we worked and had our last harmony lesson. To-day I had a singing lesson, and Mother, Mrs. Alves went off again about my voice. I talked to her as sensibly as I could about it and told her I had no idea I had a voice. She gave me several pieces that I have taken, and said "Now you may sing those when anyone asks you". Imagine in 15 lessons.

I got another book of songs to-day — all German, by Schumann. I have three dear little English ones that you will love, and I am singing a lot of music from "St. Paul". It is an oratorio.

She said for me to sit down and write you that I had one of the most beautiful voices she ever trained. She said that I had the talent to bring out the voice, too. She says "That is the best Xmas present you will get". Wasn't that nice of her?

I work like everything for her, for she is so interested in me. She hasn't given Gladys any encouragement and she feels badly about it, but I tell her to stick at it till it comes. Her voice is contralto, while mine is soprano. To-day was Gladys' birthday. We just celebrated it by having an ice-cream. It was so near Xmas that we did not give her anything. I am giving her a little German bible for Xmas, and Edna a calendar. We are all pulling at our expenses to keep them down. My singing lessons are my big drawing card, as regards money, but you will surely know that it is worth it. I would rather stay a shorter time and have a good teacher.

We are so comfortably settled here. I would give anything if you could walk in and see us. There is not one objectionable person in the pension and Fraulein Schröter is very careful of us all. We are all under her supervision, just as if we were in a boarding school. She never sleeps until we are all in.

To-night I went to the opera, from 6-8. It was just sweet — *Hans und Gretle*[1] by Humperdinck. Miss McKenzie and I went in the top gallery for 85 pfennigs — 20 cents. It was a dear opera. It is a children's opera. The others wouldn't be bothered going. I feel that it is a duty as well as a pleasure for it helps me so much with my voice. Miss McKenzie said to-night "Oh, let us drink in this orchestra, for we shall never hear anything like it in America". It is a grand thing to hear so many instruments.

It is now very near eleven, and I know you would rather think I was in bed than sitting here writing. I will write you all about Xmas, and what we do and get.

I am thinking about F'ton most of the time now but when I get back to hard work I won't have so much time.

All kinds of love,

Helen

XXXIII

Friday night
Dec. 26, 1913.

My Dearest Ones:-

I have just finished eating one of Germany's oranges (the first I have had) and it did remind me of dear old Nan and the many we have sucked together — such talks we did have.

Well Xmas is over, and we did have a grand time. Of course we must admit that we did think

---

[1] *Hänsel und Gretel*, 1893.

of home most of the time but we were kept busy and that kept the "lonesome" away pretty well.

The day before Xmas was a horrible day — wet, cold and not a bit like Xmas. We were out most of the day, and saw all the shops and the big crowds. It was very interesting. You know everyone in Germany has a tree, even the poorest person. The maids here in the pension had one in their room. It is their custom. They don't put the presents on the tree but decorate it beautifully and lay the presents around it, or on a table. It is all lighted with candles and has all kinds of draperies.

Christmas Eve we did not have our celebration here for Fraulein Schröter had to go to her mother's (she is over 90). We stayed here and had some fun singing and acting out.

The McAdams sent us each a bust of a musician and Queen gave us each a nice framed picture — mine was of the Kaiser and his wife. Then we got all kinds of cards and letters from everyone. You would be surprised to know how many friends we have here. It is wonderful how soon one makes them.

Xmas day — yesterday, we had a big dinner of goose, cranberry sauce, apple sauce, vegetables, etc. It was lovely.

We went walking most of the day for it was fine — just like a fall day — no snow or ice now. Then in the evening we all dressed up to kill for supper and I wore my blue dress with the train. Everyone said it was swell.

After supper we all sang "Stille Nacht, Heilige Nacht!"[1] It is so pretty and I am sure you know at least the tune. They always sing it in Germany at Xmas.

Then we went into the dining room and saw the immense tree, all lighted and all the presents lying around on a table. Now we had great fun over them, for Fraulein Schröter had written each of our names on a piece of paper, and shuffled them up. We each drew one and the one we drew we had to buy a present for, not to exceed 1 mark (25 cents) in price. Well, I wish you could have seen the things we gave each other. They were all funny, and we had to make up a piece of poetry to put in with the present.

I got Gladys and bought her an imitation diamond ring, and wrote a violent declaration of love in my poem. It was so funny. She had to stand up and read it out in front of us all. She never dreamed it was me, and asked everyone if they were guilty. Wasn't it funny? She drew my name too and wrote a long poem about me and gave me a jabot.

Then when those were all distributed we were given a parcel, which was merely a card rolled up in a dozen wrappings telling us to search in a certain room for a parcel. We all made a dive for the different rooms for our parcels, and when we got to the middle of those parcels we were directed elsewhere. Finally after searching upstairs and down we all got our parcels and what did I find but a beautiful paper knife and pen knife combined. It was lovely. Fraulein Schröter gave us all some little gift like that, and they all had a poem too. We ended up by having candy, fruit and apples and we all said we had enjoyed it fine.

This morning I got seven long letters, and cards, and Mother I received your dear letter. I always want to keep it for it is the nicest one you have written me. It made me feel good all day. You are so interested in all my operas and work that it certainly helps more than anyone knows.

To-day I have gone over everything that I could, as regards clothes, and mended, darned and moved hooks and eyes and have my room in great shape. I have worked hard, and I wish you could run in and see how neat my room looks. We have everything ready to start for Dresden to-morrow morning at 8.44. I wanted everything to be in order when I came back.

---

[1] "Silent Night".

Ida McA. and Queen were up to-day and they said they had had handkies from you. They were tickled to death with them. It must have been a lot of bother for you to get them all. Mother I have not received my cake yet or Della's gift. Likely they will come when I am away. I got myself a pair of opera glasses from you all.

Oh yes, Mut, dear, and Kath, I am going to write you a big long letter when I come back from Dresden. I want to thank you a thousand times for the mon. I tell you it looked good to me. I shall tell you what I buy with it in Dresden.

I haven't received Anna's letter yet. They will all come in time I know for the mails are slow here, and yesterday and to-day there has only been one mail. They have two Xmas Days here you know, 25th and 26th.

We expect now to stay in Dresden till Sunday night but don't know how long it will take to see the place. Imagine us seeing the Sistine Madonna. We are going to stay at the same place that the McAdams did when they were there 8 yrs. ago. The Kings are going too, and we are going to have one big time. It is such a chance to go with the Parlows, for Miss Parlow is an artist and will know everything about the pictures.

Now dear ones it is after eleven, and I must get to bed for we must be up very early in the morning. If you don't get a letter very soon don't worry for we will be too busy sight-seeing, to write I imagine.

I often think of you, and wonder if any of you have ever been sick since I came away. Please tell me if you have for I always want to know everything. I shall be good while away in every way, and act as nice and politely and truly as I can.

With all kinds of love to everyone of you.

> Good Night!
> Helen

XXXIV

> 4 Sophien Platz
> Leipzig, Germany
> Dec. 29, 1913.

My Dearest Home Ones:-

It is Monday afternoon and I am back from Dresden. Mrs. King and I came last night together. Now I must tell you all about our wonderful visit.

We left here at 8.44 a.m. and arrived in Dresden somewhat after ten. There were six of us, Mrs. and Miss Parlow, Mrs. King, and Edna, Gladys and myself.

We had written for rooms, but when we arrived there were none at the pension we wrote to, and the lady sent us to another lovely place — 1st étage. It was lovely. We had three rooms — Mrs. and Miss Parlow were in one, Gladys and Edna in another and Mrs. King and I in the third. We each had our own beds of course.

Immediately we started out sightseeing, and ended up at the Gallery. There we stayed till two o'clock and then went home to dinner. After dinner we were all pretty tired so did not get out again till about four. Gladys had sore feet and didn't get one thing out of the day hardly. We had to go with her till she got a large pair of boots. Mrs. Parlow's feet gave out too, and they were a great pair.

I felt mighty punk after dinner too, but would not give in for anything. We went out to the Dresden China store, and Mother, Anna, Kath, you should have seen the dishes. I never saw anything so grand in my life. It was a wholesale place where all the big Toronto firms buy. You could get things for wholesale prices there. We stayed there till tea-time and rushed back. I took a cup of tea in one gulp and Mrs. King and I started on the run to the theatre. We could only get seats for $2.50 or else 60 cents for standing room. We chose the latter — and will you believe it, we stood for five hours — from 6 to eleven. The opera was *The Meistersingers*.[1] We were up in the fourth gallery. Edna & Miss Parlow went too, but Gladys & Mrs. P. would not stand it, and stayed home.

Well I never heard such music, or saw such scenery before. It was certainly grand. The theatre itself is beautiful and is all white inside, with gold trimmings.

You must read the story of the *Meistersinger* Mother in my book of operas. Then you can imagine how wonderful it must be. They have almost perfect scenery, and the trees etc. are all real. The costumes are wonderful — and there are often about 75 or 100 people walking around the stage. It is all beyond anything I ever dreamed of.

We were all just about dead when it was over, but had a good supper when we went home, and had a good night's sleep. I could have gone twice the pace that I did but my usual visitor arrived when I reached Dresden and I had to be as easy as possible.

Sunday morning we went to the Gallery again, and dear ones, I can't describe it to you in any way. You can't imagine what the Sistine Madonna is like.[2] We sat and gazed at it for ever so long. Then Battoni's Magdalena[3] was wonderful also. I could tell you all about them all, but I have work to do, so must leave it till I come back, and I can show you all the cards, and you will enjoy it so much better.

In the afternoon Gladys went over to Shaw's to stay till to-day. We met Hilda in the morning. She is just a kid and doesn't know much about Dresden yet. They have only been here since September. I couldn't be bothered going about with them when I had Mrs. King, who is an M.A. to go with. She has travelled a lot, and knows so much. We were together so much. You would like her just as well as Irma. She is lame (one foot longer than the other), but she is so sweet, and is as good as gold. I wrote you how wealthy her father is. Well, she wouldn't spend one cent more than she had to. Our accounts were just about the same, only I bought more cards and china than she did, for she may go back again with Mr. King.

Edna, Mrs. K & I went out Sunday afternoon to see the city. It was pouring rain, but we got on a car and stood on the back and saw all the sights. We went clear around the circuit for 20 pfennigs (4 cents). Then we took another line and did the same thing for 4 cents. In this way we saw all the main points of interest, and crossed the Elbe four times over four different bridges. It is a large river and is the nicest I have ever seen.

We saw the King's Palace, and all the public buildings, statues and gardens. There are also beautiful residences there. We were pretty tired when we got back. Mrs. King and I decided that we had seen

---

[1] *Die Meistersinger von Nürnberg*, Richard Wagner, 1868.

[2] By Raphael (1483-1520). It survived the Allied bombing of Dresden in 1945, was taken to the Soviet Union at the end of the war, and was returned to Dresden in the nineteen-fifties.

[3] Pompeo Batoni (1708-1787); titled variously the *Penitent Magdalene* or *Saint Mary Magdalene*, this was destroyed in the bombing of Dresden in February 1945.

Souvenir Card of the *Sistine Madonna* purchased by Helen
(Collection of the Lochhead Family)

Dresden very well, and that it would be useless to stay there any longer, and spend money when we have to pay just the same here in Leipzig — whether we are here or not. Edna wanted to come too, but had promised Gladys she would wait, so she had to stay. It seemed mean, when she had seen all the main things.

We left there at 7.10 and got here shortly after nine and we were just tired out completely. What do you think of our expenses though? Isn't that pretty good?

I have a singing lesson to-morrow and I wanted to be prepared for it, so I worked this morning and must get back to it now.

I found Della's lovely tie & Mother's violets. They were just sweet, and I love them so much. The cake also arrived safe and sound, and I was tickled to death to get it, but don't bother sending more for it was so expensive for you to pay so much.

I am going to frost it when I get my chafing dish and we will have a great time. Many, many thanks.

I can't begin to tell you about Dresden in a letter. It is foolish to try. You will just have to wait till I come back. I shall write more very soon but must run now, for I am going to hear Aida to-night, and must study it, as well as practise. I am going with the two Scotch girls here. They are from St. Andrews, and have a wonderful home there. They have invited me there on their way home.

Now dear ones, adieu for now, Heaps of Love

Hoping you are all well,

Helen

P.S. I feel fine now and am going to dig in hard at my work.

Diary of the year 1914.

January 1st. Thursday.

Here we are in Leipzig. having completed one term's work at our music. Our holidays are being spent rather quietly. with the exception of a two days trip to Dresden. On new years' eve. Fraulein Schröter gave us a party. Those who were here for xmas were there. and about five or six Roumanians who were friends of the two German girls. young herr Schröter was present also. We had games and punch and cake were served. The toast to the new year was drunk. and we all wandered off to bed. I confess that my thoughts were in new Brunswick considerably but I did enjoy the

First Page of Helen's Short 1914 Diary.

(Collection of the Lochhead Family)

Diary

January 1 to February 28, 1914

January 1st, Thursday

Here we are in Leipzig, having completed one term's work at our music. Our holidays are being spent rather quietly, with the exception of a two days trip to Dresden.

On New Years' Eve, Fraulein Schröter gave us a party. Those who were here for Xmas were there, and about five or six Roumanians who were friends of the two German girls. Young Herr Schröter was present also. We had games and punch and cake were served. The toast to the New Year was drunk, and we all wandered off to bed. I confess that my thoughts were in New Brunswick considerably but I did enjoy the experience, for it was so different from any I had ever had.

New Year's morning, Gladys (whom I must call G, here-after, to economise on space) Miss Beattie, Irma Shaw (who was down from Dresden for a few days) Mr. Cohen, and I went for a skate, at the Tennis Platz. It was no fun, for there was only an inch of ice and one would strike each occasionally and make very fancy figures.

The rest of the day I spent quietly at home, the others having gone to the Rodelbahn[1] to slide.

January 2nd, Friday

In order to take the afternoon off I worked all morning at warbling and spieling. In the afternoon, Ruby, Ella, Mr. Cohen and I went "Rodeling". We had to go on a car to Gundorf, 20Pf., and then walk about a mile and a half. It was grand, though, and we had some fine slides. In spite of the fact that there was a red-cross man there, we managed not to need him and did not have one dump. Weren't we cold and wet when we got home, though, at 7:30 (late for supper).

January 3rd, Saturday

At ten o'clock I was practising, and worked hard for G had been at it real early, and I did not want her to out-do me. I worked till one.

In the afternoon at two, we went down to that corner near the Supreme Court House and found two sleighs awaiting us, with two good-natured drivers. Fraulein Tiele, Mrs. Cohen, Mr. Cohen, Allie and Lottie were in one; while Ruby, Ella, Edna, G. and I were in the other. We went through

---

[1] A toboggan run.

MORITZ ROSENTHAL

Moritz Rosenthal (souvenir postcard)
(Collection of the Lochhead Family)

the woods to Connewitz, and took a little café by storm, there, and almost frightened the waiter to death, for fear we would break his poor electric piano to pieces to see the works. The coffee was no good so we hustled back to the sleighs and came back home (2 marks! but it was worth it!).

I worked till seven and Gladys and I amused Herr Schröter after supper.

N.B. I then had a bath in the bathtub!

Sunday, January 4th

After reading some very interesting Canadian mail, we started off to church, arriving five minutes late as usual.

Everyone being away for their holidays, things seemed rather slower than usual, but Mr. Sterne gave us a real good "English sermon".

In the afternoon Mr. and Mrs. King came over for afternoon tea, and stayed till after six. Edna and I had a lesson on photography in the evening up in Mr. Luck's room.

Monday, January 5th

At last my letter from Liverpool has arrived and it won't be long until the sender will be here. Two weeks is pretty long though when you are simply waiting.

Our "infant class" in harmony started to-day, and dear old Daddy Schreck tried to pound into our heads the difference between a cadential 6/4 and a passing 6/4.

All the talent of the pension was combined to-night to try to afford amusement for the crowd (that is for what is here of the crowd). In about a week every instrument in the house will be strained to the utmost, from 7 till 7 at night. Poor things!

Tuesday, January 6th

My singing lesson was good, for I received two new songs (Schumann's Dichterliebe!).[1]

Mrs. and Miss Jones came around to see us in the afternoon.

In the evening I darned stockings, and listened to the Misses Beattie's account of their trip to Oberhof, with Mr. Cohen (will that trip to London and Berlin ever get ended?).

[1] *Dichterliebe*, or *The Poet's Love*, a song cycle by Robert Schumann.

Wednesday, January 7th

Red Letter Day!

We heard D'Albert play in the Gewandhaus.[1] He played one of his own concerts, and also a Liszt concert. It was simply splendid. Nikisch conducted. There was a piece by Schönberg that the orchestra played which was hissed.[2] Who knows it may be famous some day like some of the other great things which people have hissed.

A busy afternoon followed, for Edna, Muriel Hunt and I went to *Figaro*.[3] It was very neat, and pretty typically Mozart.

I was in the seventh heaven when Susanna sang "Endlich naht sich die Stunde".

Thursday, January 8th

Two lessons, as usual, which takes up all the day. To-night we have had a big time organising an orchestra consisting of Haeberlin Hills and the Canadian Frauleins, yours-truly taking the part of Nikisch. Mr. & Mrs. King, Mrs. and Miss Parlow, acted as a very appreciative audience. We hope to be heard from later in the season.

Friday, January 9th

One day nearer the fifteenth! It has been dark and dreary most of the day. I worked and had a lesson.

At half-past three Edna, Maida Parlow, and I went down to see the art stores. We saw two of the modern paintings of the Kubists and Futurists exhibited in a window. They were very similar to the Schönberg concert that we heard in the Gewandhaus on Wednesday. We will all have to develop some to appreciate their work.

To-night I have heard Pussini's *Madame Butterfly*.[4] Oh what music! The scenery was good and the voices very fair, for here. I did enjoy it but was homesick when I saw the two American suits on the Consul and Pinkerton. I really can't imagine an American man doing such a thing as he is supposed to, and I don't think he is typical of any class of Americans, as I heard some one say to-day.

The "Star-Spangled Banner" was brought into the harmony very cleverly.

Saturday, January 10th

There was a general rehearsal for a private lesson in piano. Then after dinner was the usual rush to harmony. After supper we were all in my room for a musical evening, but we just fooled — no genuine music.

Sunday, Jan. 11th

The day was brightened by four letters from home — Maida Parlow did our hair very nicely in

---

[1] Eugen D'Albert (1864-1932), composer and pianist, was born in Scotland, spent much of his early career in Germany, and became a citizen of Switzerland in 1914.

[2] Arnold Schönberg or Schoenberg (1874-1951), Austrian composer and music theorist, who emigrated to the US in 1934; his music was designated "degenerate art" by the Nazi party.

[3] *Le nozze di Figaro*, The Marriage of Figaro, Mozart, 1786.

[4] *Madama Butterfly*, Giacomo Puccini, 1904.

the afternoon and Gladys, Edna, Mr. Haeberlin and I went to the Sevcik Quartet in the evening.[1] It was a great inspiration. Hans Bruck played with them.

                                                                Monday, Jan. 12th

I dropped the primary class in Harmony, so I can work much more now. The Parlows went at noon to-day. We were all sorry to have them go. We went skating in the evening. Mr. Lochhead was there and we skated and came home together.

                                                                Tuesday, Jan. 13th

My singing was good and I got some new songs. I worked in the afternoon, and Miss Beattie, Mrs. King, Muriel and I went to the *Tales of Hoffman* in the evening.[2] It was very good, but not what I had expected. The "Barcarole" was about the only thing in it. I thought it was too tragic to be beautiful.

                                                                Wednesday, Jan. 14th

Gewandhaus day — Fifth Symphony — Beethoven, Nikisch conducted it without a note.[3] Elena Gerhard[4] was in the Gallery. There was an American dance in the evening but I didn't go for Will comes to-morrow and I didn't think it quite fair to run off that way. Ella and I went to the Casino and saw Neilson act in *Engelein*. It was sweet, and she acted perfectly.[5]

                                                                Thursday, Jan. 15th

Will's Visit!
Well how can I ever describe it.
Thursday night saw an excited girl facing the platform waiting for the 8.40 train — dressed in a navy blue suit, black furs, & black hat with a yellow feather.
A taxi carried us to Pension Schröter and a hearty welcome followed, after which an exciting time was had trying to alarm the five etages in the house opposite to let Will in. The affair ended disastrously in Will having to take a room here, for the night. Horrors! Me waking and rousing Fraulein S. out at 11:30.
Rather an exciting week and a half was spent, in seeing Leipzig, and trying to work at the same time — I must say it was strenuous.
We visited also the principal cafés, Casa Francais, Panorama, Bauer, and dear little Bourssia; also the Elkline Kellar and the Carleton Restaurant shall not fade from my memory very soon (especially the price 60 pfennigs for one apple).
I saw *Mignon*,[6] from a stall in Erste Rang,[7] another modern play given for the first time (from

---

[1] The Ševčík Quartet, a Polish string quartet founded in 1903.
[2] *Les contes d'Hoffmann*, Jacques Offenbach, 1881.
[3] Without a score.
[4] Elena Gerhardt (1883-1961), German mezzo-soprano, former Leipzig Conservatory student who often sang with the Leipzig Opera and worked with Nikisch; she emigrated to the UK in 1934.
[5] A silent movie starring Asta Nielsen.
[6] *Mignon*, Ambroise Thomas, 1866, revised 1870.
[7] The first rows.

Zweite Rang) and also had my beloved Case[1] in *Falstaff* from "Balcon".[2] A trip to Corso followed[3] and the American dress suit took the cake. We sat in front of the orchestra but did not remain long. I was never so embarrassed in my life. We felt much more at home at the Panorama afterwards.

Mrs. King entertained us very nicely at tea on Sunday night, and we had very pleasant times going around.

Will then went to Wien,[4] Hamburg, Munich and called around here on his way to Frankfort — for two days.

We three girls were sorry to see him go without us, but I was glad when the strain was over and I could settle down to work and think out a new lot of plans.

It is wonderful how every plan one makes can be turned upside down in one glance, almost.

* * *

After Will went I saw a grand opera *Acté*, (the first performance given in Leipzig). The composer was there and it was received very well.[5] The dancing was the main feature — it being centred around Nero's time. The half of Pension Schröter occupied a section of Zweite Rang.

Tristan and Isolde, Rigoletto,[6] I also heard, the former for the second time. Urlus was not singing but the guest was fairly good.

Then the Russian Ballet was grand, especially the "Dying Swan", danced by a pupil of Pavlova's.[7] The "Carnival", was also fine.

At the Gewandhaus, *Das Paradies und Die Peri*, (an oratorio by Schumann) was very well put on. Case and Joeger singing two principal parts.

Rosenthal[8] was splendid also with a Chopin piano concert and splendid encores.

The Bohemian Quartette played their last concert of the season with Lamond at the piano.[9] I went with Mr. Lochhead.

The next night I heard Elena Gerhard and she was simply divine. As an encore she sang Schumann's "Nussbaum".

The climax of the concert season was Schönberg's *Gurralieder* in Albert Halle.[10] He conducted an orchestra of 150, and a choir of 600, with about a half dozen soloists. I never saw such applauding in my life. It was simply wonderful. The crowd went wild over him. He will certainly be on the Bach-Beethoven list if I am any judge.

My birthday passed off rather slowly, for I had a headache — but I never received such attention or such beautiful flowers, and gifts before. Everyone remembered me and it was mighty nice when I was sick!

---

[1] Obscure. Oddly enough, there was in the second half of the twentieth century a singer, Stan Case, who sang Falstaff, but he was not born until 1959.

[2] *Balkon*: the balcony.

[3] Possibly a theatre or cabaret?

[4] Vienna.

[5] *Acté*, Juan Manén, 1903.

[6] *Rigoletto*, Guiseppe Verdi, 1851.

[7] Anna Pavlova (1881-1931), famous Russian ballerina.

[8] Pianist Moriz Rosenthal (1862-1946), a pupil of Liszt; Jewish and born in the Austro-Hungarian empire, he emigrated to the US before the Second World War.

[9] Scottish pianist Frederic Lamond (1868-1948), another pupil of Liszt.

[10] The *Gurre-Lieder*, which had had its premiere in Vienna in 1913.

Pension Schröter
Leipzig, den *jan. 7* 1914.
Sophienplatz 4

my dearest Ones:— it is
wednesday, and we are
back at work, now,
and don't have much
time to write letters.
Our harmony, takes
so long to do, and
then so many lessons.
It just keeps us on
the jump.
I received mother's
dear letter Sunday,
and each one seems
to get better than
the last. They are
far better than mine

Letter on *Pension Schröter* Letterhead

(Mount Allison Archives, Lochhead Fonds, 8701.)

LETTERS, 1914

XXXV

4 Sophien Platz
Leipzig, Germany
January 3, 1914

My Dearest Ones:-

Old 1913 is gone, and here we are three days in the new year.

This week has been so busy that I haven't had a chance to write to you. When I do write, I like to tell you everything, so I always wait till I have a long time ahead of me to write. Then I generally forget a lot of things that I want to tell you. It is so hard to remember everything.

Well Wednesday I had a great treat in hearing Elena Gerhard sing, in the Gewandhaus. She is Nikisch's sweetheart, and he has a wife besides. He conducted the orchestra, and played her accompaniments on the piano. It was some interesting to watch them.

Mrs. King and I had seats in the sixth row from the front, and we saw it all. It was in the Gewandhaus.

She was the daughter of a Leipzig policeman. Her voice was perfect. I never heard anything like it.

Well, Tuesday morning. Gladys came back and brought Irma Shaw with her. She is a dear little thing and we have had heaps of fun with her. She is really too young to be over here, for she does not take it seriously enough, I think.

Her father came down for her yesterday and he is very nice. He reminded me so much of Father that I was as homesick as could be. When he talked I could just imagine it was father. They are spoiling her I think, for they have heaps of money.

We have not been killing ourselves working this week, but have been doing a little to keep up our technique.

New Year's Eve. Fraulein Schröter gave us a lovely time. She gave us a party. We played games, and had all kinds of fun. We heard the old year ring out, and it made me think of you people, but we had so much fun that we could not get very lonesome.

New Year's morning. Gladys, Miss Beatty, Irma, and I went skating, and also Mr. Cohen (a Jew, who stays here). The ice was rotten but we had a skate just the same.

Then yesterday we had one grand time. I worked all morning, and then we took a street car and rode for about four miles to Gundorf, (a suburb of Leipzig). Then we had to walk about two miles to what they call the "Rodelbahn". That is where there is a big hill, and we hired two sleds, and you should have seen us go. It was swell. There were crowds there and I tell you it was simply grand. I wore my old sailor suit, my red coat, that white hood affair that I bought in Saint John, my white gloves, and wasn't I a swell.

We have nothing like it home, and think of the hills that go to waste. It is not half as high as ours, but they make use of everything here.

Last night it rained, and so that snow was packed down somewhat to-day. They have not had so much snow in twenty-five years, and now there is not more than four or five inches.

Hardly any of the people in the pension had ever been in a sleigh, so to-day Fraulein Schröter arranged for two sleighs for us to go for a ride — five in each sleigh. It was grand, and we have just come back. We went away out to Connewitz, (another suburb) and had a cup of coffee at a lovely café.

It made me think how little I appreciated old New Brunswick — where we can drive so much. The sleighs are funny here — the driver sits behind, and drives. I just wish you could have seen us sailing through the woods. Of course all the snow in the city is taken away, and we had to walk quite a way to get a sleigh. The two Scotch girls had never had a ride before and they were wild over it.

On Wednesday we start in work for certain. I have done a lot of work so far to-day, and am going right at it, as soon as I finish this.

Oh yes, I got a dear little vanity box from Gladys for Xmas. It is sweet — you wear it on a chain. Jim sent me a lovely book, and I had a dear booklet from Miss Paull, from New York. Then I had heaps of cards and letters from everyone. Thank Aunt Jeanie for her dear handkerchief — Mrs. Peter McDonald sent us each a dear wash-rag that she worked. I expect to write to her to-morrow. Wasn't it nice of her?

Will sent me chocolates, and let me tell you about Arthur Andrew — he called for the florists here to send me flowers (he wrote me about it) and they evidently did not get the message right or something, for they did not arrive. Ha! Ha! I suppose he will take a trip over to see about it.

I have a chance to send this to the mail, so bye-bye dear ones for now. Fraulein Schröter sends best wishes for 1914. She is sweet to us. All kinds of love, and I am a good girl.

Helen

P.S. I always think how you would like a thing before I do it. Don't worry, for we get along fine and expect to work like everything this term.

XXXVI

4 Sophien Platz
Leipzig, Germany
January 7, 1914

My Dearest Ones:-

It is Wednesday, and we are back at work, now, and don't have much time to write letters.

Our harmony, takes so long to do, and then so many lessons. It just keeps us on the jump.

I received Mother's dear letter Sunday, and each one seems to get better than the last. They are far better than mine now, for I really don't get time to write half decently.

Anna, dear, a thousand thanks for your dear handkerchiefs. They are sweet.

Mut, you know I think of you and Kath whenever I go to the opera, for I took your money to get my glasses. They are swell — pearl.

Mother, don't worry about my Xmas present from you and Father, for I got as much or more than any of the others, and I think I am getting my share of presents in getting this year over here.

We all had to draw ninety dollars the other day, for our board, and Con. fee. It nearly broke my heart but, I just had to do it. I hate to think of you dear ones working so hard to keep me over here. However I shall try to pay you back if possible by the pleasure you will get from my training, especially in voice.

I have the loveliest songs you ever heard — now I can sing Schumann's and they are beautiful. Mrs. Alves is certainly bringing me along.

Thursday morning. I must finish this and mail it on my way to my piano lesson.

Yesterday was one big day — we went to the Gewandhaus in the morning and heard D'Albert play with the orchestra and Nikisch conducted. You can't imagine what he was like. It was perfect. He is about the greatest pianist of the day, and is Liszt's pupil. He is French, and he played one of his own concerts, (that is a piece with the orchestra of 100 men). Everyone went wild over him. Then last night Edna, Miss Hunt and I went to *Figaro*, by Mozart. It was lovely. We sat in Dritte Rang (highest Gallery), and it only cost us 85 pfennigs (about 22 cents).

I heard My Aria sung, and it was sung just the way Mrs. Alves told me to sing it, so she must be about perfect. I can imagine it so much better after hearing the opera, and the piece sung.

I saw May and Ida yesterday. They were tickled to death with their handkerchiefs.

May is taking a few singing lessons. I guess, they did not tell even Annie, for about a month. Her teacher can't touch Mrs. Alves, so I am not worrying about her getting ahead of me in voice. I bet I shall keep ahead in that for it certainly is my talent.

Ida heard me sing and she went wild about it, and only sang a little English song.

Will expects to be here next week. I will write you every single place I go, and all about it. Don't worry, for you know I would not do anything foolish or that you would not like.

All kinds of love, Helen.

XXXVII

4 Sophien Platz
Leipzig, Germany
January 11, 1914

My Dearest Mother & Father:

I have written to Anna and George, and to Will and Kath so you two dear old souls are going to have a letter all to yourselves this time. I don't have much time to write here for there is so much going on and so many things to do.

To-night we went to hear the Sevcik String Quartett.[1] It was grand. They had a great pianist with them. It just made me want to get right home and to work at my technique. That is the main thing, and it rests entirely with the pupil. The teacher can only tell one what to do, and you just have to dig in.

I am going at it with an awful vim this week, and hope to accomplish a lot.

I got four letters from Mother to-day, and they were all grand telling about Stell and Anna J. I was glad to hear it all, for I think about you all so much.

Mrs. and Miss Parlow have been here for a few days. They leave to-morrow for Italy, and sail for Canada the 29th Jan.

They have invited me to Toronto to visit them, and they have a swell son — a Forestry grad from Toronto and a friend of Arnold Shives. They are very educated and nice — great friends of the Kings.

Now Mother, dear, you needn't think Will had one thing to do with my not going to Italy. I could not spare the time for such a long trip, and it would have been an awful strain to travel so much and then get right down to work. Even our small trip to Dresden tired us all out, and I can't imagine what the other would have done. You want to have lots of time to travel and see things right. I am keeping my eyes wide open for a chance to go to Italy in the summer, for everyone advised me to wait till then. It is punk in the winter — just imagine Venice!

Will is not here yet, but will be along soon I suppose.

Mr. Lochhead asked me to go to another dance this week, but I have refused for Gladys and Edna are not going — and I thought it best not to go. I decide everything according to my best ability and I know you will trust me in every way. Whenever I am in doubt as to what course I am to take, I pray about it and ask Mrs. King or some older person whom I can trust.

Mrs. Jones and her daughter (Irma's friends from Halle) are here now, and she offered to chaperone me to the dance but I refused even then for fear I should not go. She is a dear woman, and was in to see us the other day.

I had a lovely letter from Irma, and she wants to tell me all about her trip so I shall go over some day I suppose, or else she will come here. They understood perfectly about my not going, although they wanted me to be with them. She thought I was wise not to go when I explained it to her.

Fraulein Lütz has never mentioned my name to Gladys, only to tell her that I was very musical.

She told me all about Edna on Saturday. She feels so sorry for her and asks me what she can do to help her. She is a true woman, and is not pulling the wool over me. She said she would rather Edna

---

[1] The Ševčík Quartet.

would go home, for she can't do anything.

I feel terribly about it, and don't dare breathe it to her. Don't you let on for your life.

She says she likes Edna, but she has no idea of rhythm or concentration (two very important things).

I am digging away, and, if spared, I want to conquer my technique, and I have the other naturally.

My voice is coming fine, and I am doing all I can, so don't worry your dear hearts about me, but look forward to next winter when we will be together and you can enjoy all the music I learn.

Hoping you are all well, and not working too hard. I think about that awful ice so much. Do be careful Papa.

Love, to you both, and trust me for I won't fail you. It is 25 minutes to twelve so excuse writing.

Helen

XXXVIII

4 Sophien Platz
Leipzig, Germany
January 11, 1914

My Dearest Anna and George:

I want to thank you both many times for your dear remembrances.

I did not get the notice from the "Philistine" till the other day, telling who sent it to me. I thought of Daddy and was quite sure he was the guilty one.

Then the three handkies arrived the other day. Many thanks. They are very dainty and I shall carry them only on state occasions.

I am so sorry about your parcel not getting off, but cheer up, it will come before the end of the year. I didn't want to run any risk of your not getting the things. Will, will take the small things back anyway and mail them from there to you.

I want to bring you and the kiddies heaps of little things when I come back, so if you like the rubber goods (aprons) that you will receive, let me know and I will get you more.

Well, Stell is with you by this time I suppose. Mother wrote me all about her clothes and gifts. You will like her I am sure and she will learn lots from you I bet (make a bow please.)

We are working like — now, and expect to from now on.

We are hearing all kinds of operas, and concerts, and really it is grand. This week we have heard D'Albert play in the Gewandhaus, and also heard *Figaro* and *Madame Butterfly* at the opera.

To-night we are to hear the Sevcik String Quartett. I have heard the Bohemian, and am anxious to compare the two.

I wish you could hear all the grand music with me. I shall do my best to describe it all to you when I get back.

You will have to come down to Seaside again and we will talk it all over. I think about our summer together so much, and I did enjoy every bit of it. I must send a card to the street car conductor. I am sure he would appreciate it.

I have had cards from Carrie, Agnes, and Eva Linton. Please thank the former two, for really I never get a chance to write. Someone comes popping in with a funny story or something of the kind and the letters are left till the next time.

I have just been in Miss Parlow's room, and she has dressed my hair for the concert to-night. She is a Toronto girl, and she and her mother are just here for a day or two. They leave for home on the Twenty-ninth.

Now dear ones, I could write to you all day, but I want to write Kath and Will a note, and then Mother's, so I have enough mapped out for to-day, don't you think.

I would give anything to see the kiddies. Honestly I get terribly homesick to see them whenever I see a kid on the street I think of them. They must be grown up by this time. Kiss them all for Aunty Helen, and tell them she will bring them German dolls and toys when she comes back.

Love, Helen.

XXXIX

4 Sophien Platz
Leipzig, Germany
January 17, 1914
Saturday (11 p.m.)

Dear Ones:

Here I am sitting at my desk with my blue kimona on writing to you. I am ashamed at not having written before, for I really intended to, but honestly I have been very busy, and haven't had a moment.

Will arrived Thursday night so we have been busy hustling him around to see the sights. There is so much to see here and so many places to go that it seems that we will never see half of the place. Why I have not been over more than half of it myself, and I have been here for months now.

Doesn't it seem like a year to you? It does to me, and I have seen so much in such a short time.

Now I know you are crazy to hear all about Will, so I shall just tell you all there is to know, and if I omit anything that you would like to know, just please ask me, for I want you to know every single thing that there is to know.

Mr. Haeberlin got him a room across Sophien Platz from here. It is right next to his room. I have never seen it, and he is there as Mr. Haeberlin's friend. Everyone here thinks he is just passing through on a business trip and so there is no commotion about it whatever.

Friday morning we went to the Art Gallery and had a nice morning looking at the wonderful art and sculpture. I have not begun to study it all yet.

In the afternoon I practised and Will wrote his cards and letters. We went to *Mignon* at night, and it was grand. My but I wish you could have heard the music.

We had an ice-cream afterwards, and were home before Gladys, and some of the others who were skating. (I would rather hear opera any day than skate, when I can do that in Canada).

To-day I did not see Will at all, till noon. I worked hard at my practice and he fooled around town seeing the sights.

At one o'clock, he, Mr. Hills and I went to Thomas Kirche to the Motette. I left before it was over for I had a harmony lesson. Mr. Hills took Will in the meantime all through the University and around town.

At half-past three, Gladys, Edna, Will and I went skating in the park. It was simply perfect, and we had a good skate, only all our skates were dull, and we are going to get them sharpened before the next time. We have had it very cold here, and all the ponds and places are frozen. It is a penetrating cold which goes through your very bones. I don't mind New Brunswick cold nearly as much.

To-night we had a big crowd to supper, and the Beatties, Schröters, Dearns, and we Canadians had a dance in the hall. It was great fun. Mr. Haeberlin came over about 9:30 and he and Will left shortly after 10, and then Gladys and I had our usual little chat and now she has gone in to patch her pants (she wears a pair about a day and then they are worn out).

We have great times laughing about getting fat.

Mother dear, your lovely letters came to-day — also one from Aunt Nin, Della, and a card from Mrs. Tubery Kierstead. She is a dear. You should go to see her, mother.

I enjoy Mother's letters so much — so please write when you can. I would come straight home if I didn't get mail — and Father must write once in a while for I do love to hear.

I hope Anna has received my Xmas things. If not please let me know for I must see the man about it, if she hasn't.

Now to-morrow we expect to go to church — and then to Mrs. King's for afternoon tea. I do like her so much, and it is certainly mutual. It will be great to know her and the Parlows in Toronto.

Mrs. K., Miss Beattie, Miss Hunt and I were at the *Tales of Hoffman* — Tuesday. It was good but could not touch *Mignon*. I play some of the music from the latter, and I am going to learn some of the arias to sing from it. At the Gewandhaus Wednesday, I heard the wonderful fifth symphony of Beethoven's. It was fine — next week there is a good singer so we expect to go.

Now dear ones don't worry about Will — for I have been perfectly frank with him in everything and have not put myself under the slightest obligation. I try to pay wherever possible and we all go places together and anyway I am not at all keen on settling down to one fellow. I want to see more, and know the world better. There is plenty of time yet, and I haven't the slightest intention of being engaged. Now that is final, so don't worry.

I get lovely letters from all the boys, and Will knows it, and so I am not deceiving anyone. He is a mighty decent lad, but I really think he is too old for me. However I am not worrying about that subject now for I must work, and bring home some results.

As far as I know now, I will come back and teach a while, and have a look around, and perhaps take another trip over here, again, to see more.

I expect to travel next summer, if I find some nice people to go with and if I accomplish what I want to. I shall be home in September but if not, I must make myself stay till I succeed, — although I do get lonesome lots of times — you and Father will just have to go back with me, so that I can act as interpreter for you. You could never get along in a foreign country alone without a guide.

It is nearing twelve so I must say "night-night" for now. I shall write in the middle of the week though so don't worry. I am fine, and am doing what I think is right.

Love, Helen

XL

4 Sophien Platz
Leipzig Germany
Tuesday,
Jan. 27, 1914

My Dearest Ones:-

I did not write on Sunday for Will had not gone, and I thought it would be better to wait till he went, so that I could write you everything.

He went last night at 8:40, to Dresden. From there he will go to Vienna, Frankfurt, Nurnberg,[1] Munich, and other places. From these places he will go to Paris, and spend a week or so there. Then he expects to spend a week anyway in London, and will stop off at about a dozen other places between there and Liverpool. He has many other firms to see, so he will likely be over here till March. Then he will sail for Canada, and you will see him and hear all you want to know about me.

He will be home a week or two before he goes up likely, for he will have heaps of business to see to. He said he would ring you up before he went up, or else write and let you know what evening he will be up. Of course he will only be in Fredericton one night, and go back next morning so you must have all your questions ready. He took a little parcel to Edna's mother, so when he lets you know that he is coming you can let Mrs. Baird know (if you want to) and you can all have a talk about Leipzig. Gladys' mother isn't in Fredericton, and I would ask Mrs. MacDon. up for she would publish it all around and perhaps Mrs. Baird would. You do just as you like about it.

Now I have sent several little things to you — two silk shades for a lamp or electric light (typically German). I want you to take your choice Mother and give the other one to Kath. I thought perhaps the one with the colours would go well with our parlor, but you take the one you like.

I have sent the rubber things to Anna, so you roll them up, and if you like the rubber apron I will get you one too. Then the Dutch pins and handkies are for the kiddies, and one handkerchief for you Mother.

The little salt and pepper shakers are for you Mother, and I got them in Amsterdam. They are sweet I think. You fill them from the bottom — I have a little Dutch shoe in the same china for my bureau. Then the table cover is for you also. That was what I wanted to give you Xmas, but was afraid to send it. It only cost $1.50 so I think it was pretty reasonable. It is all hand work — made in the mountains here. It isn't just the shape I wanted or the pattern, but I didn't have time to look around. Now I would love to have sent more but I wouldn't ask Will to take it, for he bought so many things for his own people. As it was, I considered that he took enough.

He was very kind to me, in every way, and I enjoyed his visit. We parted the best of friends, but no more, and we may never be.

I am so interested in my work that I don't bother about getting married, anyway I want several years to look around yet, and I told Will that. He was rather disappointed but understood perfectly my point of view.

He took me to the opera, and any place I wanted to go, and I think he is a perfect gentleman in every sense of the word.

We were very careful how we acted, and no one here knows that he came here to see me.

---

[1] Nürnberg, Nuremberg.

Everyone thought it was chiefly a business trip.

He entertained himself all day, and I worked, so I am not behind by any means.

It was great to see someone from home, and we all enjoyed his visit very much. He will tell you anything you want to know, for he saw all the places that I go, and met most of the people in the American colony. He went to church, with me, and saw every place that we go to lessons, and shopping, and to the bank and even the dentist's.

I am glad in a way though that he has gone, for I didn't want him to be here two weeks. We went down and called on the McAdams, and they were out so we left our cards, and so we did our duty. That was yesterday, so they can't say I didn't go to see them. I would have been more particular about them seeing him, only they said so much about liking Jim better, after the day in Montreal, that I just didn't bother myself too much about them seeing him.

We didn't do one thing that could in any way be misunderstood and as I said before, Will is one fine chap. However he is not the man for me. I want education, and a profession, if possible. You know I can't let Anna have the laugh on me, so I have to keep busy to keep up the race.

We can talk it all over when I get home for there is heaps of time.

Fraulein Lütz told me Saturday at my private lesson that she did want me to stay two years, so I may try it, but am not sure yet. She said it was well worth it, for I was very musical, and then when I go back I can get twice the money for lessons. She said Gladys could not interpret but she thinks perhaps it will come out as she grows older. My whole feeling is right she says, so that is a good deal to work on. I asked her plainly what she thought and she told me very encouraging things. She is still discouraged about Edna, though and says that she is too old now to do anything.

I am digging away at my voice. Will was pleased with it and my piano too, but he does not appreciate it like a person who cares about art, and music.

He is too practical for anything very high in music, but he tries his best to appreciate it.

My German is coming, but I have not been studying much lately — now I am going to settle down to it, and work hard.

Mother's letter came Saturday. I was so glad to get it. We don't get much mail now for we are too busy to write — Cary Thomas wrote me a lovely letter and asked me to be her bridesmaid for her wedding next August. My but I would love to be there but if anyone takes a trip you, Mother, and Father are going to be the ones. I do wish you could come over and go back with me. We would travel on a cattle boat or a lumber boat if you would only come. We could have a grand time together, and you will never come if you don't come when I am here.

I would stay till August or September and that is the most perfect time to travel here. Think it over and let me know what you think. I will write more often now, when Will is gone, for I shall have much more time. I hope you will not be worried for not hearing more often, lately, for I really haven't had a moment.

Will took dozens of pictures and he will take them up for you to see. He will lend you the films.

I hope you are all well, and happy. I think about you all so much. It won't be long now, so I must work and make the best of my time.

All kinds of love, Helen

XLI

4 Sophien Platz
Leipzig, Germany
Feb. 1, 1914

My Dearest Home Ones:

Wasn't I glad to get your two dear letters to-day, one from Mother and Anna, and Kath's a day or so ago. It is grand to get mail over here, and Mother, dear, I look for your letters just as much as you watch for that faired haired cass[?] postie.

Yes, Papa, I want a birthday present from you, and it is nothing more or less than a letter, now it won't cost us more than five cents and if there is any excess postage I shall pay it at this end.

For Mother's present, I am going to have a bath every month in the bathtub, now when you reckon up that it costs 10 cents for a bath, here, that counts up in two years. It is the greatest luxury I can have here, for it is so hard to do, with a sponge bath, after being so warm practising. Now don't be alarmed at my wanting to have a bath, for I really enjoy them more than anything here, except my meals. I had a grand one last night and changed all my clothes, and darned my stockings. If I ever get back home I bet I shall live in the bath tub. They say you never miss the water till the well runs dry, so I guess that's the way with me.

My last epistle was all about the Hon. Sir William Skinner. Well this one will not be, for I have at last freed my mind of all boys, and have become resigned to the fate of an old maid. I can earn a good living by teaching Anna's and Will's kids to warble and play the piano, so I guess that is the best thing to do.

Well this week we have worked real hard, and heard some good concerts too.

Must go now!

More later!

Monday morning!

Back at Schröter's again at eight o'clock. Now I have had my coffee and Brötchen[1] and must get to work, for I have a lesson at eleven.

It was a perfect walk over this morning, and the streets were crowded. Everyone goes to work so early here, and school goes in at eight.

I could write more but must get back to work.

Love to you all! Helen

---

[1] Buns or rolls.

XLII

4 Sophien Platz
Leipzig, Germany
Feb. 9th, 1914

My Dearest Ones:

Here it is Monday night and your letter has not been written. Well it is simply because I have not had time, so I will try to make up for it all in this one. Mother's letter came this morning and one from Harry, I tell you I was glad to get them. Mother, don't tire yourself writing, for you have so much work to do, and then you have Anna to write to, too. I just love to get your letters though, so write just whenever you feel like it.

Now for the pictures. These are two we took Xmas Eve, and I think they are grand. They were taken with Mr. Hill's camera. Now I have tried to write all particulars on the back of the group, as to names.

The pictures were taken in the dining room, and that is where we eat. Of course you can't tell anything about the room for it was all upset for the night.

Fraulein Schröter looks nice, I think.

I can assure you that I never looked better in my life than that night, but you would never know it to look at the picture. I wore my blue dress with the train. Edna has her eyes closed too. It is not because my eyes are weak for they are not. Gladys has to wear glasses and her eyes trouble her lots, but still in a picture she can keep hers open.

Of course half of the pension was away when this was taken and you don't see all the crowd, but it will give you an idea.

Everyone of them are nice, and some are perfect geniuses. The girl in the black dress is a pupil of Teich's. She gives concerts.

The picture of the tree is good, but Hills took two pictures on one film, and you will notice my lamp and table if you turn the picture side-ways.

The tree was wonderful though, and I shall always remember it. Fraulein Schröter and the other kiddie are at the side.

So much for the picture. I am enclosing one for Anna too, so you will each have one of the group. If you want to know anything about them ask me, and I will tell you.

Now last week was busy, I can tell you. Will came back from Vienna, via Leipzig. I wrote and told him not to come, but he just came Monday and went away Tuesday night. I did not give in an inch and have not the slightest intention of doing either. He is in Paris now, and will soon be sailing I suppose.

I just worked right ahead, and never stopped anything for him.

Tuesday night the whole of Pension Schröter almost went to a new opera *Octé*.[1] It was a grand thing. The scene was laid in the time of Nero and the dancing wonderful. It was the first time it had been given here, and the composer was there, and came out and bowed after the last act. He was a Spaniard.

Wednesday morning. The Gewandhaus concert was splendid. Nikisch conducted his favourite symphony without a note.

---

[1] *Acté* by Manén.

I stayed with Mrs. King Wednesday night. He is getting along fine now, and will be out of the hospital real soon we think.

I just love Mrs. K. She is just like a mother to me. We are both so glad that we both expect to be here part of next year at least.

I really feel as if I ought to go home, and it all rests with my voice, what I shall do. Mrs. Alves will be here till August anyway, so there is time enough to plan yet.

I am getting all kinds of compliments on my voice, so it must be doing well. Anyway I am working away at it, and have two new Italian songs. I have not had any before these, but they are beautiful and you will love them. I have had about thirty German songs so, you will have lots to hear. Then of course the English ones are not nearly so hard.

At my piano I am working most, as Mother says technique is the principal thing, and that is what I am striving to get. It means slow practice. I had a great private lesson in it on Saturday and I tell you my fingers are improving. They are much fatter and stronger.

I am determined to stick it out here, until I have something to show for my money, and then I will teach.

Annie McA. said she wrote you to-day, so she told you, I am sure that I was out skating with May on Saturday.

But let me tell you a joke! Ida borrowed my skates and started out to have a spin on the pond in Johanna Park. I missed the performance much to my regret, but it is reported that she went around three times and then succumbed to it. (Old maids for you, every time. Never too late to try!)

Anyway they have been very nice to me lately, and can't seem to do enough for me.

We are having a mask party in the pension here Saturday night — Fraulein S. is giving it, and I am going as "Madame Butterfly".

May loaned me a butterfly for my hair, and one of the girls is going to lend me a kimona. I will write you all about it later.

Yesterday Mrs. James and her daughter were here to tea with us. I made tea in my little pot, and we had your lovely fruit cake, and some other cakes and bread and butter. We all stuffed in on it.

Miss Daly was here too. She has entertained us. In the evening everyone came into my room and we had a great sing. (My voice being the leading Soprano Ahem!)

Well I haven't said half I wanted to, but I must not write any more to-night. I shall try to write in the middle of the week too.

Mother, dear, don't worry about me — for I am fine, and working just as hard as I can. My teachers are good, and I am sure I am improving in every way.

I shall stay as long as I can stand it to leave you two dear old souls alone. If I do stay next year it will only be till Xmas. I think — so we will hope to all be together then anyway. With all kinds of love, From your poor little "baby" in Germany.

　　　　　　　　　　　　　　　Helen

XLIII

4 Sophien Platz
Leipzig, Germany
Feb. 11, 1914
Wednesday noon!

Dearest Mother:-

I have just about ten minutes to write you a little mid-week letter, for a card does not seem the same to you as a letter, I know.

This morning I did not go to the Gewandhaus, for it was a violinist and I thought I would save my two marks for a pianist or vocalist. Then I always miss so much time from my practice.

I came home from Mrs. King's and started in to work like everything, and I have had a great chance for everyone except the blind boy and I are out. I have already done two hours piano, and about a half hour vocal.

Right after dinner I have a harmony lesson, and then I will hustle back at it again.

Yesterday I worked very hard too for I had a vocal lesson, and got in four hours piano practice besides.

I have not been out to opera this week yet but expect to hear the *Meistersinger* on Friday. I think a little rest from so much going out, is good, and then I appreciate it much more when I do go.

To-night Mr. Lochhead is coming in. He is the McGill boy I wrote you about. His father is a professor in McDonald College, and I think he is a very nice boy. He asked me to go to another big dance on the 19th but I refused, for I don't like to dance with lots of the boys here, and you have to when you go to a dance where they are.

Herr Schröter, the fraulein's nephew has invited me to go to a very "chic ball" on the twenty-sixth, with his aunt as chaperone, but I will not think of going. I just want to be friendly with the Germans, and no more.

Now don't you think me wise in refusing to go? I bet you most girls would jump at the chance. Well I can have all the dancing I want home, and don't come over here to get that.

Oh yes! My little English girl, Muriel Hunt, wants me to go to England to see her in the summer. They may go to the Isle of Wight for the summer, and it is simply grand there. Wouldn't it be fine? She is a perfect girl in every way, and the 25 yr. old. Then the Beattie girls have invited me to St. Andrews, Scotland, and you know the finest golf courses in the world are there. They are very wealthy and are nice too.

There goes the dinner gong, so I must away. This is just a note to tell you we are all well, and working like -.

Heaps of love to every one of you. Enclosed is Anna's picture of Xmas party.

Helen

Pension Schröter Maskenfest
Grant Lochhead and Helen in upper left, sailor and geisha.

(Mount Allison Archives, Lochhead Fonds, 8701.)

XLIV

4 Sophien Platz
Leipzig, Germany
Sunday Night
Feb. 15, 1914

My Dearest Ones:-

Here it is after ten, as usual and your letter has not been written. We three girls always sit up late Sunday night to write home, for there doesn't seem to be any other time during the day.

Well we are all pretty tired to-night, for our big mask ball came off last night. It was a grand success, and now I must tell you about it. Edna is writing home too, so we are liking writing the same things about the big affair.

We all had to get up costume, so I chose a Japanese geisha girl. I borrowed a kimona, and had my hair done up on top of my head, with two chrysanthemums, and little fans stuck in it. We had masks on, and I didn't know hardly a soul in the pension. There were a lot of strangers too — Fraulein Schröter's nephews, and their friends. In all there was about 30 or 35 here.

We had some English people too — Mr. Stephen, Miss Beattie's friend, Mr. Lochhead, and Mr. Luck came down for a while. Edna was an Indian girl, and Gladys too, but they didn't know that the other was going to be it. They both looked well.

We had pictures taken so we will send you some if they are any good. Then you can see all the costumes, for I really could not begin to describe them all to you.

They cleared out the longest room and the hall for dancing, and they had a man to play the piano. We did have a grand time, and I wish you could see me dancing around the German way. You would laugh. I have become quite accustomed to it, now though and get along nicely.

We had salad, lemonade, fruit, cake, and two other drinks which I did not taste. The Germans smoke and drink punch at a great rate, but it never worries me a particle. I just refuse to do either, for I haven't the slightest desire to do such things. The very nice girls here smoke and the Beattie girls do too, and dear little Miss Hunt, but I would not touch one of the dirty things to my lips.

Well I was determined not to miss church to-day on account of the big time, so I was up at eleven, and in church at half-past and I was the only one out of the pension who went (except two Catholics). We had a lovely sermon, and I would not want to have missed it.

I wrote to Earle this afternoon, for I had a lovely letter from him to-day, also one from Mother, and one from Jim Wathen. I am so glad, Mother, that you are making a new table cloth, for we did need one didn't we? You must have a lot of nice things like that when I get back, and we will have a little tea or something of the sort. I am just aching to get into a kitchen again and do some cooking, for I love it so. I would like to cook enough for those hungry college girls, even. The time will soon slip around though and I hope you will fight down the lonesomeness like I have to. It is mighty hard sometimes, but I say to myself what a wonderful chance it is for me over here, and dig in.

To-night Edna, Mr. Lochhead and I went to the Bohemian Quartet. Friedburg (Liszt's pupil)[1] played with them. This was their last appearance this year, and I have enjoyed their concerts so much. We were home about ten, and now we are writing away for dear life.

---

[1] It is uncertain to whom she is referring by "Friedburg"; see f.n. page 57.

Group at the Pension Schröter Maskenfest
(Mount Allison Archives, Lochhead Fonds, 8701.)

The Canadians, l. to r. Mr. Luck (?), Edna Baird, Helen, Grant Lochhead.
Front: Gladys Grant.
(Mount Allison Archives, Lochhead Fonds, 8701.)

Mr. Roadman and Mr. Harper were in, on Friday. They came in to hear some lectures, and so I couldn't see them much. They were very nice and Mr. H. wants us to get up a party to go to Italy at Easter. He thinks his Aunt from Eng. will go too. Wouldn't it be grand? I must go down there, for it is such a great country. Let me know what you think?

It would not be an expensive trip, for the Roadmans did it very reasonable they said. Harper did not go with them — only Middleton.

Well I must run away to bed for I have a lesson to-morrow morning, and must get up early, to practise up my technique.

I have been looking for Papa's letter, but it has not arrived. Mut, I wish you would drop a line too, once in a while, for I love to get mail, from you all, and poor Mother has to write so often, that I don't see how she ever gets time to write so much.

I am gradually dropping my large correspondence for I find time only for your letters, so if my friends get cross they are not worth thinking about, when they know I am so busy.

Well dear ones, I hope you are all well, and not worrying about me, for I am doing the best I can, and trying to look after myself in every way. I ask Mrs. King anything I want to know, and she is always very kind in telling me what she knows.

Love and kisses to you all.

I do hope Kath is well. I shall write her soon.

Helen

XLV

4 Sophien Platz
Leipzig, Germany
Wednesday Evening
9:30 p.m.
Feb. 18, 1914

My Dearest Mut:-

Here is a letter for your own self. I know you won't write to me till I write you an answer to your letter.

I have just left the bunch of tangling, one-stepping, Bostoning[1] Germans to come and have a chat with you before I go to bed.

Everyone is practising up for to-morrow night when the big masken Fest[2] comes off. I am not going for I belong to the labouring class now, and am afraid of tiring my melba-like warble[3] for my lesson the next day. It seems a shame to miss such a chance to see such a mixed crowd in fancy dress.

We are getting along fine here, but sometimes old New Brunswick appears mighty good, as we

---

[1] The one-step and the Boston are dances.
[2] *Maskenfest*: a masked festival.
[3] Dame Nellie Melba (1861-1931), Australian operatic soprano.

think about it. I am bound to stick it out though till I have some class to my technique. Then Canada for me, and I shall always be content. This is no place for natural ordinary mortals, but more for the long haired, wooly ones.

Night before last though I heard Elena Gerhardt sing. She is about the best here — and I never heard anything so beautiful as her voice. She sang before in the Gewandhaus and was so good that I went to hear her in her own concert. She sang one of my pieces.

Then last night I heard a great oratorio in the Gewandhaus for 10 cents — Nikisch conducting — just imagine such a thing. I keep wishing all the time that you could hear some of the good stuff. It is beyond anything I ever dreamed of.

To-day I have done over four hours work, besides my lesson, and am pretty tired to-night. To-morrow morning I have a piano lesson at 11, and must get up early to have my technique good. Really I don't get time to breathe here. There is something doing all the time. We can't read much and that is my great regret for I do love to read about music and Germany.

We read aloud some and now we are at present reading "Inside the Cup" by Winston Churchill.[1] It is good.

Mut, I wish you would borrow Billy Laskey's camera and take some pictures for me. I have not a sign of a picture of Mother, nor Kath, nor Mickey Boy, and I would just love them if you would. I get so lonesome for I have so few pictures, only yours and Father's. I have written to Anna for one of her, but she is too busy with the judge to stop to have her picture taken.

Oh yes, you might take one of Celia, if you have any left, and Mary Sykes.

By the way, please remember me to all my friends, Billy Laskey — Billy Golden — Fletch, Earn, Charley Edge, and you know — anyone whom you like and think I would remember them.

I bet you are the happy boy now, — and I am sure happy for you, and hope and pray that everything will come off in fine style. I wish I could be home for it, and it will make me all the more lonesome when I hear about it all. Nevertheless I must think of the future, for I speak now to be the musical instructor of the family. Between the Massies and Vans, I think I can keep the pot boiling.

Now Mut, don't forget the pictures will you? and I will send you a lot of Leipzig too.

Be good, and you will be happy, and please write me a note once in a while, for I think about you so much, and how little I saw of you in your dear home before I left. I would sure like to drop in now and spend the evening telling you all my adventures, for they are interesting I assure you.

It will take years to tell you all.

Well Bye-Bye for now. Love and kisses to all, and tell dear Mother I am well and happy and get lonesome sometimes to see her.

Helen

---

[1] Not Winston (S.) Churchill, the British statesman and historian, but the American novelist Winston Churchill (1871-1947), author of *The Inside of the Cup* (1913).

Elena Gerhardt (souvenir postcard)
(Collection of the Lochhead Family)

XLVI

4 Sophien Platz
Leipzig, Germany
Feb. 22, 1914

My Dearest Home Ones:-

On Wednesday I wrote to Mut, and hope he has delivered all the news to you. To tell the truth there is not much to tell you except work, for that is all I am doing now. I haven't been out to a concert this week, only to the Pictures last night. They were splendid, and we heard the new Edison talking machine, and they played three pieces in English. Well I was never so tickled in my life. They had a picture entitled "A College Reunion", and a crowd of boys came in and sang all the old college songs and played on all kinds of instruments. Of course the Germans could not understand it, and we did have the laugh on them. It was the first thing we have heard in English since we have been here. The Beatties, a friend of theirs, Gladys, Edna and I went. It gives you an idea of the German life to see the picture shows, but we go very seldom.

This morning I got up about nine, had breakfast, and went through my room from top to bottom, tidied up my clothes, tables, bureau drawers, and I just wish you could walk in and see how sweet and cosy it is. Then we went to church and had a fine sermon, and nice singing. It is a perfect day, and I feel like staying out all the time, but must write letters — for we are going to hear *Tristan and Isolde* to-night, and won't be home till late.

Oh I have so much to tell you, and I don't know where to begin.

First of all my work — I had a private lesson yesterday, and I had a heart to heart talk with Fraulein Lutz. I asked her when I could possibly make my prefung[1] (the shortest possible time). She thought it all out, and told me that she thought I could make it a year from this Easter — that is a year from this March. I was simply overjoyed for it is such a short time to do it in.

She said she was sure about the piano part, and that if I worked hard on the German, I could get the other subjects all right.

She said that Edna and Gladys couldn't possibly make theirs then — and that I was degrees ahead of them. She says it was no mistake in my coming over here, but she is very doubtful about the others. She says I am "clever", and in her broken English said that I was a "lyrical person", not in the least sentimental.

Now dear ones you will just simply have to let me write this to you, for I haven't anyone else to tell it to, for it is all about myself. This is exactly as she said it.

She said I must have one month of complete rest in the summer, in order to do the work, for it is very strenuous.

I must get a private tutor for my German, so that I can attend classes after Easter. Mr. Luck is going to get me one.

Now, I tell you it is a might big proposition but I am willing to tackle it if you people say the word. It all rests with you. I will be lonesome here alone, but will stick it out with Mrs. King. Then I would have my big certificate and could teach anywhere.

I want to take more in voice too, for I am doing so well in that, but I could never teach it, and so must stick to the piano.

---

[1] *Prüfung*: examination.

LEIPZIG. Gewandhaus.

The conductor of the orchestra. nikisch

mendel-sohn

The Gewandhaus, with inset of the conductor Nikisch, annotated by Helen.

(Mount Allison Archives, Lochhead Fonds, 8701.)

Mr. Lieppert, Mrs. Alves' best pupil came to me yesterday at choir practice, and told me that my voice had increased to twice its former size, and he said the quality was wonderful. He is a big bug, and has been offered everything in America. He said he wished that I could go back to New York in August with the Alves family and he, and study there. I might do that, but I would rather finish my piano. He was away from her a year and it didn't effect [sic] his voice in the least, so I will be all right till I go back. I won't have time to take voice next year anyway, with all my piano.

Now I want all of your opinions and can we afford it? The latter is the main thing.

If Mother came over we could live cheaper by having a room and cooking our own meals, but I wouldn't ask you to leave dear old Papa, for he would be so lonesome.

If we could afford it I wish you could come over to go back with me, or to see me, while I am here.

After August my awful singing bill will be off and it will not seem so much money.

I do on as little as I can, and spend all on seeing and hearing.

Now this is all I can write to-day for I have heaps of letters to write. (Oh yes, Mother, Irma Roadman expects another arrival). They expect to be in England at the time. She is such a dear. I may go out soon, for they will be leaving in May, I think.

Oh another thing! I had one fine letter from Hib — confessing everything — and telling me all kinds of things. He said I had more sense than any girl he ever met. Ha! Ha! Poor boy, he seems to have it bad, but he can just get over it, for the way he acted before. He isn't worrying me any. I like to think that he didn't do the throwing over, for I have a hand in it, now.

Well dear ones, I must really close. We expect Canadian mail to-morrow.

We are all well and happy.

All kinds of Love.

Helen

XLVII

4 Sophien Platz
Leipzig, Germany
March 2, 1914

Dearest Ones:-

Here it is Monday, and your letter is not written. I am ashamed, but really I haven't had a moment to write. Yesterday there was someone in the whole day, and I would not stay up late to write for I don't think it is right to miss my sleep.

Saturday was my birthday, and I just want to tell you what they all gave me. Why I never had such a big time in my life. The only drawback was that I had a sore throat and a headache in the afternoon. I lay on my bed most of the afternoon, and did not rush around, and so it was all gone yesterday.

Well I never got such greetings in my life — roses — chocolates — etc. Gladys gave me a 1/2 doz. roses and a bunch of violets, Edna, a box of lovely fancy cakes, Mina Shearer — two beautiful handkerchiefs — her sister in London (who was here for a while) three beautiful handkies (blue, pink, lavender, the latest), Allie and Lottie Dearn — a collar (lace). Will — flowers, chocolates, telegram, and a dear clock for my writing desk — wasn't it nice of him? and I only write him once in an age. Mrs. Cohen (Jewess, in the pension) a lovely pot of flowers. Fraulein Kroll (with whom I speak German) a pot of flowers, Muriel Hunt, a pot of flowers, and a little German boy who comes here to see us all (he is only 16 or 17) a bunch of flowers. They made candy — and arranged a dance for me in the evening but I did not dance, but went to bed early and had a good sleep.

Yesterday they had my special pudding, the one I like best, at dinner, and lovely fowl too. I hadn't the slightest idea of getting anything like that, and it was just one surprise after another. I certainly have made some good life friends here.

Allie Dearn bathed my head all the afternoon that it ached. She is a dear girl, and I just love her. She helps me all the time with my harmony. She is very clever, and plays the violin.

I am taking special German lessons with Herr Prof. Dr. Bennewitz. Mr. Luck got him for me. He is inspector of all the Leipzig schools, and is a member of the city council. He charged 50 cents a lesson, but he is the very best, and I just got him by a miracle — he just likes to keep up a little English-speaking. He is also a Prof. of English in some school here. Mrs. King has to pay $2.50 for three lessons, and her teacher isn't half as good, so I am very lucky. He only took me for I am a B.A.

and Mr. Luck gave me a great blow up. He is very nice to us, and helps us when he can.

I have had two lessons and am coming along fine.

You should see my room now — it is sweet with so many flowers. I am better and not working hard for a day or two till my throat and cold get completely cured. It was just from my stomach. The German food makes me bilious, and we all have a little upset sometimes, but it never lasts long.

Now dear ones don't worry. I am perfectly all right but am not even deceiving you by not telling you this. I tell you everything.

I am saving as much as I can, and hope you don't think I am wasting.

Will write a great big long letter Wednesday — and tell you more details. Must run mail this now so it would go out on today's train.

Love and kisses to you all!

Helen

I have had papers, books, music, and letters from Earle, and he is certainly going some! I don't care what his father is — he is O.K. Anyway, you must go to see his mother.

When she called on you.

XLVIII

4 Sophien Platz
Leipzig, Germany
Sunday Night
March 8, 1914

My Dearest Ones:-

Here it is half past ten, and your letter is not written. Well I shall start it to-night and finish it to-morrow.

To-day I didn't get up early — nine o'clock — we went to church and did not get home till one. Then I wrote three short letters that I have owed for weeks, and then we had tea.

After tea Edna and I went over to the hospital to see Mrs. King. You know she has always been lame, and she went to the same doctor that operated on Mr. King, to see if he could help her. One leg is shorter than the other, and they are trying to draw it back into place. She had immense weights on her, and it must hurt terribly.

Now don't mention this until you hear it yourself but Edna is going over to-morrow to let the Dr. see her back. He is about the best in Germany, so if anything can be done he ought to be able to do it. She hasn't any hopes of it, but there may possibly be a chance.

Well I have been digging away, and had a private piano lesson yesterday. I dropped all my old Bach and Beethoven and got a lot of new stuff — the Moonlight Sonata, and a Beethoven Concerto. I will have to dig in now to get them up. However we are all getting tired from the winter's work, and may possibly go to the mountains at Easter for a few days — complete rest — I don't think it would be wise to do much sight seeing for we have a hard term ahead of us, after Easter. We are not

The Gewandhaus Concert Hall, Leipzig.
A postcard sent home by Helen, with the Conservatory and other points of interest marked.
(Mount Allison Archives, Lochhead Fonds, 8701.)

decided yet, for the holidays don't start till April 5th. We have two weeks.

Friday night we heard one of the most wonderful things that has been here for ever so long.

It was an immense oratorio by Schönberg, and he conducted the orchestra of a hundred and fifty, and six hundred voices with the leading soloists as well. It was the first time it has been played in Germany and the people went wild over it.[1] They brought the poor man back about fifty times. It was received with great enthusiasm and that means [something] in Leipzig. I can't begin to write you all about it, but I am sure I won't forget it soon, and will be able to relate it all when I get back. We had to pay 3 marks (45 cents) for a seat, but we would have paid $5 for the same thing in America, and then it will not be there likely for years to come.

I will not write more now, but hustle off to bed, and try and not lose my beauty sleep.

Monday morning

Well I have had my breakfast now, of brotchen, preserves and coffee, and now I must finish this letter while my room is being done. It takes them so long to finish it, when there are so many rooms to do.

I have a letter from Irma to-day, and she is coming in on Thursday morning to the Gewandhaus concert and also to say good-bye to me. My, but I hate to see her go, for we are such friends. I am sure we will always be great friends. I told you about her expecting an arrival didn't I? I don't know where she expects to be sick yet, but will write all particulars after Thursday.

I am going to work all morning till twelve and then go over to show Edna the way to the hospital.

---

[1] The *Gurre-Lieder.*

She is no good to go alone anywhere, and it is such a pity. I can go anywhere and Gladys also. Remember Calgary, Mother?

I haven't seen the McA's for a few days, but must go down to see them for they won't be here much longer. To tell the truth we won't miss them very much for we don't see enough of them.

Well I must get to work, dear ones, so I will close this uninteresting letter. I must write a better one next time, and I will likely have more to tell you.

I received Mother's two letters and Chris's. I am so glad you have had Eliza and Ida. Don't tire yourself with too much company but keep enough to keep you from being lonely. All kinds of love to you all.

Helen

Mother, I am doing a doily for your birthday but it may not arrive till later for I don't get much time to sew. I wish you a lovely birthday just the same. Also dear old Nan on March 12th. I bought a lovely photo album from you for my birthday present. I am pasting all my pictures in it and it will be lovely to look at when I get back. It cost $1.75.

Postcard view of Kaiser Wilhelmstrasse, Leipzig
(Mount Allison Archives, Lochhead Fonds, 8701.)

XLIX

4 Sophien Platz
Leipzig, Germany
March 11, 1914

My Dearest Mother:-

My letter Sunday was so short and to the point that I must do my best to give you something more this time.

This is what they call a fest day, in Germany.[1] It is a day of general repentance throughout the country, and is even more solemn than Xmas. This morning we are not allowed to practise, so I decided to write you a little note, and then go for a walk in the woods with the girls. We have had spring here for a month already, and the grass is green and the leaves are almost out. It is very different from our spring weather, and they say that it always rains all April.

Almost every day I go for a walk (talking about an hour) with Fraulein Kröll. She is a Russian girl who has lived here all her life. You can see her in the picture I sent you. We converse in German and English, and it is a wonderful help to me, in my work.

I told you that I am taking two lessons a week in German with Herr. Prof. Dr. Bennewitz, didn't I? I must do that in order to attend classes at the conservatory after Easter. He is simply splendid, and there is no reason why I shouldn't learn quickly. It means that I must work pretty hard at it, but I am bound to speak German before I come back, and not be like Kathleen Hodge and Jeanie. Why Jeanie didn't know anything for having been here a year. I would be ashamed if I were she.

My singing is coming along fine, and I know you will love my songs. I can hardly wait to sing them for you. I am not a bit nervous about singing, and I am terribly so about playing. I sing before the whole place here and it never jars me a bit. I sang before Mrs. Alves' best pupil the other day, and he said I didn't realise what a voice I have.

Saturday I got everything new in piano — Beethoven Concerto — The Moonlight Sonata — and Bach's Preludes and Fugues. It means an awful lot of work, and I get discouraged many times, but still keep at it.

Everyone of Fraulein Lutz's pupils have their blue times about their music. She is very strict, and sometimes we don't know what to think of her. She is very good though, and we all know that it just means work, and longer time.

I am trying to make myself stay after Edna and Gladys go home, but it is going to be a fight. I am so afraid something happens to you or Father, that I can't seem to think of staying away longer than next August. If anything happened either of you while I am over here, I think I would hate music ever afterwards.

Of course it all depends on what I accomplish by the end of July when the Con closes. If I decide to continue with voice I shall probably go back to New York with Mrs. A. in August. If I can play well enough then, I shall get a certificate from the Con, with my teacher's opinion of my playing, etc. which should be enough to allow me to teach anywhere.

I want you and Father to see the fruits of my work, and to enjoy it, and I am not going to stay away over here so long and you two poor souls living there alone. Life is too short for that.

I want to take my M.A. degree next year if possible, and I plan (if I go home) to do it after Xmas.

---

[1] *Festtag*: a holiday or holy day. Significance uncertain; Easter was April 12th in 1914, so March 11th fell two weeks after Ash Wednesday.

It is so hard to plan over here. I think and think all the time, and pray about it all.

The only thing I can do is to let things work out themselves.

I am spending an awful lot on my lessons, but am economising in every other possible way. I am enclosing my washing [accounts] for ever since I have been here. I have reckoned it out in our money and it is $5.60 approximately since September. Now isn't that pretty good? You see Mother there is one article which costs me so much, 2 cents for every one of them, and I usually have so many as you know.

I have tried to keep my accounts of everything I spend, but I found it simply impossible. I have everything nearly up to Xmas, but since then I haven't been able to do it.

I just spend what I have to and no more, so please don't worry. If I am spending too much on lessons you just say the word, for you hear what I draw don't you?

Well it is time to go walking now, so I will close and get my coat and hat on.

I haven't told you half I intended to, but you will just have to ask if you want to know anything. I can't remember everything to tell you.

Heaps of love to you all, and write me what you think I ought to do. I am being very good and working hard.

Helen

L

4 Sophien Platz
Leipzig, Germany
Sunday afternoon
March 15, 1914

My Dear Ones:-

Yesterday brought two letters from Mother, and I certainly devoured them. I also got my usual weekly volume from Earle. Besides that I got a letter from Irma and one from Mr. Harper. Letter day is a big time here.

I wrote you Wednesday. Well Thursday Irma came in, and I met her at 9:06 in the morning. Helen James took her to their house and from there to the Gewandhaus. I came home and worked till half past twelve and then went down and brought her up here to dinner. We had dinner and after a little rest, started out, to do some shopping before her train went at 4:10. We had a lovely cup of cocoa at a little cafe before she left. We are such great chums, for Irma is very young. She wrote me a note next day, thanking me for giving her such a lovely time in Leipzig. I haven't done anything like she has for me. She said that she and Mr. R. were planning on the good times we would have when I go out to their home in Ohio to visit them. Wouldn't it be lovely?

Well she told me that Mr. Harper has decided to go to Italy at Easter, and has his trip all planned out. I was immediately anxious to go, for it is a perfect time to go to Italy, and there are special rates all over. One can travel over every part of Switzerland on boats and trains (travelling all day if you want to) for ten days, for 10 dollars. Think of it! The prices are awfully cheap. It is a chance of a life time - that is all!

I coaxed Edna and Gladys to go, but they haven't the cash, they say. Edna would go, I think. If she wasn't having her back treated. She is crazy to go.

However I hunted around, and found a dear little American girl who says she will go — Miss Taylor. She is much older than I am, but is very short. We are going to try to get someone else to go too, if we can, but if not we simply must go ourselves. It is the only chance I shall have, for you can't go there in the summer on account of the heat.

The whole trip will be under a hundred dollars, and we shall be gone three or four weeks. We get reductions on our board here, so it isn't so bad. Then I arranged with Fraulein Lutz about my lessons. I shall only miss about a week from the Con and that is nothing. We leave here, with Mr. Harper, the 30th of March, and will be back the fourth week in April. He has studied the trip for months, and knows exactly what we are to see, etc. It is just like taking a guide. You needn't worry about us going with him, for he is one of the finest gentlemen I ever met. Irma said she would trust me to the end of the world with him, but of course I wouldn't think of going alone, and we are doing our best to get some older lady to go.

Mrs. King would go if it wasn't for her leg, and I can't wait, but must go when I have holidays.

I know you will be crazy about my going, for it has always been my dream. We will be ten days in Rome, two or three in Venice and Florence, Milan and Naples will also be visited. We are not going to rush and get all tired out, but we are going to travel very cheaply, and stay at Y.W.C.A. and Y.M.C.A. places. They are all over Italy.

We girls could never go alone to Italy. It isn't safe, and think of going with such a beautiful man. He is as good as gold, and reminds me so much of Dr. Smith.

If, however, you get this letter before March 30th, and decide that you would rather I wouldn't go, simply cable me, and I won't be in the least disappointed. I have thought it all over, and decided according to my best judgement and that is all I can do. When alone Gladys and Edna are crazy to go, but can't. When Mother said she would like me to go, I thought that I never could go with better company. If anything happens that Miss Taylor can't go, I shan't go either unless I can find someone else to go with. If I do go I shall write you all particulars along the way, and don't worry about me, for I am in as safe hands as could be found. You can see that by his face.

So much for Italy! We heard two great operas the other night — *Cavalleria Rusticana,*[1] and *Bajazzo*[2] — two Italian operas. We stood in the highest gallery for 20 cents. I was terribly tired afterwards but we couldn't get seats and had to stand or not hear it.

We are digging away at our music, I haven't time to read this over. Please excuse mistakes.

Helen

---

[1] By Pietro Mascagni, 1890.
[2] By Rugiero Leoncavallo, 1892.

LI

4 Sophien Platz
Leipzig, Germany
Monday, March 23

My Dearest Mother, Father, Will and Anna:-

Oh yes, before I forget it — send me some Spruce Gum. I am dying for some, for Harry's supply has run out some months ago. He thought he gave me enough to last two years. I guess.

Well I have almost given up the Italian trip, for Miss Taylor can't go, and Edna does not feel she can afford it from her back. I hate to miss it, but unless I find some other nice person I shall not think of going. The McA's said it would be perfectly right for two girls to go with Mr. H. so I felt fine about it — but no one has the craze to go that I have.

I will get another chance though, perhaps before I go home.

The McA's sail April 25th. I was out to church with them yesterday and Ida and Queen came up in the afternoon. Mr. Lochhead was making me a call at the time, and so they met him, and will be able to tell you all about him.

He hasn't been over for months, for he has been working very hard. He has his B.A. and M.Sc. from McGill and has almost completed his course here. He is very clever, and a nice boy. We sang hymns, and talked about the lovely Sundays at our homes in Canada compared with the German Sunday, which is so un-Christian. I am going to Hoffman's *Tales*, at the opera with him this week. I have heard it once, but it will stand hearing twice.

Mr. Harper will be very disappointed about our not going to Italy, and I will too. If I can only find someone to go with — there is a week yet.

I am working very hard, and am digging into my pieces for my prefung.[1] I am going to stick to it as long as I can stand it to stay away from you dear ones.

I may stay a few months in England on my way back to have my voice finished by one of the big bugs in London. What do you think about it? My little English friend thinks it is a good idea. If I do, you Mother and Father will have to come over and see England, Scotland and Ireland with me.

The McA's think I am going home this summer, with the girls but I won't if all is well home. I shall stay and stick it out here.

It is perfectly safe, and I will have Mrs. King, who would do anything in the world for me. She has done more than anyone for me, together with Irma.

The McA's were tickled to death with Father's letter. I told them I was jealous, and they thought it a big joke.

Dear Ones it is nearly three and I have so much work to do, — must close for now. I am working like sin and haven't time to worry. Am getting French as well as German from my teacher. Love to all, of you, and a kiss for dear little Mary, from Aunty Helen.

I forgot to tell you that I was weighed and it was 141 lbs. I got weighed on two different scales, and it was the same. Isn't that grand?

---

[1] *Prüfung.*

LII

4 Sophien Platz
Leipzig, Germany
March 25, 1914

My Dearest Home Ones:-

It is Wednesday morning, and my room isn't finished yet so I shall write a few lines to you, to tell you about the glorious time I had last night.

Yesterday morning Fraulein Schröter came into my room and asked me if I would like to go to a big affair in aid of Germany's colonies, with she and her younger nephew (not the one who asked me before). This one is an officer in the army, and is one fine boy. He has been around here so much that we all know him well, and know that he is true and good.

I considered it perfectly all right to go when Fraulein Schröter would go too, so I accepted.

I wore my yellow dress, and Fraulein Schröter had a lovely black and white evening dress. Herr Schröter wore his uniform, for they all have to wear them. He is a university boy, but had to stop and put in his two years in the army, the way every boy has to do.

Well we went to the immense hall where the affair was held (at the Zoological Gardens) and I can't begin to tell you what it was all like. There was a great programme of all kinds of singing, dancing, and costume affairs.

There were numerous booths all over the place where they sold cake, ice, beer and every kind of stuff to eat.

Then there were people dressed in costumes and they went about among the crowds selling cards, etc, from the colonies, and flowers, and everything was designed to bring in a big lot of money. For instance they didn't give back any change, and that brought in an extra supply of money, for nobody ever had the right change to pay for anything.

Well they bought me ices, cakes, lemonade, cards, flowers, and treated me like a Queen. I never saw such kindness. They tried their best to give me a good time and they succeeded all right. It was such an interesting sight to see all the people and the dresses. It would take me years to tell you about it. I was the only live American there, I think, and I was like a cat in a strange garret, except for the Schröters. They were so pleased that I enjoyed it, and said I must write you all about it.

We had three or four dances after the programme and came home at 1:30. I was asleep by 2, and feel fine to-day. Not the least bit tired.

It does you good to get out like that to see and hear something entirely new.

Everyone else here is jealous because I had the opportunity of going. I can't seem to help them asking me, so what are you going to do about it?

After Dinner!

I have worked like sin all morning, and have done so much. I am not a bit tired, and expect to work all afternoon, and go to hear Lambine play to-night. He is Miss Sheares' teacher.

The McA's are coming up to-morrow night to see us, for Edna and I may possibly go to Italy on Monday with Harper. Edna has almost decided to go, but is not sure yet.

It will be one grand trip and you need not say one word as to who we are with — simply say that we went in a party — for it is nobody's business.

When the McA's say it is perfectly all right, I say so too. They asked two old Scotch ladies about it, and they said we would miss a big chance by not going.

I will write you all the particulars on Sunday.

I hope you are not worrying Mother and Father, and that dear Father's cold is better. Do be careful and not work too hard. I do think about you all so much, and think of the chance you are giving me. I am trying to make the best of it, and hope you will be pleased with my work.

I will write Will and Kath as soon as I get a chance, and dear old Nan and George. I think about you all, every day, and hope that you will all be spared, till I get back. Don't worry about us in Italy. We are in the best of hands.

Love, Helen

LIII

Munich, Germany
Tuesday, March 31, 1914

Dearest Ones!

Here I am in Munich having come from Leipzig to Nürnberg yesterday. Had the most wonderful afternoon there and saw everything. It was very very interesting. I have just one moment to write and must go to breakfast. We arrived here at 10:50 last night. Had a good night's rest. Leaving at 8:20 this morning for Venice — the city of my dreams. I will write you volumes from there, but just wrote this to let you know what a wonderful time we are having. Edna and I get along fine.

Love from us both.

Helen

LIV

Venice, Italy
April 1, 1914

My Dearest Family:-

Now I must write you everything in particular about our trip. Of course I can't begin to tell you all we have seen for it would certainly take years. I would like to keep this letter, however, so that we can read it over together when I get back and then I can fill it all out.

Venice, the Bridge of Sighs.
(Mount Allison Archives, Lochhead Fonds, 8701.)

We three left Leipzig, on Monday morning at 8:20, and we had a great send-off. Four of the girls came down to see us off.

We arrived in Nürnberg at 1:15 and after checking our grips we started off to see the sights. Mr. H. had read a lot on the city and it was more than interesting.

We saw the old old buildings which are the oldest in Germany. It is so quaint and you feel as if you had stepped back a century.

We visited the old churches and the wonderful square with its market. Then we went to Dürer's house.[1] He was a great painter in the time of Luther. His house was very interesting.

---

[1] Albrecht Dürer (1471-1528).

We then went up to the castle where we had one grand view of the city. There we saw all the old instruments of torture of all centuries, and we have cards of them so that you will be able to hear all about them.

From there we went to Hans Sachs' house and saw all his old relics.[1] He is the main character in DIE MEISTERSINGER (Wagner's Opera). You must read about him, Mother.

Then we went to the dearest old inn where Dürer, Hans Sachs and a heap of others used to go to drink beer. It was the quaintest place I ever saw. We had a genuine German dish of sauerkraut and worst[2] — just what the old guys used to eat. My! I would not have missed it for anything.

We went leisurely down to the station then — having paid our hotel bill, and took the train for Munich, arriving there at 10:50.

We walked up to the Christian Hospiz and they didn't have rooms for us so we found a lovely pension right across the street.

We had a fine rest and in the morning we had our cup of coffee and a couple of brötchen (bread), and started out for the train at 8:30. Well I simply can't describe the scenery that we saw on our trip from Munich to Venice. It took all day, except for an hour and a half that we had in Bozen-Gries, to change cars.

We travelled through Tyrol, Bavaria, and saw the Bavarian Alps. They were wonderful and dotted all along with old castles and monasteries. We met lovely couples on the train, one of which was from Dresden. They told us all kinds of information about Italy, etc, and it made the journey fine. We went from Bozen-Gries down to Trient, and from there down to here, was the most beautiful scenery I ever saw — Mountains — every one snowcapped. There was one brute of a peak, and what do you suppose it had on the very top of it — a fort. It was between Italy and Austria, so if there was ever war the Austrians could see what was going on. We saw our first Italian lake, at sunset. It was surrounded by mountains and was so pretty with the evening shades in the sky.

We arrived here at 10:15, and had our first glimpse of this dear place "by the light of the silvery moon". It was not very large but I always dreamed of Venice by moonlight.

We had some fun making them understand our German, but as Mr. H. speaks it very well we got along all right, and an old chattering Italian showed us our way to the boat which was to take us to our hospiz. Well we then had our first glimpse of the Grand Canal, as we slide rapidly along. We were not in a gondola but a steam launch affair which would take us quicker than the gondola. It was a wonderful sight. We landed at a little landing place, and started to go through the narrowest streets I ever saw, and over dear little bridges. Finally we came out on a square, where we found our hospiz. It is an old castle of the 14th century. It is the quaintest old place you ever saw. Edna and I have two beds and they are right along side of each other.

We had a good old laugh about it all last night and then went to bed and had a good rest. We didn't get up till nine this morning to be sure and not be tired.

We started out at about ten, and really I can't begin to tell you all we have seen to-day. Why it will take years to tell you all about Venice. It is grand — and no noise — no street cars, etc. You would all love it.

We spent the morning in St. Mark's and it is a great old place.[3] We heard the priest rattling off his Latin.

This afternoon we started out bright and early and went through the wonderful Doge's Palace. It

---

[1] A poet and *Meistersinger* or master singer (1494-1576).
[2] *Wurst*: sausage.
[3] St. Mark's Basilica.

must have been grand when it was new. There is the largest oil painting in the world there.

We had a great look at the sea from the balcony.

Then we took a gondola and our dream came true as we slid up the Grand Canal. It was great. How I wished you were all there. We saw all the palaces, etc — where Byron, Browning, Wagner etc lived. We stopped at the glass factory and saw them making the mosaic pins, etc. I bought a little sample of the wonderful work for 50 cents. Then we went on and saw the Rialto Bridge, and sailed under the Bridge of Sighs. It was just grand. Then we came to the Venetian lace factory. We went in and saw them weaving and making all kinds of lace. I bought two little doilies of it, as small and cheap as possible 75 centimes each — about 20 cents.

Well then I went up in the immense tower and saw the view of all the country around at sunset. It was the finest imaginable. You go up in an elevator and then walk around a place at the top, where you can see for miles and miles — out to sea, and all around. To-night we have been out walking by the canal in the moonlight and we saw all the ships and gondolas lighted and the people were all singing. Oh, but it is one grand country. You must all come over and see it. I will write every time I get a moment. Hope you are all well and not worrying. I am doing this cheaply as I can.

Helen

Venice: In a Gondola on the Grand Canal.
(Helen on left.)

(Mount Allison Archives, Lochhead Fonds, 8701.)

LV

Rome, Italy
April 6, 1914
Monday Night!

My Dearest Ones!

Here it is Monday and your letter is not off yet. Edna and I have certainly done our best to get a letter written, but it is simply impossible, when we are seeing so much. Now I must start right in to tell you all we have been doing, for it will take hours. I did not go out to-night, for I knew if I did your letter would not get off and you will worry if you don't hear. I was tired anyway, and will write you and then go to bed and get rested for to-morrow.

Well our last day in Venice was grand. We spent the morning in the Academy of Arts. There were wonderful paintings there, chief of which was the "Assumption" by Titian.[1] We stayed there all morning. After dinner, we took a little steamer called a "vaporetta" and sailed away over to the island of Lido. It is the most fashionable sea resort in Italy, and all the people go there, — including Kaiser Wilhelm.

It is right in the Adriatic Sea. We went down on the beach for a while and sat and watched the boats pass in and out. A very swift hydro-plane passed by, going about 100 miles an hour. The many coloured sail boats were lovely. Then we went up in the immense tea piazza and had a cup of tea, with the water splashing up, underneath us. The pavillion is built out, so that the water comes up under it.

We sat there till about five and then went back to dear old Venice. The whole trip did not cost much over a quarter.

When we got back we decided to leave the next morning, for it looked a wee bit like rain, and we didn't want our wonderful dream spoiled, for Venice is not much in rainy weather.

It turned out to be a fine night though, and we went out to shop and get a few things to remember our visit by. I have some beautiful Venetian glass ware and I had it mailed to Germany, so I would not break it. My but it was cheap, and as pretty as you can imagine. I tell you, Mother, our house will be very fine when we fix it up with all my junk. I just wished you could be here to help me choose some good samples of the glass, but I think my choice was pretty good. We saw how they made it and that makes it very interesting.

Well at seven in the morning we left dear old Venice. Oh yes I forgot to say that the Kaiser's yaucht (I can't spell this word right) was in the harbour, and the Kaiserin[2] arrived the day we left. My but the boat looked lovely in the harbour! Pure white and gold!

Our trip to Rome took all day till six o'clock, but it was very interesting and we were not so very tired. At Bologna we just happened to meet one of Heber's professors and his wife, and a young girl travelling to Florence. We just happened to meet them in the station, and it seemed so funny, in such a big place. They are lovely people — Mr. and Mrs. Akers, and a Miss Ottis, who is studying in the university at Göttingen (where Lou and Gordon were). We talked steadily till they left at Florence.

---

[1] Sixteenth-century painter.
[2] Augusta Viktoria, wife of Wilhelm II.

Helen , Piazza San Marco, Venice, 1914
(Mount Allison Archives, Lochhead Fonds, 8701.)

Our train came right through to Rome. We started out when we arrived to hunt a pension, but had quite a lot of trouble, as every place was full. However, we found a dandy place at last, and stayed there the first day — Saturday. All the people were American millionaires, I guess —(by their gowns), and as we only had our plain travelling suits (I am wearing my blue suit, and my old last summer hat that I wore away) so we decided to find a place where we didn't have to bother so much about dress.

We went to a place where Irma stayed when she was here. They gave us our meals, and Heber, a room (they only had one with one little bed), and the landlady got Edna and I this dear room right around the corner from there. It is lovely, and the lady speaks German so I am quite at home here.

Well now for what we have seen. I can't begin to tell you half of it, for we are on the go all day and night. We have seen twice as much as most people do, for Harper keeps us trotting to keep up to him. We are doing it on the minimum cash also.

Saturday we went to the Vatican Museum in the morning. It is wonderful. I can't tell you half of it, now, but I intend to study more about it. In the afternoon we went to see the Catacombs where all the early Christians were buried. They were grand, but cold (cut out of solid rock). We then went to St. Clement's church,[1] and saw where they are excavating two churches underneath the modern one. They date away back before Christ. My but it was interesting.

Then we went over to St. John Lateran's Church,[2] where the stairs of marble are that the catholics worship so. They were supposed to have been those that Christ walked down after Pilate's judgement — They were brought here from Jerusalem.

The marble was so worn that a layer of wood had to be put over them. All Catholics and in fact,

---

[1] Basilica of St. Clement, built circa 1100.
[2] Basilica of St. John Lateran, rebuilt in its present form in the sixteenth to eighteenth centuries.

anyone, who ascends these steps must do it on their knees. The Cath. say a prayer on each step and there are twenty-eight of them. Old men and women and boys and even kiddies were going up. They are given a thousand years indulgence for doing this. Luther when he was a Catholic went up half way, and suddenly the thought came to him of how shallow the custom was, and he jumped up and ran down the rest of the steps, crying "the just shall live by faith". Heber went up on his knees, just because Luther did this, but Edna and I would not. We just watched. It is a very noted spot in Rome.

In the evening we just wandered around and went to bed pretty tired.

Sunday morning we spent in St. Peter's — Palm Sunday. I never saw such a beautiful building in my life. We heard that wonderful cardinal give mass. The Pope is not well now. The sculpture and painting in the place is marvellous.

In the afternoon we went to the old Forum, and roamed around all the old ruins, of ancient Rome. It was fine. We met a man there from whom we wanted to get some information. Heber always asks and asks till he finds out what he wants. Anyway we asked him about an old ruin, and Heber said "Sprechen Sie Deutsch?" (speak German?). He said "yes, I speak German and English." Then H. asked about the ruin, and the man said "yes, I am a Roman, but I don't know much about Rome and its ruins. I am here to meet a girl, and I don't see her. I am very sorry." Well I can't write it as funny as it sounded, but we just roared. He was pacing up and down like an animal, and we walked up so leisurely with Baedeker,[1] to enquire.

We have hot times asking where our places are. It is the only way to get around.

To-day we went back to visit another Section of the new Vatican. You know it contains over 3000 rooms. We saw much of Michael Angelo's[2] and Raphael's[3] work — the former's in the wonderful Sistine Chapel. Oh I have volumes to tell you about that one little place.

We went out the Appian Way[4] this afternoon and saw the Baths of Caracella,[5] the tombs of the Scipios,[6] Quo Vadis Church,[7] the old wall, and gate, and came back to another old church — San Rubro — where another of Michael Angelo's wonderful pieces of sculpture is.

We went over to the Town and took a picture, and then came home. I am tired after such a long day, and I must get away to bed, to be rested for to-morrow, when we go to finish up the Vatican. Edna and Heber are wandering around somewhere, but I just said I was going to write to you dear ones who have given me this wonderful opportunity.

I just hope that I will be able to make you happy with my tales when I get back. I am going to make as many notes as possible so that I can refer to them when I am telling you all the particulars.

I get so homesick for you all sometimes that I just about die, but I make myself forget it, and try to get the most out of my opportunity.

We leave here Wednesday or Thursday for Florence, as far as we know now, then to Milan and Switzerland and then old Leipzig again.

I do hope you dear ones are not worrying about me, for we are perfectly all right, and as far as Heber is concerned — he is as harmless as a Grandfather. We like him fine, and he is very good to

---

[1] A long-running series of guidebooks.

[2] Michelangelo, Renaissance painter and sculptor, 1475-1564.

[3] Renaissance painter, 1483-1520.

[4] Via Appia, a famous Roman road.

[5] Ruins of early third century A.D. Roman baths.

[6] Tomb of the Scipio family used from the third century B.C. to the first century A.D.

[7] Church of St Mary in Palmis; a seventeenth-century church near Rome on the spot where, by tradition, Christ appeared to St. Peter as he was escaping persecution in Rome.

us, but he is quite old maidish, and there is no danger of Edna and I falling in love with him.

I didn't get your answer to my letter asking if I might come to Italy, but I knew you would be willing, and it is such a wonderful chance to get down here, that we wouldn't have missed it for anything. The place is full of English travelling people. We hear English wherever we go.

Well, dear ones, I must close for now, hoping that you are all as well as can be, and not worrying about me.

I will write whenever I get a moment, but I am here to see, and see I must. I will drop you cards though, so don't worry.

Here's all my love for you all, Anna, and her dear family, and Mut and his dear family, and Grampie and Grannie.

All the kisses imaginable,

                                                                        Helen

LVI

                                                    4 Sophien Platz
                                                    Leipzig Germany
                                                    April 22, 1914

My Dear Miss McAdams, May, and Queen:-

We were so pleased to get your lovely letters in Rome, and we appreciated your kindness so much especially when you were so busy. I suppose Edna is writing you the same thing, but I shall tell you, in case that she didn't, that we took our mail out to the Colosseum to read it. Wasn't that romantic? It was great to get mail when we were in dear old Rome anyway.

Edna and I agreed to take a country each to describe to you. My choice was Switzerland, if I could make a choice, so I said I would try to describe it to you, in some small way. She liked Venice more than any place she saw, and so I thought she had better describe it to you.

We were rather tired after our Italian trip, for it was mainly trips to Galleries, and even though it is very enjoyable, I must confess that at times, it is rather tiresome.

We longed for some grand natural scenery. This we saw first, as we approached Como, on our way from Milan one evening at sunset. The cloud effects were so wonderful that we actually could not tell which were mountains and which clouds. We arrived at Lake Como, about nine at night, and after a short walk around, to see the lights on the water, and the little twinkling lights on the mountain sides, we went to bed to get a lovely rest.

In the morning we got up early, and wrapped up in the warmest things we had, and went out for a morning's sail on Lake Como. We saw the wonderful summer foliage along the shore, and every tree seemed to be covered with bloom. We noticed this much more in the Italian Lake district than in Switzerland — because it is farther south, I suppose. The little villas along the lake were beautiful, and we had a lovely sail, around to all the little villages along the shore.

We all decided we would like to remain at Como, but alas, our holidays were already nearly gone, so we left at noon, for the other lakes — Lugano, and Maggiore.

We crossed the first and got a pretty fair idea of what it was like.

Then we took a side trip to Lucarno which is at the end of Lake Maggiore. We had time enough there to take a walk around, and take some pictures, before our train left. It is another great summer resort, and we were very much tempted to remain there when we saw the empty row boats along the lake shore, and the busy games of tennis which were being engaged in by the tourists.

However we were glad to get along to our chief object of interest — the Alpine pass.

It was most interesting when we went through the St. Gothard's tunnel — twenty minutes long.[1]

We climbed right up mountains, and over high trestles and it made us wonder whether we would ever get down again or not.

It was dark when we finally pulled into our station at Flüelen. Here we planned to spend the night, and we had a very unique experience, for the ordinary tourist — that was in staying in a genuine Swiss home, all night. We saw the Swiss life, and had a glimpse at their characters, which we never could have had at a hotel.

They were very kind to us, and we loved all the Swiss after our one night in this little home. In the morning we started on a six-mile walk up the wonderful Axen Strasse — perhaps you have heard about it.[2] It is cut right out of the rock, and you look out at the wonderful mountains, and Lake Lucerne at your feet. It was one wonderful view, and at the end of our walk, we were rewarded by a glimpse of Tell's Chapel,[3] down by the lake. We hated to leave this interesting spot, but as we had a long walk home, we had to walk very smartly to get back for dinner. On the way home we bought some of the Idyl-Weis (flower of Switzerland)[4] from an old man who had gathered it away up on the mountain tops.

Right after dinner we took the boat and sailed the whole length of the lake down to Lucerne. It was the loveliest sail I ever had in my life, and the mountains were so wonderful rising right out of the water, and going up beyond the clouds.

We stayed out on deck all that trip, and wasn't it funny, that we didn't get sea-sick like I did on the way over! I was too busy sight-seeing I guess. At Lucerne we saw Wagner's house, and really May, it is no wonder he wrote such operas if he wrote them at this wonderful place. From Lucerne we went by train through another pass, where they had to go up the mountain by means of cog-wheels.

We climbed away up to where the snow was and then went down on the other side of the valley to Brienz.

It was then getting late, and we were anxious to get on the water before the sun went down.

We took the boat there, and were on board till nine o'clock. I wish you could have seen the red tinge on the alps after sunset. They were marvellous. Then they got dimmer and finally we could only see a huge mass coming out of the darkness.

The lights in the little villages scattered all over were very pretty, and then we came to Interlaken, that wonderful summer resort of the American multi-millionaires.

---

[1] The Gotthard Tunnel, built between 1872 and 1888, takes the railway under the St. Gotthard Pass in the Swiss Alps.

[2] The Axenstrasse is a Swiss road built in the 1860s, protected from rockfalls and avalanches by tunnels and galleries along much of its length.

[3] A small chapel on the lakeshore marking the place where legend has it William Tell escaped from his captor Gessler.

[4] Edelweiss; *Leontopodium alpinum*.

We stayed at a German Hospiz there and enjoyed it very much.

In the morning we climbed half-way up a big hill, and had a glimpse of the wonderful Jungfrau —(second highest of the Alps). It was one huge mass of ice and was veiled partly by mist and clouds. It was a great view, from this point, and we hated to leave it.

After visiting several other places there we left at two o'clock for Bern, by train. Our two hours there were spent in trying to get a general idea of the Swiss capital.

It is very modern, and did not seem to be as picturesque as the smaller towns. We visited their church and found quite an interesting contrast between it and the Italian.

When we arrived in Geneva at eight that night, we were all pretty tired, and did not see much.

In the morning, we took a beautiful steamer, for a lake trip. It was a perfect day, and we were out from eight in the morning till about two in the afternoon.

On this lake we visited all the famous watering places, and we enjoyed the sail so much —(an orchestra and a soloist helping out with the scene).

We arrived at Terretet, took a street car from Chillon, and had dinner at a restaurant right above the castle.

It is the loveliest old place imaginable, and certainly must have inspired Byron.[1]

We went on to Martigny, where we expected to get a train going down to foot of Mont Blanc. This train does not start till May 1st so we had to stay in Martigny till eight that night. We used the time by wandering up to an old Roman tower on a high cliff, where we got a splendid view of the valleys and mountains around.

We went back to Vevery for the night, and saw beautiful Lake Geneva in the morning.

A long train ride brought us to Neuhausen where we saw the famous Rhine falls. They are very beautiful, tumbling down over the big rocks.[2]

Another train ride brought us to Stuttgart where we spent the night, and travelled all the next day, up to Leipzig — that was yesterday.

We certainly had one grand trip, and how much I wish you had been with us. Don't you think we saw a lot in such a short time?

We are rather tired but it was a wonderful change. We ought to be able to work now.

I hope you have enjoyed your trip so far, and that you will have a very pleasant and calm voyage, over to dear old Canada. Mother is looking forward to your coming so much.

I also wrote Jim, and I feel sure he will be down to see you in Montreal. Please give him my kindest regards.

Haven't I written a very rough description of our trip? It seems there is so much more to write about it, that it would take me years to tell you all about it. I shall not forget it soon, though and I can tell you some interesting details when I come back.

Again I wish you all kinds of good luck on your trip, and we shall be anxiously awaiting the news of your arrival in dear old New Brunswick. Remember all my kisses and hugs for dear Mother and Father and much love for you all, from,

                                                        Helen

---

[1] Byron's 1816 poem "The Prisoner of Chillon" is set at Chillon Castle, on Lake Geneva.
[2] The Rhine Falls are the largest waterfall in Europe.

LVII

4 Sophien Platz
Leipzig, Germany
Dear Old Leipzig Once More!
April 22, 1914

My Dearest Home Ones and Western Ones:

Here we are back again in Leipzig, and we are both sitting here writing to you dear ones in old New Brunswick. How we would love to see you all, and talk things over. It is so much more satisfactory than writing.

We arrived home last night, and you should have seen how glad every one was to see us. It seemed good to get back even if we did have such a good time on our trip.

Well, we both got stacks of mail, and I never enjoyed anything so much as sitting in my lovely little room, chewing Mut's spruce gum, and reading all Mother's letters and Papa's most welcome one too. Mother, dear, I was so worried about you being sick, and I felt like taking the next boat home, for fear you might want me. Be sure and tell me everything, now, for I must know. I hate to think of either of you being sick, and if anything ever happened to you, when I might have been there to help you, I should never get over it. Be sure and cable me, at anytime when you feel I should come. Mut, dear, I ask this of you, as a favour for neither Mother nor Father would want me to leave till it might be too late.

I hope you are well again, and both enjoying the wonderful spring.

I haven't written you a letter for years, it seems to me. Well we just didn't have one moment for anything but sight seeing, and we certainly had one grand trip. Just imagine we only had two very small showers in three weeks and one day. The weather was perfect, every day, and we had everything in our favour.

I think I wrote you all particulars up to my last day in Rome, didn't I? Well, I can't begin to tell you all I saw and heard in that wonderful city.

I shall have to save all the particulars to tell you when I get back for I could never write them all.

The last night we were in Rome we heard an Opera *Mephistophole,*[1] and I wish you could have heard the Italian voices. They were grand. They are certainly better than the German. They are more emotional, and put so much feeling in their voices.

Well we left in the morning for Florence, and arrived about five o'clock. As I said on my cards, we had a lovely hospiz there to stay at. The people were all Germans and you can't imagine how much at home we felt.

Now it would be simply impossible for me to write you everything that we saw and did in Florence. We were there five days, and I could have stayed five weeks, and never thought twice about it. I think I liked it better than any place I was in.

Oh yes, I forgot to say that we only got our meals at the Hospiz, for they had no rooms (busy season!) and we had rooms at a real Italian house — the family was away at the seashore, and let the rooms when they were away. Their dear old servant was so nice to us. She had been with them for

---

[1] *Mefistofele,* Arrigo Boito, 1868.

fifteen years. It was a great treat to live in such a place.

Florence was just beautiful with all its spring foliage and we had full moon when we were there.

We spent one morning in the Uffizi Gallery,[1] another in the Pitti Gallery,[2] and I couldn't begin to describe them to you. I have copies of some of the pictures I liked, so you will be able to enjoy them too. Another morning we spent in the Academy where we saw wonderful work in statuary by Michael Angelo. Oh but it was wonderful.

Then we had that wonderful time, the evening we went out with the American Vice Consul —(Edna wrote all about that, so you likely have heard it).

He was a class mate of Heber's and then we met the same night, Miss Spalding, who travelled all the rest of the trip with us. I can't begin to tell you what a night we had. First a dinner in an old Kellar[3] — then moving pictures — and lastly another café with real ice-cream. It was all fine.

We had a great time one afternoon up on Piazza Michael Angelo (a hill overlooking the city). We had tea up there and visited a dear church up there too.

Another day, we went up on Filesio hill, where we visited the old Franciscan monastery. We walked most of the way back and the scenery was grand. The hill was just dotted with Italian villas.

Oh Mother if you could only have seen the shops in Florence. Well I wanted to buy so much, but I didn't. I just thought I must save for my work. I only bought one waist for myself — all hand work, for two dollars. It is beautiful. They have the most beautiful hand embroidered things I ever saw.

I have the address, and I know a lovely lady there (one of the girls here gave me a letter of introduction to her) so if we want anything we can send and get it.

They had the most beautiful five o'clock tea cloth I ever saw in my life — hand made lace and embroidery. I almost took it, but decided to wait till I could talk to you about it. It was 8 dollars and in Canada would cost 20 I should say. It is ahead of anything I have ever seen.

I hated to leave Florence, more than any place, I think. We had five days there, and we certainly saw a lot.

Miss Spalding and the three of us left in the morning for Milan, and arrived there about eight at night. We went out to see the wonderful cathedral after night, and I never saw anything so beautiful as it is. It is just like a piece of magnificent lace. There are about six thousand statues in and out of the building. It is so large, and grand. I was crazy to hear the organ, but it was not played when we were there.

In the morning we spent all the time in the cathedral, and climbed 500 steps to the highest tower. It gave a great view.

In the afternoon we went to see that wonderful picture of Leonardo de Vinci's[4]—"The Last Supper". It must have been grand in its day, but even yet it is beyond most of the modern efforts.

We left at about five or six for the Italian Lake District.

We went right to Como, and spent the night there. In the morning we had a beautiful sail on the lake. Then we left at noon, and travelled over to see the other two Italian lakes — Lugano, and Maggiore. They were all so blue, and the mountains in the background were just like you saw on the post-cards. The lakes were just dotted along the shores with beautiful summer villas, and little villages.

---

[1] A sixteenth-century palace housing a collection of paintings and sculptures largely collected by the Medicis; it became an art gallery open to the public in the second half of the eighteenth century.

[2] The fifteenth-century Palazzo Pitti.

[3] German: cellar. Possibly a wine cellar turned café?

[4] Leonardo da Vinci (1452-1519).

We went on to reach dear old Switzerland by ten at night. To do this we had to go through the St. Gothard's Pass. It was the most exciting experience I ever had. We were in a tunnel for twenty minutes.

We spent the night at Flüelen and we stayed at a real Alpine home. They were lovely to us.

In the morning we took our six mile walk that I told you about up the Axen St. It was beautiful. We visited the William Tell Chapel down by the lake. It was a beautiful spot.

On the afternoon we sailed down Lake Lucerne the whole way, and arrived at Lucerne about four. Then we went through a pass in the mountains where we were drawn up the mountains by a cog-rail. We were up to the snow, and it was cold, but very interesting.

We ended up by a sail down another lake (at sunset) to Interlaken where we stayed all night and the next morning we climbed away up a hill to see the Jungfrau (second largest mountain in the Alps). It was almost hidden in clouds but we caught a glimpse of it, anyway.

Interlaken is a wonderful summer place, and we saw the great hotels, one of which has its private theatre, etc. The stores there were made very attractive to attract the tourists. I didn't buy much, for I thought the prices were high.

Well, we went from there to Bern, and spent a couple of hours there looking at the capital. I didn't like it as well as the smaller places. It is more modern. We went on then to Geneva, and spent the night there.

The next morning was spent by a sail down the lake to Terretet. It was one grand sail with orchestra, etc. The mountains were grand along the banks. We landed and went by streetcar up to Chillon, where we saw the wonderful castle, which Byron wrote of. It was very picturesque. Didn't I send you a card of it? I forget.

Well we went on to Martigny to try to get up to the foot of Mont Blanc. The railway was not running so we had to stay there till the evening and then we went back to a place on Lake Geneva for the night — Vevey.

In the morning Miss Spalding left us for she had to get back to Paris to her work there (she has a year off from teaching in America). She was lovely to us, and we hated to see her go.

Well we then started up towards Leipzig, and we took in the wonderful Rhine Falls. On the way, we had to stay in Stuttgart all night to break up the journey. Then we had to travel all the next day and we arrived here at night.

I started this letter Wednesday, I think and have been adding bits whenever I have had a moment. I haven't had any time to write particulars, and I am so sorry for I do want you to know all about everything I saw.

I landed right back in time for work and I had so many things to do, that I am not caught up yet.

Our trip was one wonderful dream, and we did it on $100, with extras, as closely as we can figure. Heber did everything to do the journey cheaply and that is why I missed Naples — he felt he couldn't afford it, and it was impossible for we two girls to go alone. I have it all to look forward to, the next time I go, though, and I must not complain for we had the best trip possible.

Our whole trip through Switzerland (lakes, railways and everything) only cost $10, and we could have travelled ten more days on our ticket. It is the most wonderful ticket I ever heard of.

Don't you think we saw a lot in five days? We saw everything well too. We travelled third class on every line that had such cars, and we did it on half the price. We never could have done it alone, and Heber was very very kind to us in every way. He is one fine fellow, in lots of ways. We feel very much indebted to him, but hope to entertain him some in our rooms, and pay up for it.

Everyone here thought it was perfectly right for us to go with him and we never felt the least embarrassed being with him, for he is such a gentleman and a good boy. It is nice to say though that we had our chaperone, and then there is nothing to be said by anyone.

When we got back our rooms had been all cleaned, curtains washed, etc., and it was great to get settled down again.

I am planning all kinds of work for this term, and I hope to get enough done (if I work very hard) to come home in the summer, if I feel I should go. I want to be with you dear ones, so that you may enjoy my accomplishments, for I am doing it all chiefly for you, and I want you to have the benefit of it.

I am trying to pick up lots of little things for the house, Mother, and I shall try to get nice things in England on the way home. I am so anxious to help you fix up the house. Won't we have a great time doing it?

Now I am so sleepy that I can't write any more. It is late now, and I must get up early.

I shall tell you more about my trip in each letter, as I think it over. All kinds of love,

Helen

LVIII

4 Sophien Platz
Leipzig, Germany
Wednesday Morning 7.30
April 29, 1914

Dearest Ones!

I was the first up this morning, so I shall have my room done first, and that means that I get to work early. There is a lot of scheming to be done if you want to get along in this world, isn't there?

Well, now for the news! I told you a little about my trip in my last letter, but I could never write it all to you. It was the most wonderful experience I ever had, and I want to thank you dear ones for it. I just wish I could give you the benefit of it now, but I have all my cards, and pictures, and they will keep me from forgetting. Wasn't it wonderful that we did it on such a small sum? We never could have done it, if Heber had not been managing the wheel.

When we got back it was "right to work" for us, and I have been very busy.

You know, perhaps through Edna, that poor Mrs. Luck died when we were away. It was a relief to everyone for she was just a skeleton at the last.

One afternoon Mr. and Mrs. King and Mr. Luck and I went to the Messa (a big affair like our Exhibition).[1] It was great fun, and we laughed all the time. You can buy all kinds of laces and stationery very cheap, but I am not buying much now, after having had my trip.

Sunday night we were over at Mrs. King's to supper, and we took our cards and told her all about our trip. She gave us the best supper you ever tasted — and Mother dear, she had potato salad. It was simply great. I haven't had any for months, and I was terribly hungry for it.

---

[1] *Messe*: here, a sort of fair.

Well I have taken on all my extra subjects in German — Pedagogic (teaching), Form, History, Ear Training. It is going to be pretty hard but I am going to try it anyway.

Mr. Luck knows the woman that May got all her hints from, and he is going to take me out to see her. May tried to keep it away from me, but she didn't succeed. They are so afraid I'll go back and teach, that they don't know what to do. Don't use them mean on that account for it doesn't bother me in the least. Don't let on to a soul though that I am going to do it, for even Glad. and Edna don't know yet.

Mother dear, I am enclosing Hib's letter that I got a couple of days ago, and it is for you alone to read, and you may tell what you choose out of it. I don't like to have a private letter read by anyone but you, and then you can tell what you think best — I don't think it is fair to any boy to show his letters to anyone but your mother.

I haven't answered it yet, and don't know yet what I shall say. What do you think? There will never be anything to it, for I shall never marry a man who drinks if I can help it. There are other nice boys, and they think far more of me than Hib does.

I feel sorry for him, but there is a kind of satisfaction in knowing he didn't throw me over.

Now don't worry for I am not, in the least.

I must get away to work. It is high time.

If you want to know anything at all, just ask and it will be easy for me to remember what you want to know.

I forget when I sit down to write just like dear old Nan.

With all kinds of love to you all and a big kiss for Mary, and each of my little Westerners, from,

Aunty Helen

LIX

4 Sophien Platz
Leipzig, Germany
Sunday, May 10/14

My Dear Home Ones!

Here is another Sunday, and how quickly the time is flying. I can't realise it. Just think how busy I was this time last year getting ready for Encenia and do you remember how sore my eyes were, and how anxious I was over my exams. It seems just like yesterday to me. I am glad that I am not home the first closing after I was through for I know I should be lonesome. I can't help thinking about it, even over here.

Well I am digging away with all my might, and I am anxious to hear what you say about next year. I am not going to make any changes till I hear.

Gladys, Edna and I have been singing hymns, and Sunday pieces. It is now ten and I have only a few moments to write, for I don't want to sit up late.

Well this week what have I been doing — I heard the *Merry Wives of Windsor* in English on Friday night. Mr. Lochhead took me. He is very nice, and it is so nice to have such a friend here. He

Postcard of König-Albert-Park (King Albert Park), Leipzig
(Mount Allison Archives, Lochhead Fonds, 8701.)

is chased everywhere, but comes to see me, where he is not coaxed to come. We went for a great walk yesterday, also, after my lessons were all over.

He is working very hard now, and I don't see much of him.

Oh yes, the Lesleys — Heber's friends arrived Friday, and I was out with them for a while in the morning. They were very nice, and will mean much to me. They are just like Earle and Irma Roadman.

We danced Wednesday night in the Pension with the Germans, and enjoyed it very much. It is so interesting to study the different customs of the different countries. I am enclosing a picture of F. Schröter's nephew, (the soldier), for you to see. Be sure and send it back or he would think I didn't appreciate the fact that he gave it to me. He is a college boy, but had to leave off to finish up his military course. He is very keen in my direction but I have told him a thing or two that opened his eyes. You know, over here it is a great honour for a man to pay attention to a girl and especially if the man is anybody worth noticing. The girls advertise in the papers every day for men. It is a mere business proposition with most of them. Why it is a hard & fast rule that no lieutenant can ever think of marrying a girl unless she has $25,000 in her own name. Isn't that awful? They don't pay the men enough to allow them to marry a poor girl.

Well to go back to what I was saying about this week — another night we were around at King's and made ice cream. They have a freezer, and supply the ice, sugar, flavouring, etc., and we three club together and get some cream 30 cents, and go up there and make it. That is so much nicer than going to a café and we have heaps of fun.

I had a letter from Will, and he said you two dear ones looked very lonesome, and he thought you wanted me to come home in August. Is that right? He said Mic looked very lonesome, and I would just like to have him over here with me. He must be company for you. He also said that you served a lovely lunch, Mother, and he seemed quite taken up with his visit. I write about once or twice a month to him now — I really haven't time to write more.

I have a piano lesson to-morrow, so I must get up early. I am at my German too, and am trying to do as much of everything as I can.

I am going to have my old green suit let out if I can, this week, to wear every day. I do miss it so. I wish you could see it on me. It is the funniest sight imaginable (only the skirt). The coat is fine. I am looking forward to having my two new cotton dresses. You remember, Mother, I was short on the summer dresses last summer, and so I need them this summer.

There is a dance next Saturday, given by the Colony (American) and I may go, but don't know what to wear yet — it is just informal and they wear plain summer dresses. I must press out my hamburg, and the others.

The McA's must be home by now. I should think. Don't let them ever worry your dear head again, Mother, for you know we shall not have to depend on May for my getting to Germany again. Just let them say or do, or act as they please, and don't let them walk on you. They are fine if you keep them in their place.

Well my eyes are tired from writing, and I must go to bed, to be up with the birds in the morning. I hope you are all well, and happy, and not worrying about me, for I am fine.

Remember me to everyone, the girls — all my aunts and uncles, Earn and Fletch, the Jacksons, Celia, Mary Sykes, and the "Wedalls" (By the way, how is Charles?), Mr. Estey, old Mrs. King, and Mrs. Wright and all the people who live along the street, whom we speak to on the way to church.

Don't work too hard, but plan to come over to go back with me.

All kinds of Love. Be sure and return the picture by next mail. I will send Nan a snap of him if she is interested.

Helen

LX

4 Sophien Platz
Leipzig, Germany
Thursday, May 14/14

My Dear Ones!

Your cable here, and how it frightened me, you can never imagine. I was sure something had happened Mother or Father. I was very much relieved to find it was about my work, for it is a minor matter.

Well I can't imagine what ever made you cable. Of course I know the McA's are at the base of it all, and I suppose they have terrified you, Mother, by some outlandish yarn. Whatever it may be, I can't imagine.

I have done nothing but think ever since I got the cable, and I have decided that Mrs. Grant must have got Gladys' letter and immediately come down and told you that Glad had Teich, and I didn't.

Naturally that would worry you, and I am very sorry about it. But you just tell May, or Mrs. G. or anyone you like that I have never tried for him, and that I would be ashamed to have to lie to get him, like Gladys did. I don't intend to try anything of that sort, for it never pays. She got him just out of F. Lutz's good will. If the latter had said one word, she would not have got Teich at all. The two of them are one. I can't imagine what a letter Gladys has written home. Edna and I have found out that she exaggerates everything, and we never know what to believe.

Well I got your cable in the morning, and I worried all morning to know what to do about it. Right after dinner I put on my hat and went right over to Lutz with the cable. I knew that in order to ever get him I must get her help. She was as nice as could be about it and said, there is not the slightest chance of your not getting Teich, and I shall do all in my power to help you get him. She said, you are better than Miss Grant, and he will take you quicker than he did her.

You see I didn't try for Teich for I wanted to hear from you telling me whether you really wanted me to stay next year or not. If I make my prefung[1] as planned, I must do it under Lutz, for Teich, always keeps his pupils for years and years before he lets them make a prefung, under him directly. However he signs my diploma when I get it, (having made my prefung under Lutz), and it carries the same force as if I had made it under him, as far as a position or anything of that sort is concerned.

Now if you talk it over and decide you would rather I should take from Teich, I shall take your letter, which you must write (one of you, it doesn't matter which one) to Lutz, and she said she would promise me that I could get Teich. I would then finish up at the Con. this year with Lutz, (for I have paid my last term's money), and take privately from Teich also. Then if you want me to stay next year, I would just take privately all the time with Teich, up till Xmas. That would give me enough piano, and then if you didn't want me to come home, I would go to Paris, and get some finishing touches on my voice. I like this last idea very much, and the only thing that would be missing would be my diploma (of couse I get a certificate for one year at the Con. which is signed by Teich), and that would do for teaching.

Now Lutz has been doing her very best for me, and I have made wonderful progress, everyone says. (May never heard me play, so how does she know).

I was playing my game very carefully, and knowing that I was getting all I possibly could now, my technique must be worked up you know, and Lutz takes much more care on that than Teich does.

I am dying to take from Teich, and don't be mistaken about that, but unless I don't make my prefung, I can't do it.

Now Lutz said if you decided on getting this letter that you would rather I should go to Teich, just cable me one word "Private". That word will mean that I am to get Teich, and plan on taking privately from him next year. You might add "no prefung" if you want to, and I will show her the wire, and that will be all there is needed. If you would rather I should make my prefung, wire "Conservatorium" and I shall know that you want me to stay in the Con.

If you can wait to write a letter it would be much better, anyway, for then I can show it to her and she will know that you have decided, and it will clear me.

Don't say anything in it about my doing as I please about it. Just write a very short letter and to the point, saying that you have decided that you would rather I had a few private lessons with Teich than to make my prefung, and that you have absolutely nothing against my present teacher, but would just like me to have a few lessons with Teich before I come home.

Now can you get all that? There is no rush about it, at all, for I have got more work than I can

---

[1] *Prüfung.*

handle now, and am digging in with all my might. Don't run away with the idea that I am loafing, no matter what the McA's say.

Now let us drop this question, and let me open your eyes on the McAdams a bit. They are being laughed at here for sure. They left one place, secretly, and had their luggage sneaked out without the people knowing it. They never said "Good-Bye", (just left a note on the table, saying they were leaving very hurriedly.) Did you hear of such rot? Everybody laughs about them. We put up with a lot from them I can tell you, and the people here laugh when we mention our "chaperons", and say, they are not worthy of the name. They didn't know a thing about us, for they were only around about 10 times the whole year.

Now I parted perfectly friendly with them and I am not holding any grudge at all, but if they are telling you things, just be easy in what you believe. I am afraid of them, after things they have done, so be friendly and not bother your heads about them.

Lutz told me (not in connection with what I was asking her about myself) that Teich said May played like a foolish person. That was what she said in her broken English, but in other words she meant that she couldn't play well at all. That is this last time she was here, so what about all the yarns they told us about her being his assistant, etc.

Now this isn't spite or jealousy, just plain facts. You can think what you like.

If I get Teich, I am going to do it right anyway, and that is all I have to answer for.

You just write or cable like I have told you, and I shall act accordingly.

The whole thing hinges on whether you want me to stay more than next year.

I would make a prefung next Easter, and would take privately with Teich till summer, (just pieces, no technique).

If not, I shall go privately with him till Xmas, and if I don't go to Paris, then I can come home for New Year's.

If you want me to come home with the girls, just cable, to that effect, and I will get a few lessons with Teich before I come home.

Don't worry! That is the main thing. I am doing my best and you simply must not let anybody or anything worry you.

More Sunday. I have taken time off my practice to write this.

All kinds of love to you all.

Send a slow cable gram. It only costs half. I only paid $1.25 for mine. It comes in 2 days at the latest.

Helen

LXI

4 Sophien Platz
Leipzig, Germany
Tuesday, May 21/14

My Dear Ones:

I had no less than four lessons yesterday, (three of which were in German), so you can imagine that I had no time to write. To-day is a holiday (a holy day) and we can't practise. I had a lesson in singing, though and it went fine. Then I went around to King's for a while before dinner. They told me that I might go wherever they go this summer if I stayed over. Wouldn't it be lovely?

They were making lemon water ice, and asked me to dinner, but I had not told F. Schröter, so I came home, and we had ice cream here for dessert.

This afternoon there is nothing to do in the house, so Mr. Lochhead and I are going for a walk. He is very nice, and helps me with my German. His Mother and Father expect to come over this summer for a trip. Imagine he is only 23 and expects to get his Dr. degree this August — he already has a B.A. and a M.Sc. I tell you, a girl finds out how much brains are worth, when you run across a fellow like that.

Heber asked me to go out with him and the Leslies, but I had promised to go walking with Mr. L. first. He asked Edna to go then, and I felt awfully cheap about it, for she knew she was second in the invitation.

We are planning on going out on Monday, though, for there is another holiday (King's birthday) [the King of Saxony's]. It is a great rest to get away from the piano for a little while, some days.

Well I got dear Mother's two letters yesterday, and how I enjoy them. I look forward to them all week. I am very much afraid you have been working too hard, Mother, when you had those awful shingles. Doesn't it come from being over-heated? I am so worried about you.

I am also very much worried over the fact that Willie and Anna want me to come home. There must be some good reason why they want me to come home, or surely they would never be so selfish as to deny me anything without a good reason.

Now, Mother dear, please be honest with me, and tell me if you are saving and working too hard, for you know, I only know what you tell me, for Anna and Will write so seldom.

I have a mighty hard fight to stay over here, sometimes, and I think I must go right back home, but it passes away, with fighting and then I realise that it is so necessary for me to stay here, till I get something to show for my work. The first year is just a tearing down of the old foundations, and you just get started on the building of something new, at the end of the first year. The second year you see what improvement can be accomplished.

I should be perfectly satisfied to come home and work myself, if you think it best for me to do so. I have now had almost my $1000, for the last time I went to the bank, I discovered that I had only $130 left.

That is a lot of money and I am perfectly satisfied with it as my share, for an education. I have $5000 worth of knowledge though from my stay here, and I wouldn't give it up for twice that money.

I am awfully sorry about Anna, and I think she and George are very silly to endanger her health, with having so many children.

She has lots of time to have them yet, and it to me seems very dangerous to have them so fast. However, it is their own business, and I wouldn't want you to send her this letter, for it might make her feel badly.

Now if I stay next year, I shall need more money, and if not I shall only need enough to come home on. I would advise you to renew my letter of credit, and it is always perfectly safe. I asked at the bank here, and they said you might just tell them at the B. of N.S. [Bank of Nova Scotia] how much you wanted it renewed for, and they would see to it. I don't need hardly anything till fall, if you want me to stay over, and if your money is low, just give me what you can spare, and for goodness sakes be honest with me about it, for I surely take you at your word.

I would give anything to see you two dear ones to-day but I am willing to stick it out here, to give you both something to be proud of, when I get back. Don't think I am going to lead a butterfly existence when I get back either. I am going to get my M.A. when I come back, and I will be too busy for social gossip. I hate it anyway and I hope my ideals will never let me descend to such a level.

Must get ready to go out now, more later!

Here it is Friday and your letter is not off yet. I have been so rushed that I forgot about mailing it. You will get it and the Sunday one together likely. Please be honest with me about the money and everything for it is worrying me. I am spending as little as I can. We have all spent more than we expected to even saving as much as we can. Next year will be much cheaper for me.

Love,
Helen

LXII

4 Sophien Platz
Leipzig, Germany
Out in the Garden,
Tuesday afternoon.
May 28, 1914

Dearest Ones!

I must write you a little note to-day, before I go out to tea. Mrs. Flint has invited us out to afternoon tea, and for some music too. She just had us up about a week or two ago, and here we are invited up again. They will be great to me if I stay next year.

We all had a wonderful time last night at the American dance. It was very informal and we all enjoyed it so much. Gladys, Serdice (a Roumanian), Edna, Mina Shearer, Lochhead and I all went together from here. Don't ever mention Serdice's name to Mrs. G. for I don't believe she has ever told her Mother half about him.

We had our supper of ham and eggs out there, and then danced till half past eleven. It was held in a little café in the woods, and we had it for the evening.

The nightingales sing out there, but we did not have time to go out doors to hear them. We are planning on going out just to hear them some night. They only sing in Germany I guess.

Monday Morning!

A big crowd surrounded me yesterday, and I could not write another word. We all got together in a group and had our picture taken.

Well Glad. and Edna could not go to Flint's after all, for they had forgotten that they had invited Mabel Moore and Ella Beattie in to tea here. I went to save the reputation of the crowd.

We had a lovely afternoon, and I helped serve. It made me homesick to be serving at a tea, here in Germany. They had the best sandwiches, cake, and biscuits, candies, and tea that you ever saw.

They served everything well too, so I have some new ideas. When you serve tea, have a tray like the one we gave Anna, with a doilie on it and a little pitcher of cream, a sugar bowl, and a little dish like the one Gladys gave you, full of lemon sliced very fine. You put one cup and saucer on the tray and take it to someone, and let them take either lemon or cream. It is much nicer and easier than asking each one what they take.

If you have a big crowd, have someone pass the cups of tea around quickly, and another person follows with the cream, sugar and lemon.

After tea we had lovely music — a pupil of Mrs. Alves' sang, a pianist played, and two violinists played. It was lovely all around.

This morning I was the first out and my room is just about done, now, so I must go and get to work, for I have a lesson at eleven.

I am so anxious to get your letter or cable telling me what to do. I can't imagine what yarn the McA's have told you.

We are all well and the time is flying faster than ever. It won't be long no matter if I do stay part of next year.

How is the baby Mary? I want a picture of her, also of you all. Mut you just must get busy and take some pictures, and get Mother to have hers taken. You don't know how I would prize it Mother. Now do it just as a favour to me, and I will have a little frame for it and hang it up alongside of dear old Papa's. It gives me more inspiration in my work than anything.

Oh yes, I am low on the gum too. Just 10 cents worth. Mother I planned on sending you milk chocolate from Switzerland but the duty is terrible and I thought perhaps you would never get it.

Must get to work. All my love to you dear ones. Please don't worry about me for it bothers one when I think you worry. Love,

                                             Helen

P.S. No letter for over a week from you. I do hope you are all well.

LXIII

4 Sophien Platz
Leipzig, Germany
June 11/1914

Dearest Ones!

Just a mid-week note from Kath. So very very busy getting ready for Teich, studying German, and getting the most I can out of my singing lessons before Mrs. A. goes away. I was never so busy in all my life. Every day brings a million more things to do. When you don't hear from me, you will know it is because I am too busy. Even now I should be darning stockings or studying something, but I feel as if I must let everything go to write to you. The weather has been terrible here lately, and we have had sore throats. Mine is better now though and I am going to sing to-day. The air is very damp, and that causes it. Fraulein Schröter had it so bad that she couldn't speak. It is nice to-day, though and I hope to be able to warble right along now.

Mother's letter here to-day. I am glad you are pleased at my getting Teich, and you want me to stay — Well I want to do what you think best. If I go home when the girls do, I won't have anything more than they, as far as lessons go. I should like to have some more lessons with Teich than they, then I will have a higher standing. Then I do want to stay in Paris a month anyway with Mrs. James. She is such a beautiful woman. Then I know a dear French girl who lives there. She is in my piano class. Then Muriel Hunt knows a lovely English family there, and Miss Spalding is going to be there too. It is perfectly safe for me to be there with such people.

As for the McAdams saying I can't stay here alone — Don't you see through their scheme? or are you all stone blind? They want me to come home so I won't have anything on them. They are very anxious for me to stop studying. Well just let me tell you one thing which we have never told you home people before. Now don't tell any of the Bairds or Grants, but if the McAdams were so afraid for our safety over here, what did they have us in the station all sole alone when we arrived here, and they drove off to their own pension. We started off with a cab, in this strange city to hunt up a place to stay. It was just Providence that brought us here, to this lovely pension. We couldn't speak two words of German then, and we were at the mercy of anyone.

Oh yes, they are very afraid to let us stay. After we have been here a year, but they were perfectly safe in letting us go and find a boarding house all alone.

Now if you mention this to one soul, you can't tell what the consequences will be. You must keep all such things to yourself. Just be careful, they don't fool you, that is all I want you to do.

They were very nice when we saw them during the winter, but we shall never forget our arrival here.

I wouldn't treat my worst enemy that way — especially when they knew the city — having been here before.

There are dozens and dozens of girls here all alone, and boarding in rooms without pension. If a girl is all right, there is absolutely nothing can happen her.

I feel much safer here than I did in England. The people are all so afraid of the Police here, that they would never bother you.

I have been hearing *The Ring* this week. It is simply great.[1]

---

[1] Wagner's *Ring* Cycle.

Yesterday I was out at the Austellung (Exib. of all Books from every country) — It is simply wonderful. I shall write you all about it when I get time. The two Herr Schröters took me, after my lessons at the Conservatory. It is great to talk to them for I get such practice in my German.

Now don't worry about me. Just write me all about yourselves, and I shall make myself stay till Xmas, in order to have a good grounding in my work.

Then I can work by myself, home.

All kinds of love to you all. Hope Mut is not mad because I am not coming home.

If Mother gets tired or sick, let me know by cable, and I can come home in five days. If it is only homesickness, just think of what it must be for me to be away from you all. I fight it off whenever I feel it coming.

Love, and then some.

Helen

P.S. I missed one letter. Think must have been on the poor *Empress of Ireland*.[1] My dresses are simply grand. I am not going to get a suit till I go to Paris.

LXIV

4 Sophien Platz

Leipzig, Germany

Tuesday, June 16, 1914

My Dearest Ones!

Here it is Tuesday night and your letter, not written. I have never had one moment to write to you, since I last wrote. I just work all the time, it seems. Now you must never worry when you don't hear, for I should wire you immediately if anything was wrong. No news is always good news.

Well I am alone to-night after a hard, hard day's work. The others all went to the pictures, but I stayed home to work. They called me everything for not going but I don't care, for I want to work. My German is coming fine, and I myself can feel the progress.

I was around and had a talk with Teich Saturday, at his house. He was very nice to me. I told him I did not intend making a prefung next year, so we are to start lessons the very first hour he will have which he said would be next week.

He is busy preparing the people who are leaving right away, — but he said he would give me an hour very soon. Lutz is giving me great instruction, and she is telling me what to play for him, etc. She says he will be satisfied with my technique and give me lots of nice things to play. The old boy joked and fooled with me a lot. He is a desperate old flirt, and I can imagine how May imagined he was in love with her the first time she was over here. That was a big joke.

He was engaged last year to Queenie's teacher but it is broken off now. I shall not flirt with him, you bet.

Well, everyone is still raving about the voice. Mrs. Alves told me at my last lesson she was going

---

[1] The *RMS Empress of Ireland* sank in the St. Lawrence on May 29th, 1914, after she and the Norwegian collier *S.S. Storstad* collided in the fog; it was the worst marine disaster in Canadian history, with over a thousand people drowned.

to write to you when she got a moment. She sails July 2. Upstairs in her house, a judge lives, and they were so interested in Mrs. Alves. She was up there the other night, and they asked her who I was — for they said I had a wonderful voice, and such quality — they named the hour I have my lesson and everything. Really you wouldn't believe how my voice has changed. It may all sound fishy to you, and I can't believe my ears when I hear it. Mrs. A. asked me to sing in church, but I said "no"—"not yet".

She considers me capable of anything. My songs are beautiful and you will enjoy them so much.

I got two lovely letters from Mother to-day, and I have decided to stay till Xmas for piano. Then you can hear my voice and do what you like with it. It is a problem for me to decide, but I do not try to do it alone. I have Mother's clipping in front of me now, about giving up the choice to a Higher One. Fraulein Lutz said "you must not worry about your work any more, just trust in someone higher." She is a good woman, and you must not think bad of her.

Well last week I heard the whole Ring, and Mother I wish you could have heard it. It was simply grand. Sunday was the last — *Gotterdamerung.*[1]

We had such a busy day on Sunday — in the morning we had church and communion, (the whole time I thought of you, Mother and Father — and of the example you have set to we three children). It was a very beautiful morning. Then we went to King's to tea in the afternoon and to the Opera at night. I was tired after it all, but am resting this week, (at night).

Now I must go to bed, for it has struck ten and I won't get tucked in till half past now.

I am so happy to be staying over, till Xmas. It won't be long really — just think of having Xmas turkey to-gether. You can begin to cook now, Mother. Keep busy seeing people and you won't be lonesome.

May is cool for she wants me to come home. Don't worry about her. I shall never have to ask her for lessons now, so we are quite independent.

I think of you all so much, and I never do anything that I wouldn't do if you were here, so don't worry. You must trust me.

I have all sorts of plans for when I get home. It will take me years to do all the work I have planned out.

I love to be busy. I never read an English book or paper — I am so busy.

It is so hard to do everything.

Love and kisses to you all, from,

Helen

---

[1] *Götterdämmerung.*

LXV

4 Sophien Platz
Leipzig, Germany
Monday Night
June 22/1914

My Dear People:-

I started to write to you yesterday, but was interrupted as usual. To-night I planned to write a long letter to you, and Mr. Luck came in with his banjo, and he is playing now, and Edna is amusing him, while I write. I simply must send your note in the morning, for you will be worrying.

This week I am busier than ever, and won't be able to write till Sunday. I don't think.

Just imagine — on Saturday Teich telephoned and I went to my first lesson. It was just fine, and I was not very nervous at all. He was very nice to me and told me that I played fine — He gave me a very difficult piece — that one of his good pupils is playing here in the pension. Now this week I have my harmony exam, and on Friday I have to play at my small "prefung" as they call it. Teich said it isn't anything to do, so I don't mind when he is the man who judges the playing. We just play a bit of our piece and then they stop you. Then Teich writes on my paper that he has heard me play, etc.

I am going to be working very hard this week, and I have my last singing lessons too. To-day I have had three lessons, and was at the dentist — an old crown that Doc. put on, wore out, and I have had to have another put on. Then I had another hole, and had it patched up too. I have to be careful of my teeth when I sing — for you can't sing with false teeth —

(I simply can't write when this banjo is going — I shall finish when they go).

Tuesday morning

Well, Dear Ones. It was so late when the people went last night that I was too sleepy to finish this. Now I am waiting for my coffee and must close off for now. Really — I am so rushed that I can't see straight. I expect to work all day long to-day — except for a German lesson from two to three.

The post man came in just now, and said there was a parcel for me. I am so anxious to know what it is — perhaps the gum. I am waiting patiently for a good old chew.

Well I have old Teich for sure. I felt like cabling to you, but thought it was too much money.

I got Papa's cable — there was no need of cabling for me to stay but I was glad to hear you wanted me to. I am working like everything to get all I can before I go home. I have never bought a hat yet — still wearing my old one that I wore away. I would not buy any if I had my old last summer leghorn — ask how much it would cost to send it at the customs and I never have to pay anything to get it here. If it isn't much, why send it and I won't get any new hat till I go to Paris or to England.

My new dresses are fine. I won't need any new thing till I get something to come home with.

Now my coffee is here, and cold by now, I suppose.

I must close, and really I will write you volumes when I get a moment — Have another lesson with Teich next week sometime and I have an awfully big lesson.

Don't worry about me — work never killed anyone — and I will try not to worry about you.
Lots of love,

Helen

LXVI

4 Sophien Platz
Leipzig, Germany
Sunday, June 28/1914[1]

My Dear Mother and Father:

I can write you the results of my exams, which I had on Wednesday and Friday. I could not write till I found out, for I had nothing to tell you. Now you will think I am boasting I suppose, but I came through well in both exams. I never worried or worked harder in my life for an exam, and I did not know how I came off. It has been a very trying week, but it is over now, and I am ready to dig in harder than ever. On Wednesday, I had my Harmony. It was a very hard paper, and I had four or five perfect exercises. There was only one exercise that was partly wrong, and I think I did pretty well — Our paper was much harder and more advanced than Gladys'. I am in a higher class, you know. Dr. Schreck went over all our papers with us yesterday, and I stood very well — better than Muriel Hunt — and she is very clever at it. Now I am not dreaming all this, for I waited till I knew before I wrote it to you.

Well Friday morning at 10:20 I was supposed to go to the big hall to play with six other girls. We had to wait a long time, but finally went up, and there we were confronted by a table of critics — Teich, Sidd (head violinist), Klengel (Head Cellist) the director of the Con. and a couple of others — also F. Lutz. Well everyone shook from head to foot (no poetry about it either). I thought my day had come, for sure. Every girl was nervous — and scared to death. Well I played the fourth, and had to listen to the others play first, which didn't help the nerves any.

Well when my name was called I went up and played as if I was in a dream. When I finished I hadn't any idea how I had played, or anything. Lutz said "Good" as I passed her, on my way back to my seat.

After it was over I was too much afraid to go up to her and ask her how I had done for fear it was bad. She said to one of the other girls, though, that I had played well.

Yesterday I had a lesson with her and she said I had never played it so well, in any of my lessons, and she was well pleased with it. Now arn't you pleased? That means that I shall get a good write-up on my certificate. I am so glad it is over for it is an awful strain. I had to fight hard all week over it all — but I knew you dear ones would be pleased if I did well, and so I prayed, and worked till it was over. Now I feel like I used to after a big set of exams at college.

Mother's letter came yesterday telling me to work, etc. I surely have been doing my best, and everyone here will tell you that I have been doing my best — and trying to keep my health. I am not nearly so fat now, and am getting into my clothes again. Worry soon takes the fat off. I try to keep well though and I don't eat any trash at all, to make me sick.

My voice has worried me so much — what to do with it I don't know — Lutz tried it yesterday, and she said "By all means have your voice well trained". Everyone here says the same thing.

I am finding out the best teacher in Paris, and I am seriously thinking of going over there with the Leslies in the summer, and having it tried by the best teacher. Then I would know what plans to make. They are making a very cheap trip — going down the Rhine — visiting Heidelberg, etc.

---

[1] On June 28, 1914, the heir to the Austro-Hungarian Empire, Archduke Franz Ferdinand, and his wife Sophie were assassinated in Sarajevo by Gavrilo Princip, a Bosnian-Serb nationalist.

and then to Paris. They go on to England, but I should stay there for a week or so and then come back here. I don't think I shall go to Eng. and Scotland for I have spent so much money already, that I simply will not spend so much more. I can rest here, I think, and study German and French.

Now my plans, as yet, are very uncertain, for I am trying to plan out the best way I can, to do as much as possible in the short time I have to stay.

I am worried terribly about Anna's and Will's ideas about my coming home. I am just between two fires — you know I can't possibly have as much piano as May, when she was here a whole year — then practised eight or more years, and then had another year here, especially when I have done what I have with my voice.

After Church!

We are out in the garden, after dinner, and it is hard to write when everyone is talking. To-night we are all going to *Rosencavalier* —(Strauss).[1] So I must finish your letter right away. Sunday I never have time to write, for there are so many things to do.

Well yesterday I got the letter of credit from Mut, along with a little note from him. I can't thank you people enough for renewing it and I feel badly to think I had to write and ask for more. It was my voice which made the price of the year go up so. It has been well worth it all though, and you will enjoy it all so much when I come back.

I shall plan on coming back Xmas, and then if I don't spend too much money, and Mother is not too lonesome I shall go to Paris for my voice. We can settle that later.

I can't begin to think of all I want to tell you. I think of it all when I am through with my letter.

I begin to think that Mut thinks I am over here on a pleasure trip. I can't begin to tell you how lonesome I have been all winter. Sometimes I actually thought I could not stay one moment longer. However I would not give in, and now I have conquered it pretty nearly. I have put up a hard fight. I can tell you, and I tried not to let you people know about it.

This year we have worked very very hard and it has been no easy time. Believe me it is hard for me to stay when the others leave but I feel that I must, in order to get enough to know a little bit. Really you don't get enough in one year to think twice about. I am so worried about you two dear ones being lonely. Now are you too lonely for me to stay till Xmas? Please tell me just how you feel. It is so hard for me to know what to do.

Well this week Mrs. Leslie and Mr. celebrated their first Wedding Anniversary, and Edna, the two L., Mr. Stein, Heber and I all went out with our supper. We went to a great pleasure resort called Luna Park, and had our lunch. It was perfect there and we stayed till about nine. The new moon came out and I wished on it.

There are so many muts sitting around, that I can't write for beans.

This week I can write in the middle of the week, for I won't have so many lessons, and exams.

Up in my room.

I just had to leave the garden in order to think at all. There was too much noise.

This week, on Tuesday I heard *Cavalleria Rusticana* and *Bajazzo*, with the best cast I have heard since I have been here. Edna and I were up in the top gallery, and heard the greatest artists for 20 cents.

My room is perfect and cool. It is on the shady side of the house. It is not so nice in winter. It is

---

[1] *Der Rosenkavalier*, Richard Strauss, 1911.

lovely now to practise in it. The weather here has not been hotter than we have it home, so don't let the McA's make you think it is an awful place.

I am going to work awfully hard this week, for my lesson with Teich. Please don't be lonely Mother. It makes me lonely to think you are lonely.

All my love, and thanks for the money. I shall save every cent I can, and not travel too much this summer. The gum arrived. It is great. Just send it by post and it is cheaper. I have enough to do me for months now. I hope. Please tell me to come home when you want me. That is my only request.

Helen

LXVII

4 Sophien Platz
Leipzig, Germany
Wednesday, July 1, 1914

My Dearest Mother:-

Your two lovely letters came yesterday, and I am afraid you are tiring yourself writing too often. I just long for your letters, but I don't want you to tire yourself writing.

I am the first down this morning. I guess it must be because I had a bath last night, and I was so light that I could not lie in bed long. It is a perfect day, and so cool, that we shall do a big day's work. I hope.

I was so glad to hear about the hair. I have so much here that I have saved too, that we shall have enough for a third. I should rather you would keep them Mother — for I never have time to do much with my hair here, and then it might get lost on the way. Roll it up so the moths won't get it, and use the other one yourself. I shall only need one, and I have enough now for another.[1]

Monday I had my last singing lesson, and she took your address to write to you, when she gets time.

I have had 56 lessons, which is not three quarters. It just cost me $210, and I can tell you I would not give it up for $1000 — what I have learned.

She told me how to keep up my exercises, etc., and she said there is no reason why I should go back any.

Then when I get my piano I must specialise in voice for I sing before everyone and am not a bit nervous. We shall have a little recital Mother, when I come back, and then I can get any amount of pupils. I am so glad our parlour is large, for my voice needs rather a large room to show it off — The quality, though, is the thing everyone raves over.

Mother I am afraid you really are very lonesome, and I hate to stay away from you. Your letter sounded lonesome.

Please Mother don't listen to the McAdams. I know more about Leipzig than they ever did, and who ever heard tell of such rot as about the red-lights. Of course there are such places in the city, but we are never in the vicinity where they are, and one does not stumble over such places unless one

[1] At this time, women sometimes used pads of additional hair to achieve a fashionable soft, full hairstyle.

wants to. They are in every city, but we are never in any danger for we never go out alone, at night, only to the theatre, and then, we just step on a car at the theatre door, and run up to our own door.

This city is much safer than any city in America. It is perfectly safe here in every way, and for goodness sake don't worry. I never have a soul speak to me, or bother me in any way, a bit more than at home.

Monday night we heard *Faust* and it was fine.[1] Urlus sings in *Il Travatore*[2] to-night and I hope to go if I can get a seat. He is about the best in Germany.

Now I must away to work, and get a good start.

Don't worry, and I shall come home in October if you are lonesome.

Lots of love and kisses to you all,

Helen

LXVIII

4 Sophien Platz
Leipzig, Germany
Monday, July 6/14

My Dear Mother and Father, and all the little and big VanWarts and Massies:-

I am up first on our flat this morning, and I must scratch off a line to you before the others come down.

Yesterday, I didn't have one moment to write to you, for someone was in all the day, it seemed. An Irish girl came around in the morning, a Scotch girl in the afternoon and Mr. & Mrs. King. In the evening we three girls went walking with the two Schröters.

It was half past ten when we got back so I went right to bed, so that I would be up early this morning.

I have had two letters from Mother, and you must not tire yourself writing so often. I love to hear, but I know how much you have to do, and I shall know that no news is good news.

Mother, you certainly are an inspiration to me, and I feel like working ten times as hard when I get your letters. I am doing all I can possibly stand now, especially after a whole year of it. We all look worn and tired but we are trying to stick out July, and then send our pianos back — mine for one month only. Then I shall come back and work, I think.

Don't you worry about my staying Mother. It was my own choice, for I knew that I wanted more than the other girls, in order to compete in any way. Teich is giving me all his technique, which is the greatest possible thing I could study, and he told me he wasn't doing the same course with Glad, and Edna, for there was not time.

I am working my fingers off for him. I almost sprained my wrist Saturday, so I must be careful.

Saturday, there was a big celebration, for July 4th in the café in the woods. There was a base-ball game, supper, fire-works and a dance. I went to the two latter, for I wouldn't spare the time from

---

[1] Either *Faust* by Charles Gounod, 1859 or *Faust,* by Ludwig or Louis Spohr, 1816, revised 1852.
[2] *Il Trovatore,* Guiseppe Verdi, 1853.

my work to go to the first two. Mr. Lochhead took me, and we brought Gladys home with us, Edna having left earlier, when she doesn't dance. I never had a better time at a dance. It was just till twelve and we got home rather early for a dance.

I heard great Opera last week — *Rosencavalier* — Sunday, *Faust*, Monday, and *Il Trovatore* on Wednesday. The last was simply grand. How I wish you could have heard them all.

After Dinner

I had to eat my breakfast and hustle off to work, this morning, so now I have about 15 min. to write before 3 o'clock, when we must begin to practise.

Edna and Gladys have their passage booked on the *Empress of B.*[1] for August 21. I am glad they have a good boat to go back on, even if the twin sister was sunk. I would go on the *Britain* as quick as any boat. Gladys supposes the people will be worrying when they hear that they are on that boat.

It makes me feel lonely to think of them all going — every English person will be gone from the Pension, but now I am going to show you people what stuff I am made of, and unless anything happens to my health, I shall not give in.

I may go to Eng., Scot., and Ireland with the girls, for I can't find anyone else who wants to make the trip. It would not be pleasant alone, and I would not go, for fear something might happen to me.

Of course, I am not sure yet, but I think I had better go with them. I think the Leslies will go earlier likely. The Kings are going to the Mountains (Harz) for the summer, and I may stay off there on my way back for a short time. About Sept. 1st I expect to arrive back here and work till Oct. 1st.

Now when we girls go to Paris on our way over to Eng. I am going to have my voice tried by the best teacher, and get an opinion from an outside party - if it should be very encouraging, I feel as if I should not stay here and work piano, when I am only going to stay till Xmas. I would much rather have the few months on my voice.

Now I shall be home sure by Xmas, Mother, if all goes well, for I refuse to leave you alone one moment longer. Why the time will be here in no time. I shall sail from Bremen to New York, and Mother you can come down to meet me, and Father too. I will not go away over to Eng. again. I don't think, just for the sake of sailing to St. John or Halifax.

Mrs. Alves said they would meet me, and see to me when I arrived, so I should be all right. I know lots of people in New York now — I could write Earle to tell his uncle I was coming and I would have a whole regiment down to meet me — Ha! Ha!

Dear Ones, I don't dare think of you, I just plan, and dig all the time. Everyone said I would only stay one year or six months. Well I can just show them that I haven't any chicken heart.

I hear the pianos going so I must away.

All kinds of love and kisses and really I am working to the very best of my ability. Love,

Helen

---

[1] *RMS Empress of Britain.*

LXIX

4 Sophien Platz
Leipzig, Germany
Wednesday noon
July 15/14

My Dear Ones!

Here it is Wednesday and I must write you a little mid-week note, before dinner. I have just completed three hours piano, and am writing this between, and 1:15 when we have dinner.

Yesterday I had my last harmony lesson. Really I never hated to leave a teacher so much in my life as dear old Dr. Schreck. Muriel Hunt and I each bought a picture of him, and he wrote in German "In kind remembrance" Dr. Schreck. He is a lovely man, and he was so nice to us — shook hands and wished us a pleasant vacation — He married an Eng. lady, so he is not like the Germans. They call him the second Bach here. He composes wonderful things.

Then Dr. Bennewitz goes away to-day so my German lessons are at a stop for the vacation. I may take from someone else when I come back the first of September — till he comes back in October — he has been a great help to me.

I have quite a few more lessons with Lutz yet, and one more with Teich. I got a card to-day telling me to come next Thursday.

He is very busy finishing off pupils that are leaving, and he hasn't many spare hours — but he gave me this and I shall get work to do in September when he is not here — That will give me a good start for the last two or three months.

I am still worrying about Mother — if she is too lonesome I want to come home — really she is more to me than all the music in the world, so never hesitate to tell me what you think about it — Father is out all day, and he doesn't get a chance to be lonesome.

Edna and Glad. are both going to tell you all about me and Leipzig and everything. Your minds will be much more at ease than when the McAdams went home with their tales of woe.

Mother dear, don't ever worry about me having to have lessons from May, or any such rot. Don't you know I am beyond that? All I have to do now is to practise till I get it — I know how as well as she does, and just give me time and I shall get there, if possible.

We haven't made any definite plans about our trip this summer, yet. By Sunday I hope to be able to write you more.

Last night it was very warm, and we all got on top of a bus and went all over the city — it was so cool there — that it is just as good as owning a motor car.

I would like to see some of the bunch of Canadians that are coming over to Europe this summer. Very likely we shall run across them in Eng. or Scot. Two Profs. from Univ. of Alberta are here now — Mr. Luck saw them and told me about it.

Just imagine mother, Mr. Luck is engaged to one of the Flint girls and was engaged to her two months after his wife died. We are all shocked about it, but don't say anything — the Kings think it is terrible. She is rather old, and it isn't so bad, as if she was young.

He loved his first wife too, everybody says. He just has to have a woman I guess, and it doesn't take him long to make up his mind. He has been very nice to us, and we must not talk about him — the Germans think it is terrible.

Well I must away to dinner — for I haven't any more news for you.

There is nothing going on now but work.

I am trying to find out the best singing teacher in Paris, before I go there.

Love to every one of you. Tell me everything and don't be afraid to tell me to come home. I want you all to be happy, and if I can help, please tell me.

Helen

LXX

4 Sophien Platz
Leipzig, Germany
Friday, July 24/14

My Dearest Home Ones!

Such good news as I have for you! Yesterday I had my last lesson with Teich, and it was the best lesson imaginable.

He said I played my piece "very well", and that he never dreamed I could play Schumann so well. It suits me perfectly, he thought.

He said "you are very romantic", and then we went on about my work at a great rate. He was simply lovely to me.

He said "I will give you romantic things, for they suit you so."

He gave me two very difficult pieces to work up myself in September. Then he spent half of the hour on technique and he gave me enough to keep me going for a month without stopping. It means an awful lot of work.

I have not felt well for a few days, but that fixed me fine, and I want to dig right in, instead of going away.

I must have a rest though, and so I leave next Thursday with the Leslies for our trip.

It is something to have Teich tell you all that, and it encouraged me very much. I didn't tell the girls what he said — only that I had a good lesson. It is best to keep pretty Mum.

I haven't heard from you all week, and I am very very worried that Mother is worse.

I am waiting to mail this till I hear.

When I go to England I shall pack my trunks — leave them at a place here, and if I decide to sail home I shall just write them to forward my trunks.

Everyone does that here. If there is the slightest need of my coming back, I shall, and then perhaps return again.

I arranged with Teich for a lesson on the first of October, but I can easily write him if I decide to go home.

Saturday morning!

No letter yet. Shall wait till I get one to mail this.

Was invited around to Kings' to supper last night. They thought I would be lonesome and gave me a grand time. The Shaws arrived from Dresden yesterday. They are on their way to England in their car. They are awfully nice to me, and we expect to go to the Exhibition this afternoon.

More later.

Monday Morning!

Still no letter — it is over a week now, and I am getting desperate. Perhaps it will come at eleven. If not, I shall have to mail this or you will be wild about not hearing from me.

I have had one glorious time with the Shaws.

Saturday Mr. S., Irma and I went to the Exib. in their car. It is a Mercedes — splendid car. We had a great time. Mrs. S. does not go around much for she had an operation in Dresden, and the doctor won't allow her to travel much. They go about 70 miles a day on their trip.

Well Saturday afternoon their son, Ralph, arrived and I used to know him at High School. He went to Rothesay. Sunday morning Mrs. S., Irma and I went to English church. They took us and called for us in the car.

I was around at Pension Harris with Maud Seyde to dinner. As we were eating her mother arrived from Honolulu, and she hadn't the slightest idea she was coming. I didn't stay longer for I wanted her to see her mother. I met the Shaws at 3 and we went out in the car, and went to Grimma — a very historic place about an hour's ride from here — noted in its connection with Luther. We had coffee there and then came back here at about half past five.

They were certainly very kind to me, and they had no reason to be, never knowing me before.

Ralph knows about everyone I know, and we raked out more acquaintances last night than you can imagine.

We are going to try to meet them in England — and they have even suggested my returning with them, when I leave the girls — I wouldn't like to accept such a favour. They want me to go to Dresden for next winter, but I wouldn't leave Teich for anything — there is none in Dres. like him.

They have just left for Weimar and then they make a lot of short trips and then go to Köln — where we expect to meet again.

Gladys couldn't have used them decent, I don't think, for Irma said that she didn't appreciate the trip to Berlin, with them, and that her mother was quite cut up about it.

I thanked them a thousand times for all they did for me, and tried to show my appreciation as much as I could.

They expect to be in London about the 25th of Aug. and that is when I expect to be there on my way back here.

Irma said — we are hoping to bring you back with us if we can — so wouldn't it be great? Imagine motoring through Europe — of course I should pay my own hotel bills and everything like that.

Well I am so worried about Mother — I am afraid she is worse. Perhaps it is poor old Nan — how I pity her having so much to go through.

And Mut — I can't think of him as a father at all. Wouldn't I love to see Mary. She will not know her Aunty Helen at all. Never mind we shall have some good old times together when I get back, together with Mic.

How is poor old Papa — I never hear a word from him, and I am afraid he is working himself to death.

Mr. Shaw reminded me so of him, that I was terribly lonely when I stopped to think.

To-day the Leslies and I are going to get our ticket so I can write you more particulars later.

I asked Mr. & Mrs. King and her brother over to tea to-night, to try to pay her back in some slight way for all she has done for me — I have never done a thing for her in any way.

Next year if I come back, I have a cheaper room — five marks a month cheaper. I am trying to economise in every possible way I can — so as to bring over half of the $1000 back if I possibly can.

I am not going to buy a lot of clothes for I would much rather have things that last.

Well the post is here, and no letter so I don't know what to do.

Perhaps there is no Canadian mail in. I shall ask Mr. Luck if he has had any.

Feeling fine — pack my clothes and things for the summer, and leave them here. If I get word to come home, why I shall be ready.

All kinds of love,

Helen

LXXI

Sailing down the Rhine
August 2, 1914[1]

My Dearest Ones!

Here is your little girl flying down the Rhine as quickly as possible to get away from the war. We have at last crossed the border into Holland and feel so much safer.

You have no idea in the world of the state of affairs here — we are so glad to get out of the country, and we have had to break our trip all up, in order to be safe.

I am so afraid you may have cabled me and I had all my mail sent to Cook's Paris, and now we can't go there. I am going to cable you the moment I get on safe ground in Holland or England. They have even said that Holland is mobilising. If so, we shall not be safe till we get to England.

Now I must tell you a little bit about it — we never feared the least till the evening we were in Heidelberg — The news came that the troops were mobilising, and we didn't take alarm.

The next day we started for Worms, Mannheim, and Mainz — when we arrived at Mainz, everything was in an uproar — the soldiers were all gathering and the people were wild. We met the American Consul (from Leipzig) and he said we had better move right on for all the trains would be stopped very soon. We were frightened and made preparations to sail down the Rhine to Cologne early next morning.

Well the racket in the city that night was terrible, and we were glad to sail at eight in the morning.

When we reached Cologne we were told to leave as soon as possible for everything was in an uproar.

We couldn't get out by train, so we had to take a boat going to Rotterdam. Everything was bought up on this boat and we could only get an ordinary ticket (no berth).

The boat was not allowed to leave till five this morning, on account of the war, so we had to sit up all night and we had no chance to really rest.

We started to sail this morning and we went very slowly all morning. Then this afternoon we were stopped and had to get out and be examined and transferred to another ship — They seized

---

[1] The Austro-Hungarian Empire declared war on Serbia on July 28. Russia began to mobilise in support of Serbia on the 29th, Germany, in alliance with Austria, on July 30th, and France, fearing Germany, on August 1st. Germany declared war on Russia on August 1st and on France on August 3rd. Germany invaded Belgium on August 4th. Britain and the British Empire, including Canada, declared war on Germany the same day.

all the provisions for the war.

Of course now, we are all right and out of danger, for we don't think Holland will take part.

To-morrow noon we expect to arrive in Rotterdam and catch a boat right away for England. Then we can't be touched by any old Germans or French or Russians.

I expect to meet the girls in London and if the situation gets worse I shall go home with them if I can get a passage.

It looks very serious to us now, but perhaps when we get to England, it will be cooled down.

It has been a wonderful experience, and I shall never forget it but we have been certainly frightened. We have trouble with money when there is war, you know, and it is hard to know what they will accept. We have some of all kinds of money so are pretty sure of getting along.

I couldn't begin to describe the Rhine trip to you. It has been simply grand — the old castles, and vineyards are fine.

The Leslies have been awfully kind to me and I don't know what I should ever have done without them. They can't do enough for me, and they are such good people.

They are going to look after me till I get to London to a nice place, so I am not the least bit afraid. Supper time. More later.

Helen

LXXII

80 Bath St. Y.W.C.A.
Glasgow, Scotland
Aug. 9th/1914

Well Dear Ones:-

Here it is a week since I wrote before, and what a change in the meantime — war on all sides.

You have received our cable I hope, and will not be worried. We had our passage booked on the *Saturnia*, which was to have sailed yesterday, but the Gov. took it off. Now we have to wait till another boat is put on. We are not hurrying off too soon, for we do not think it is safe, till the crush is over. There are thousands of people waiting for boats, and we are among the many.

What a lovely place we have to stay in though — the Y.W.C.A.

We only have to pay 15 shillings a week, full board, and there are only girls and women here. I am going to cable to you to-day to tell you not to worry. We are perfectly safe, and will come home as soon as it is safe.

I have all the money we need, and we shall not be short.

There are so many poor people here stranded without a cent, and then think of the poor people left in Germany — the Lucks, Kings, Flints, Mr. Lochhead and everybody.[1] We are worried to death about them.

---

[1] Grant Lochhead, who remained in Germany trying to meet with his professors for his doctoral defence, was interned and spent the war in a German prison camp at Ruhleben. His letters to Helen in the spring of 1914 while both were still in Leipzig show that their relationship developed from friendship to romance during those months; by August he was writing to his "dear dear Helen" and worrying for her safety as she tried to reach Britain.

I left Rotterdam by the last boat, and we had a horrible time getting over — but were glad enough to get here at all.

The Leslies just stayed with me all the time, and then I met the girls, and we arranged our passages for Saturday.

We have just heard that we can get passages for Wednesday, but have not decided to go, yet. We are being very careful, and hope you are not worried.

I worry all the time about you, and can't get it out of my head that nothing is wrong.

I am afraid mother is sick, and Anna, and I know you are all worried to death about me. Really I am all right and we have all given ourselves over to the Person who can guide our little ship back to Canada. He will not leave or forsake us, so I am not going to worry about anything. If it is His will that we should not reach the other shore, and see our dear ones once more, we must make up our minds to it, and say "Thy will be done".

I am not sad in this, at such a time one must think such things. When we sail we shall be taking a great risk, but will all try to be brave and not worry.

The poor soldiers (volunteers) were all at church this morning and how brave they were — my but the Scotch are brave, and so good and honest — I am proud of my Scotch ancestry — also my Dutch — they were so good in Holland.

They say, mail will go to-morrow, so we are writing on a chance — then we will sail when we think it safe.

I am praying for you dear souls. I don't know how you all are, but I hope for the best.

If you could only see us, and see how lovely we are situated among thorough Christians — we feel so safe.

I think of our poor Canadian soldiers coming over here to be killed — I imagine I know some of them.

It is not a war between the people of Germany and Eng. — only the officials — the people pay the price.

Dearest Ones, I can't write any more. We don't know what the future holds for us but there is One who does, and we need not worry, when He is our guide.

If all goes well, we shall be with you as soon as it is safe to travel.

With all my love, and kisses to my own dear Mother, Father, Anna, Willie, Kath, George, and the kiddies.

From,

your little girl who is just the same in character as when she left you last summer.

So don't worry. We must all be soldiers and fight for the right.

Helen

AFTERWORD

When I started to read *Letters from Helen* I expected to meet a young, vivacious girl, out in the world for the first time. I expected to see my grandmother in a new light, as she was as a young University of New Brunswick graduate, filled with enthusiasm and ideas, full of energy and music. I was excited to meet this young woman. I had known and loved my Grandma Lochhead very much, but she was, after all, my grandmother. I wanted to know the real Helen.

What I found in the *Letters* was my grandmother. Helen's intense musicality, her deep love of family, her sense of fun, her independence, confidence and sense of self and her toughness of spirit brought not a young girl to mind but rather, my own experience of and relationship with my grandmother, Helen. I was surprised, delighted and deeply moved to be with her again, in her letters.

The constancy of my grandmother's voice, her sense of who she was and her relationship with those she loved throughout her life reminded me of the continuum of life and the human spirit that is in us and in our families. It is something to be depended on in an undependable world. Thank you Helen, for this gift.

Sara Louise Lochhead

APPENDIX ONE

HELEN AND GRANT

Although "Mr Lochhead", a "very nice boy", only gets a few mentions in Helen's letters to her family as one of many friends, by May of 1914 she and Allan Grant Lochhead, who was finishing up his Ph.D. in bacteriology in Leipzig, were deeply in love. No hint of this slips into her letters to her parents, although her sudden change of plans and desire to stay in Leipzig for another term, through the autumn of 1914, are no doubt connected to this. In late summer and autumn, Grant would be completing his degree with his oral defence of his doctoral thesis. Quite probably, she was waiting to introduce him to the people at home in person. A sample of their letters from the outbreak of the war shows the intensity of their relationship, and also underscores Helen's continued optimism — or failure to appreciate the seriousness of the escalating political tension.

HELEN TO GRANT, JULY 31ST, 1914

Pension Schröter[1]
Leipzig,
den 31 July, 1914

My Dear Grant: -

I can just begin a note, to you now, for we are just waiting for Mr. Leslie to come, then we go to eat dinner, and from there is the station.

Isn't Heidelberg a grand old place? I have thought so much about you since I have been here. Your pictures of the castle are fine. Will you lend me the films sometime? I mean the ones of the castle only. We have been there all morning, and have walked all over the place. We did not go to your pension, for the Leslies wanted to go to some place like a Hospiz. It is right on the Hauptstrasse, so we are in the centre of things.

Yesterday after we arrived we just wandered around — Mrs. L and I. Mr. L. was at the university. We went over one bridge and down to the other and then back through the town. There was a

---

[1] Although written on Pension Schröter notepaper, internal evidence indicates this letter was written from Heidelberg.

big war scare here last night and it was real exciting. That was why I couldn't write for the Leslies wanted to stay out in the street all the time.

I sent a card this morning but I am afraid you won't get it to-day, anyway I was thinking about you, and hope the voiceless thoughts reached you.

We leave right away for Worms. Then by to-night we shall be in Mainz.

To-morrow early we sail, and hope to be in Cöln to-morrow night.

I am dying to get a letter from you, but shall have to be content till Paris — here's hoping you are not too lonesome, and are rested after those terrible exams. I don't believe I ever thanked you for coming to the train. I certainly appreciated it. Must run now.

All kinds of love, Helen.

GRANT TO HELEN, AUGUST 1ST, 1914

Hohenzollernstr.16
Leipzig
Aug. 1st, 1914

My dear, dear Helen: -

Your letter arrived to-day along with the postcard and I was delighted to get some news from you and specially in these troubled times. I do hope all is going well with you. Just now it looks as if war were going to become a reality and I am terribly worried about you for fear you are having trouble. The mail and the trains are very irregular and uncertain, in fact I feared that your letter might not reach me as they are having very strict measures specially in the Rheinland. I never wanted to be with you as much as I do right now. As it is I am certainly there with you in thought but I would like be really there to be able to help you if I could, because Germany in time of war is not the place where one would wish the person he loves best to be.

I am praying that things will go smoothly with you and that you won't meet with any trouble, and be able to carry out your original plans without interruption.

There was lots of excitement in Leipzig last night. We had our farewell celebration last night — a dinner at which the chaps in our laboratory whom I had been working with and who also passed the exams — were assembled — just about half a dozen altogether. The others were all Germans and naturally the only topic of discussion was the coming war. It wasn't such a lively affair as it might have been under ordinary circumstances so we broke up at the painfully respectable hour of ten o'clock.

Yesterday afternoon I went around to say farewell to the Misses Gow and Barnett. They intended leaving to-day or to-morrow for the Harz to spend a couple of weeks. They were kind enough to send me a card on Thursday with congrats. on the exams. I also got a card from Miss Seyde wishing me success. She also informed me that her mother paid her a "surprise" visit last Sunday. Miss Barnett still talks confidently of being able to pay a visit to Sweden. She said something about you being able to go with her, but didn't ask me to coax you, so I volunteered no information.

My Russian friend (the one who was at the Opera with me that time) left for home last night. I was awfully sorry to see him leave as I had got to like him immensely and he was perhaps the best friend I had in Leipzig. It certainly widens one's outlook to get to know people from another part of the world than your own, and it keeps one from being narrow enough to think people of another race can't possess as good qualities as those of one's own.

Yes, Helen, I do miss you, and I am getting to realize what it means not to be able to see you. I felt a whole lot lonelier as your handkerchief vanished from view Thursday morning. One thing however is buoying me up, and that is the thought of how we parted, — the thought that after having got to know each other this summer the way we have, each of us was able to say at the end — I love you — and mean it too.

You certainly have got to be a big factor in my life and since I have got to know and love you life has taken on a newer, realer meaning for me and I am going to try my best to prove as worthy as I can of the love you have given me. I know you will give me credit for being sincere. I am going to try to be patient — and work. And there's lots more I want to tell you too.

I hope you will just have a good, good time and without any trouble. I hope too that this letter reaches you safely. I will feel simply terrible if it doesn't. You will understand the reason if it doesn't reach you anyway. I may leave here in 3 or 4 days, as I may not be able to get my cash here, if "Krieg" really breaks out and then I would be stranded. I therefore may reach England earlier. Write anyway to Leipzig and be sure to leave a note, by — Montreal Star 17 Cockspur St. London, S.W. telling me all about your plans and where I can write you. Do that as soon as you are in England.

And now I won't take up any more of your good time. I will write again soon. Have no doubts — I am thinking of you and wish I could be of some use.

> Yours with love
> Grant.

GRANT TO HELEN, AUGUST 2ND, 1914

> Leipzig, Aug. 2nd, 1914.

My dear Helen: -

You haven't any idea how I have been thinking about you and wondering how you have been faring and how I have been wishing I could be with you. I wrote you yesterday to Paris and hope you get the letter all right. I do hope you are out of this country now that the trouble seems to have really started. In case that letter should possibly go astray I am trying one or two other ways to reach you, and hope they all succeed. I am afraid the postal service will be sadly interrupted and am worried lest some of your letters won't reach me and vice versa.

I expected to be a few days longer in Leipzig to see if it is worth while getting the "Arbeit"[1] printed now. Then I will probably strike out to England though I am not quite sure by what route. I am afraid the passenger service will be about all called off for the first few days of the mobilisation.

---

[1] "The Work": his doctoral thesis.

I'm afraid this letter won't be quite as long as the one I wrote yesterday, but this is mainly to show you that I am thinking more than ever about you and I am writing in the hope that you will get it in case the other one gets lost.

Try and leave your address and all other information for me at "Montreal Star", 17 Cockspur St. London S.W. as soon as you arrive in London. I do want so much to see you — more than I ever did. There is such a lot to tell you when I do see you.

I have been wondering so much where you are and if you have been experiencing much difficulty on the way.

I hope to hear from you soon and to get good news. Wish I could do something for you. — I would do anything in the world.

I am writing again soon to London.

Auf Wiedersehen. That is what I am living for.

With love,
Grant

Family tradition relates that Grant's efforts to meet with his supervisors for this thesis defence were the reason he was still in Germany when Britain and Germany went to war. He was taken prisoner and eventually interned in the civilian internment camp at Ruhleben in Spandau, outside Berlin, a race track hastily converted to prison camp, or as they were called in those days, before the word took on its darkest meaning, concentration camp. There he would spend the next four years, in the company of between four and five thousand other male British subjects, all civilian internees.

His love-letters written to Helen over those years are to be published by Sybertooth in 2011.

"But child! Don't work too much. Call at two-thirty
tomorrow. Good-bye. G."
(Card from Grant Lochhead)

(Collection of the Lochhead Family)

APPENDIX TWO

In the earliest days of the war, the media at home took a deep interest in Fredericton's straying travellers.

From *The Daily Gleaner*, August 3, 1914

Word has been received here that Mr. Chas. H. Edgecombe and Arthur Hawkes, who have been touring Europe, sailed for home on Saturday by White Star Liner *Dominion.*

No word has yet been received from Miss Helen VanWart, daughter of ex-Ald. A.H. VanWart, who is on the Continent. Her relatives don't know whether she is in Germany or France.

The Daily Gleaner, Aug. 9, 1914

A letter was received yesterday afternoon from Miss Edna Baird, daughter of Mr. H.P. Baird, of this city, who with Miss Gladys A. Grant, of Southampton, is travelling through Germany and other European countries. The letter was dated July 25th, and Miss Baird and Miss Grant were then in Paris. No mention is made in the letter of Miss Helen VanWart, daughter of ex-Ald. A.H. VanWart, of this city, whom it is expected is in London travelling with Mr. and Mrs. Leslie, two Americans.

The Daily Gleaner, Aug. 10, 1914

Wait Safe Sailing

Fredericton Girl Still in Great Britain on way from Germany

"Don't worry: waiting safe sailing," was the contents of a cablegram received this morning by ex-Ald. A.H. VanWart from his daughter Miss Helen VanWart, who with other young ladies has been trying for the past two or three weeks to get home from Great Britain after spending the past six months [sic] in Germany.

The S.S. *Saturnia*, of the Donaldson Line — not the *Laurentic* — was the steamer on which Misses VanWart and Edna Baird, of this city, and Miss Gladys Grant, of Southampton, were to have sailed form Glasgow on Saturday. The *Saturnia*, however, has been taken by the British Admiralty for naval service and will be used to transport supplies for the army and navy.

The Daily Gleaner, Aug. 21, 1914

Miss VanWart Writes of Flight from Germany

Fredericton Girl was aboard steamer from which Germans took food

----

Writes letter while sailing down Rhine

Is with Miss Baird and Miss Grant at Glasgow waiting for passage home

In a letter to her parents in this city, Miss Helen VanWart, daughter of Ald. [sic] A.H. VanWart, who is now in Glasgow, Scotland, tells of her experience in getting out of Germany when war was declared.

Miss VanWart's letter was written as she was going down the Rhine, with two American friends, Mr. and Mrs. Leslie, and she describes their experiences at different stages as being most exciting. They were stopped several times while on route to Rotterdam, Holland, and while on one of the steamers had to lie awake all night and were without food, the latter having been taken off the boat by the Germans.

The trip from Rotterdam to Glasgow was perhaps the most trying part of the journey, but with Miss Baird of this city, and Miss Grant, of Southampton, she is waiting in Glasgow for a steamer en route home. It may be possible that all three are now on a vessel bound for Canada. Miss VanWart had intended returning to Leipsig [sic], but this was impossible and she had to leave all her wearing apparel and music there in her trunks.

The Daily Gleaner, Tuesday, Aug. 24, 1914

Fredericton Girls home Wednesday

Misses VanWart, Baird and Grant arrived safely at Quebec yesterday

Miss Helen VanWart, daughter of ex-Ald. and Mrs. A.H. VanWart, Miss Edna Baird, daughter of Mr. and Mrs. H.P. Baird, both of this city, and Miss Gladys Grant, of Southampton, daughter of Gordon A. Grant, have arrived safely on Canadian soil.

A telegram received last evening from Miss Van Wart stated that all three had arrived at Quebec on the Donaldson Liner *Athenia* and would be in Fredericton on Wednesday at noon.

The three young ladies were all in Germany studying music, but previous to the outbreak of war had left that country on a tour of the continent. Miss VanWart left Germany later than the others and after a perilous journey joined them in Scotland.

The Royal Conservatorium of Music of Leipzig.

§ 1.

The object of the Conservatorium of Music at Leipzig, established with Royal authority and support, is the higher education in Music. The instruction it imparts, embraces, theoretically and practically, all branches of Music, considered as an Art and a Science.

§ 2.

The Theoretical Instruction consists of a complete course of the Theory of Music and Composition, which extends over three years. Every year at Easter and Michaelmas a new course commences, so that pupils can enter regularly twice every year. (See § 8. Foreigners.)

Those pupils who already possess sufficient preliminary theoretical knowledge, and are sufficiently capable in other respects, so that upon their admission they can at once be placed into the upper classes, can complete their theoretical Studies in a shorter time than three years. If, nevertheless, it is thought necessary, these pupils will be required to attend at the same time the lessons in the lower classes as "repetitions", so as to become thoroughly acquainted with the whole system of teaching in its full extent.

The Theoretical Instruction comprises the following subjects:

a. Harmony. Counterpoint, Canon and Fugue.

b. Form and Composition, by oral instruction and exercises, which include the following subjects: Vocal and Instrumental Composition in their various forms and treatment; Instruction and Practice in composition; Analysis of classical musical works.

c. Playing from Score, Exercise in orchestra-leading.

d. Italian Language for those who purpose devoting themselves to the higher branches of Solo-Singing.

The Theoretical Instruction further includes, courses of Lectures on Musical subjects varying annually such as, the History of Ancient and Modern Music, Aesthetics of Music, Metrics, &c.

Special classes are arranged for the instruction of lady pupils in Harmony and Composition, to enable their completing the course in two years.

§ 3.

The Practical Instruction aims at developing technical execution on one or several instruments, and in singing. It comprises the following subjects:

a. Instruction in Singing (Solo and Choral, thorough training for the Opera-stage and method of teaching).

b. Instruction in Instrumental Playing:

1. Pianoforte.
2. Organ.
3. Violin and Viola.
4. Violoncello.
5. Doublebass.
6. Wind-Instruments i. e. Flute, Hautboy, French Horn, Clarionet, Bassoon, Horn, Cornet, Trombone.

Extract from Helen's copy of the Conservatory Propsectus *(Collection of the Lochhead Family)*

No pupil, however, will be admitted for a shorter period than one year; and those who leave the Institution for any reason whatever (except in case of sickness to be certified by a Physician) before the expiration of that time, must pay the fee for the whole year, to do which jointly with their parents or guardians, they must bind themselves upon admission, according to the form of declaration appended (see p. 23).

§ 8.

Pupils as a rule, can be received into the Institution at Easter and Michaelmas only, at which terms a new course commences in all the lower classes. The day of preliminary examination, and reception is each time made known through the principal home and foreign newspapers and musical journals. Foreigners, however, living at a distance, will be admitted at other times, provided they have already acquired sufficient theoretical and practical knowledge to enable them to join the classes at the point already reached.

§ 9.

Pupils, who desire to be admitted must have the following qualifications:

a. They must possess sufficient general education to be able to understand and to follow a regular lecture.

b. They must possess real talent, and preliminary musical knowledge.

c. Those only who possess a good and promising voice, are allowed to devote themselves to the higher branches of singing.

d. Pupils who are not yet of age, must before admission, bring with them, the written permission of their parents or guardians. (See form p. 23.)

7. Recitation.
8. Practice in **Quartett- and Orchestral Playing.**
9. **Solo-playing, with accompaniment, and Ensemble-playing.**
10. Practice in **Public Performance.**

§ 4.

The Public Practice Evenings which, as a rule, are held once or twice a week, afford the pupils an opportunity of practice in public performance.

§ 5.

The supreme direction and administration of the Institution are in the hands of the Directors named at the end of this prospectus who form the Council.

The staff of Masters at present consists of those whose names and the branches they teach are given at the end of these pages. Besides these, an Inspector is appointed, whose duty it is to see that all the orders of the Council and Masters are strictly carried out, that the lessons are regularly attended to by the students, and that order is preserved in the working of the Institution.

§ 6.

Lady pupils are instructed in separate classes, excepting, of course, the general practice of Ensemble Playing, Choral Singing, Orchestral Performances etc. etc.

§ 7.

The complete course of the Theory of Music, as mentioned in §. 2., occupies three years, which time can be reduced only under the conditions there stated. For the duration of practical instruction no fixed time can be named, for the greater or less amount of general and technical progress depends entirely upon the talent and diligence of the pupil.

(Collection of the Lochhead Family)

e. Foreign pupils must be provided with a Passport, or similar document, valid for the duration of their stay.

f. No impediment is placed in the way of those who, being of more advanced age, or married, desire to visit the Royal Conservatorium of Music with a view to cultivating their love for music.

§ 10.

Every pupil applying for admission to the Conservatorium must first undergo an examination by a Commission appointed for that purpose, by whom it will be ascertained whether he (or she) possesses the talent and education necessary for reception, and who will determine which classes the student is to join. To enable the Examiners to form their judgment, each pupil must bring and play some well practiced pieces of music not necessarily of great difficulty. Those who have already made attempts at composition, should send copies of their productions to the Council (post-free) before their admission, or, at least, lay them before the Examiners at the preliminary examination.

§ 11.

Rules of Discipline.

1) The pupils of the Royal Conservatorium of Music must submit to the rules of the institute and obey the orders of the Council and of their masters.

2) Pupils are admitted into the Conservatorium after passing a preliminary examination, their admission being declared by the Council and they personally signing their names in the book of registry.

3) Every pupil will receive a pass-card on being admitted, which must be returned to the Council on leaving the Conservatorium. Should such pass-card be lost, the fact should immediately be notified to the Council. The fee for a duplicate is 1 ℳ.

4) Pupils are not permitted to choose their masters. The Council alone has to decide by which masters they shall be taught, and can only take into consideration the desires of a pupil regarding the choice of masters in so far as they may appear possible and expedient.

5) All pupils are obliged to attend the classes in which, besides the principal subject they intend to study, the following subjects are dealt with, viz.:
   1. Theory. Ladies may receive permission to discontinue the further study of theory after finishing the course of harmony.
   2. Choral Singing, provided the pupil shows ability.
   3. Orchestral Playing for pupils in the more advanced classes for wind- or string-instruments.
   4. Ensemble Playing for more advanced pupils.
   5. History and aesthetics of Music.

6) No lessons may be missed without sufficient excuse. Cases of illness should be immediately brought to the notice of the Council in writing.

7) Pupils are not allowed to take private lessons from any teachers not giving instruction at the Conservatory, without special permission from the Council.

8) Pupils may not take part in concerts of any description, in other orchestras or choral societies in or out of Leipzig except upon special permission from the Council.

9) Only those pupils that have attained the required degree of artistic excellence will be admitted as candidates to take part in the annual public examinations before Easter. Any wishes regarding admission to such examinations should be addressed to the respective master, who will lay them before the Council for further decision. Any other desires should be submitted to the president of the Council.

10) The pupils performing are not allowed to respond to a call in the public concerts (examinations) or the private practice-evenings.

11) The pupils are earnestly recommended to attend the regular Friday-evening-musical performances, and those occurring at times on Tuesday from 6—8. The performances must not be disturbed by entering or leaving the hall, by changing seats, talking, etc. Applause must never exceed the limits of decency and moderation.

12) Pupils are required to give 6 weeks' notice to the Council, before leaving the Conservatory. The terms for leaving the institute are Easter and the end of July.

13) In case of any moral irregularity or infringement of the above regulations, the offender will be severely reprimanded by the Council, will forfeit all privileges he or she may enjoy, or be dismissed from the Conservatorium. Offenses against rule 11 will be punished by temporary or permanent exclusion from the private practice evenings. The customary testimonial will not be given to those so dismissed and any fees paid, or due for the current half year, will be neither returned nor cancelled.

§ 12.

The lessons continue throughout the year, with the exception of Sundays and Holidays, and of the vacations to be fixed by the Council. For the present these vacations are as follows:

a. At Easter, from Palm-Sunday to the end of Easter-Week.

b. Whitsuntide, from Saturday preceding the festival to the end of the Whitsun-Week.

c. Summer-Holidays: 2 months, August and September.

d. At Christmas: from December 23rd to January 2nd inclusive.

The Summer-Term begins as before on Monday after the Easter-Week and closes at the end of July; the Winter-Term begins on the 1st October and ends on Saturday before Palm-Sunday.

§ 13.

Towards Easter of each year Public Examinations will be held, in some of which the compositions of advanced pupils will be performed. Also towards the end of the Summer-Term there are examinations which are not public and of which those pupils will partake that have chosen one instrument or singing as their principal subject and have not yet made their appearance in a private practice evening.

§ 14.

On leaving the Institution the students receive from the Council a testimonial (§. 11. ¶ 9.), in which the time spent at the Conservatorium, their attention to study, the progress made, as well as their moral conduct during the time of their stay at Leipzig are faithfully stated. A fee of three Marks is charged for this certificate which contains in extenso the remarks of all the teachers.

Nobody is recognised as a pupil legally dismissed by the Institute that is deficient of such certificate.

§ 15.

The annual tuition-fee is Marks 360.—, which includes instruction

1. in one principal subject, such as: playing on the piano or organ, string- or wind-instrument,
2. in theory (theory of harmony, counterpoint, canon, fugue, form, composition),
3. in choral singing,
4. in ensemble and orchestral playing for advanced pupils,
5. in the history and æsthetics of music.

(Collection of the Lochhead Family)

Special remarks.

The expense of rooms and living vary naturally according to personal demands. A single furnished room can be had for 20—40 marks a month whereas 25—50 marks is usually paid for a sitting-room together with bedroom. For those who prefer living in Pension, full opportunity is offered either in independent Pensions or with private families. Full board and lodging are provided in this case as well as attention to rooms and clothing. The usual price of Pensions varies from 90—120 marks a month according to the size and position of rooms. This sum has also been accepted by the Society of Leipzig Pension Proprietresses. The council is always willing to suggest Pensions which can be recommended. The usual charge for the monthly hire of an upright piano ranges from 8—10 marks, for a grand piano from 15—20 marks according to the quality of the instruments.

There are numerous establishments where instruments as well as musical works of all sorts can be hired.

All inquiries and applications must be addressed, post-paid, as follows:

An

das Directorium des Königl. Conservatoriums der Musik

zu Leipzig.

For solo-singing as a chief subject together with the above-mentioned subjects, including classes for the attainment of absolute pitch, piano-playing and lessons in Italian, the annual fee is Marks 420.—. For every other subject of tuition a fee of Marks 60.— per annum is due. Pupils who have chosen the theory of music as their principal subject, are entitled to instruction on the piano, in playing from score and conducting, free of additional charge.

The fees are payable in 3 terms, and in advance: at Easter, Michaelmas and Christmas, at the "Bureau" of the Institution. Besides this, each pupil has to pay an additional entrance-fee of Marks 10.—. Those pupils intending to study the organ are at liberty to practise on the organs of the Institution on payment of Marks —.50 (6 d 12 cents) per hour.

§ 16.

Pupils have to find their own instruments, music, and books necessary for their studies; but the instruments used in the Conservatorium for the lessons are provided by the Institution. Foreigners who do not bring a pianoforte of their own can easily hire one in Leipzig.

Index

Other books published by Sybertooth Inc.

www.sybertooth.ca

Love on the Marsh: A Long Poem
by Douglas Lochhead
ISBN: 9780973950533

Love on the Marsh, a long poem in 100 stanzas, is described by Lochhead as "an extension of *High Marsh Road*" and "brother and sister to it". The diary-like entries, a form to which Lochhead has frequently returned over the years, can also be compared to his work in *The Panic Field*. By turns earthy and ethereal, a pilgrimage through a landscape of grass and sky and tumultuous emotions, *Love on the Marsh* revisits the High Marsh Road with a new eye and finds in it the self-examining, self-discovering heart.

Looking into Trees: Poems
by Douglas Lochhead
ISBN: 9780981024431

"What Lochhead's poems achieve, virtually effortlessly, is an aural and imagist immediacy without sacrificing the richness of layering. Metaphors are repeated, and there is a cyclical nature to these connections - we keep returning to dreams and prayers, memory and the insistence of love - but the immediacy is tangible. These poems engage the senses and the heart." - Heather Craig, *The Telegraph Journal*

The Captain Star Omnibus
By Steven Appleby
ISBN: 9780973950564

From the creator of the cult-classic *Captain Star* TV cartoon series: the first collection of comic strips tracing the strange but illustrious career of Captain Jim Star – the greatest hero any world has ever known – from its surreal beginnings to its improbable middle. Witness his triumphs, learn from his words of wisdom, and meet his crew on the *Boiling Hell*: Navigator Black, Officer Scarlette, and Atomic Engine Stoker "Limbs" Jones.

Quests and Kingdoms
A Grown-Up's Guide to Children's Fantasy Literature
By K.V. Johansen
ISBN-10: 0968802443 • ISBN-13: 9780968802441

"... this is not only a fine reference tool but a finely-written book...This is undoubtedly a seminal work guaranteed to stimulate discussion on children's literature..." –*Books in Canada*

"What truly amazes, though, is Johansen's reliability and depth of knowledge...and her accuracy with facts... The sheer volume of knowledge on display here could earn Johansen honors for scholarship. This is a truly useful reference book..." -*Mythprint* (Bulletin of the Mythopoeic Society)

"...a lively, thoughtful read, and a useful reference volume." - *Terri Windling*

Beyond Window-Dressing?
Canadian Children's Fantasy at the Millennium
By K.V. Johansen
ISBN: 9780968802458

"*Beyond Window-Dressing* should be of particular interest to public and school librarians, and academic librarians in institutions offering courses in children's literature. It should serve as an inspirational tool for seeking out, selecting, and retaining exemplary fantasy literature in our library collections." –The Canadian Library Association's journal *Feliciter*

"I applaud the honesty and forthrightness of her analyses. Far too often, reviews of children's books provide little more than vague plot summaries with very little, if any, questioning of the aesthetic or literary value of a text. Not so with Johansen's analyses. She has her opinions and she quite adroitly defends them. She establishes clear criteria for what she considers a valid and valuable fantasy, and judges each text accordingly. And, I must admit, I found her criticism of even some of Canada's literary icons both refreshing and, more significantly, quite convincing." –*Canadian Literature*

Torrie and the Dragonslayers, by K.V. Johansen
ISBN: 9780981024400

Once there was a prince who set off on a quest for a magic sword. He ran into a bit of trouble with a sorcerer, who didn't like trespassers, and the sorcerer's wolf-headed guards ....

Once there was a young woman who decided to run away from home ....

Luckily for the prince, who was in her father's dungeon by then, she decided to rescue him first. Luckily for both of them, Torrie came along as well.

"An excellent read from a delightful series. Definitely recommended to fans of fantasy, adventure, or medievalistic stories." - *Mad Tales*

"Another excellent installment of the Torrie adventures. Johansen has a magical gift for creating delightful tales of ancient lore... Johansen's novels are fast-paced, high action and adventure stories which intertwine strong characters of both sexes with ancient lore and a quest which allows good to prevail over evil. *Torrie and the Dragonslayers* will have high appeal for both male and female readers..." - Sharon Armstrong, *Resource Links*

Forthcoming in 2010:
The Black Box: A Cassandra Virus Novel, by K.V. Johansen
ISBN: 9780986497407

A near-future science fiction spy thriller. Teens Jordan O'Blenis and Helen Chan-Fisher go undercover at an archaeological dig to discover the cause of the mysterious interference that is not only disrupting communication and navigation systems, but hijacking a top secret experimental space relay satellite developed by Jordan's scientist sister Cassie to transmit its own encrypted signals.

Kingdom of Trolls, by Rae Bridgman
ISBN: 9780986497414

Spin Wil's black medallion—and you'll find the medallion's silver arrow and triangle turn into a five-pointed star. With each new adventure, another tiny gold symbol glimmers on the magical medallion. What do the symbols mean? All cousins Wil and Sophie know is that an ancient and nasty secret society—none other than the Serpent's Chain—wants

its black medallion back.

✧ ✧

Donald Jack
By 3-time Leacock award winner Donald Jack: *The Bandy Papers* series, about First World War ace Bartholomew Bandy.

It's Me Again: Volume III of The Bandy Papers
ISBN-10: 097395051X • ISBN-13: 9780973950519

In this classic novel of the First World War, ace pilot Bartholomew Bandy struggles against his adjutant, his adjutant's pigeon, a defective parachute design, a new German bi-plane, and the Bolshevik army, managing to get promoted to general in the process…

Me Bandy, You Cissie: Volume IV of The Bandy Papers
ISBN: 9780973950571
(winner of the Leacock Medal for Humour)

The Great War may be finished, but Bartholomew Bandy isn't. After not quite succeeding in defeating communism in Russia, he returns to the New World, but what with carrying airmail and trying to start his own aviation business while dodging flappers and bootleggers, Bandy hardly has time to be a silent movie star... This edition includes the radio play "Banner's Headline".

Me Too: Volume V of the Bandy Papers
ISBN: 9780981024486

Back home in Gallop to set up an aircraft company, Bandy finds himself having to get involved in all sorts of unsavoury business, from rum-running to running for Parliament.

This One's On Me: Volume VI of The Bandy Papers
ISBN 9780973950557

It's 1924, and Bandy is making a solo flight across the Atlantic in the Gander, a seaplane of his own design. Not for fame though – he's fleeing from arrest for train robbery, from his job as Minister of Defence, and from his would-be assassin and friend George Garanine.

Me So Far: Volume VII of The Bandy Papers
ISBN: 9780973950502

Bandy has finally found a secure post-war job, as commander of the Maharajah of Jhamjarh's new air force. The only problem is, the British Raj are not so happy with him for setting up a rival air power inside British India.

Hitler Versus Me: Volume VIII of the Bandy Papers
(includes the novelette "Where Did Rafe Madison Go?")
ISBN-10: 0968802486 • ISBN-13: 9780968802489

It's 1940, and the intrepid air ace of WWI is eager to join the fight against Germany. Unfortunately, everyone seems to think Bandy is too old to be flying Spitfires, and should go quietly into retirement to polish his medals. Bandy, however, has other ideas, and uses his friends and/or enemies in high places to manoeuvre himself into the Battle of Britain.

Stalin Versus Me: Volume IX of The Bandy Papers
ISBN-10: 0968802478 • ISBN-13: 9780968802472

In the aftermath of the Normandy invasion, Bandy continues to bob through the ranks like a cork at sea, persecuted by one of his pilots and pursued by Gwinny, who just can't understand why her attempt to have him convicted of treason has soured their relationship.

And also:
The Canvas Barricade
ISBN-10: 0968802494 • ISBN-13: 9780968802496

In print for the first time, Donald Jack's comedy *The Canvas Barricade* was the first modern play performed on the main stage of the Stratford Festival (1961). Misty Woodenbridge has rejected the materialism of modern society for life in a tent by the Ottawa River, where he lives as carefree as the fabled grasshopper, eating stolen apples and painting masterpieces. But as summer draws to an end, Misty must choose between starving in his tent and moving to the city with his fiancée. Meanwhile, his in-laws-to-be smell a cash cow when a mysterious art buyer begins snapping up Misty's work – naturally they keep the money. Out of consideration for Misty's artistic ideals, of course…

www.ingramcontent.com/pod-product-compliance
Lightning Source LLC
Chambersburg PA
CBHW080331270326
41927CB00014B/3173